France in Revolution 1776–1830

Sally Waller

Series Editors
Martin Collier
Erica Lewis

HEINEMANN ADVANCED HISTORY

Heinemann Educational Publishers
Halley Court, Jordan Hill, Oxford, OX2 8EJ
a division of Reed Educational & Professional Publishing Ltd
Heinemann is a registered trademark of Reed Educational & Professional Publishing Ltd

OXFORD MELBOURNE AUCKLAND
JOHANNESBURG BLANTYRE GABORONE
IBADAN PORTSMOUTH NH (USA) CHICAGO

© Sally Waller 2002

First published 2002

ISBN 0 435 32732 1
04 03 02
10 9 8 7 6 5 4 3 2 1

Designed, illustrated and typeset by Wyvern 21 Ltd, Bristol

Printed and bound in Great Britain by The Bath Press Ltd, Bath

Index compiled by Ian D. Crane

Photographic acknowledgements
The authors and publisher would like to thank the following for permission to reproduce photographs:
AKG London: 121; AKG London/Palais de Versailles, Musee Historique: 49; Bridgeman Art Library: 106;
BAL/Giraudon: 5, 29, 35, 57, 147; BAL/Lauros-Giraudon: 8, 154, 183; BAL/Louvre, Paris: 87, 104, 134; BAL/Musee
de la Ville de Paris, Musee Carnavalet: 25; BAL/Prado, Madrid: 197; BAL/Roger-Viollet, Paris: 160; BAL/The
Stapleton Collection: 149; Collection Violelet: 172; Hulton: 67, 165; Mansell/Timepix/Rex Features: 185; Mary
Evans Picture Library: 23; The Trustees of the Victoria and Albert Museum: 190

Cover photograph: © Leonard de Selva/Corbis. Painting shows the death of Louis XVI in 1793.

Picture research by Veneta Bullen

Written source acknowledgements
The author and publisher gratefully acknowledge the following publications from which written sources in the book
are drawn. In some sentences the wording or sentence structure has been simplified:
M. Broers, *Europe under Napoleon 1799–1815* (Arnold, 1996): 137A
W. Doyle, *The Oxford History of the French Revolution* (Oxford University Press, 1990): 79B
P. Geyl, *Napoleon: For and Against* (Cape, 1949): 201A, 201B
M. Lyons, *Napoleon Bonaparte and the Legacy of the French Revolution* (Macmillan, 1994): 202C
R.R. Palmer, *The World of the French Revolution* (Allen and Unwin, 1971): 204A
G. Rudé, *The Crowd in the French Revolution* (Clarendon Press, 1965): 204B
A. Stiles, *Napoleon, France and Europe* (Hodder and Stoughton, 1993): 202D
D. Townson, *France in Revolution* (Hodder and Stoughton, 1990): 78A
G.A. Williams, *Artisans and Sans-Culottes* (Libris, 1988): 204C
D.G. Wright, *Revolution and Terror in France 1789–95* (Longman, 1974): 79C

CONTENTS

HOW TO USE THIS BOOK

This book is divided into three parts. The first two sections are designed for AS level students and explain what happened in France in the years 1774 to 1830. The first part deals with the period of the French Revolution and explains the factors which contributed to that revolution and the outcome of events to 1799. It provides students with detailed information, presented in a clear and accessible fashion, and raises some issues for debate. The second part carries the topic forward with a descriptive analysis of Napoleonic and Bourbon France, culminating in the establishment of the July monarchy. Each part and chapter is self-contained and the summary questions and assessment sections will challenge the student to use and digest the information presented and analyse, prioritise and explain important aspects of the subject.

The A2 part on Revolutionary, Napoleonic and Bourbon France is rather different in style. In this part the emphasis is on analysis and certain key themes have been chosen which will provoke students to consider major areas of debate. Students are introduced to historiographical enquiry and are encouraged to question the interpretation of events. Whilst this section is based on the same period as the AS parts, its thematic approach assumes that the basic chronology has already been absorbed. Students are therefore advised to read the relevant chapters of the AS parts before tackling the A2 part. For those AS level students who wish to extend their knowledge of the subject, the A2 part will also offer valuable insights. The Assessment section, based on the A2 requirements of the various examination boards, provides additional guidance.

AS SECTION: THE FRENCH REVOLUTION 1774–99

INTRODUCTION

What was the French Revolution?

The French Revolution was not a single event but a series of developments over a number of years. Arthur Young, an English traveller in Paris wrote, on 27 June 1789, 'The whole business now seems over and the revolution complete'. Little did he know that the revolution was, in fact, only just beginning. What began as a protest against royal rule in France, grew into a movement that destroyed French government and society as it had been known, and then spread its new ideas of 'liberty, equality and fraternity' far beyond the borders of France. The king was removed, the old aristocracy overthrown, the Church weakened and traditional privileges and controls abandoned. Napoleon officially proclaimed the end of the revolution in December 1799 but, even then, it could only be said that the most momentous revolutionary events were over.

The French Revolution was sparked off by a financial crisis in France. By August 1788, after a series of exhausting wars, France was bankrupt. An **Estates-General** was called to consent to a new system of taxation in May 1789. However, criticism of the monarchy and the old system of government and society had become so widespread during the years of struggle from 1774, that the representatives of the **Third Estate** broke away to declare themselves the National Assembly and to take an oath not to disperse until the inequalities of the old regime had been destroyed. The fall of the Bastille, on 14 July, was mainly symbolic, but it helped show how the ordinary men and women of France, and in particular those of Paris, had grown determined to force change. The abolition of feudalism (privileges), on 4 August 1789, and the Declaration of the Rights of Man and the Citizen, on 26 August, marked two momentous steps along the road to greater liberty and helped drive the revolution forwards.

The old independent status of the church was destroyed as its property was nationalised and the clergy required to take an oath to the state under the new Civil Constitution of 12 July 1790. By April 1792, France had declared war on Austria and, in September, proclaimed a **republic**. Counter-revolution led to a period known as the Terror, from 1793 to 1794, as France became more embroiled in war and uncertain how to maintain the revolution at home. This was a period of radical experimentation, and there was even an attempt at dechristianisation. However, the man most associated with these uncertain times, Robespierre, would eventually fall victim to the guillotine himself and, after July 1794, the Terror ceased. 1795 saw the setting up of the Directory and the rise of Napoleon Bonaparte, whose achievements as a general abroad enabled him to conduct a successful **coup** in November 1799 and establish the Consulate.

The importance of the French Revolution

The French Revolution is a fascinating period of history to study, because it brought about a change in attitudes that is fundamental to our understanding of all modern history. The revolutionaries proved that they could change a system of institutions, customs and beliefs, which had been accepted for generations as created by God. Once it had been shown that an age-old system of government and society could be overthrown, men would never again accept that their lot was beyond change and improvement.

The revolution was not, however, simply a process by which the old ways were overturned. As the revolution progressed and gained momentum, the old forces fought back. So the period is one of revolution and counter-revolution, change and regression, compromise and experiment. This partly explains why the revolution lasted so long and involved so many different experiments in government. It also helps explain why the revolution lapsed into the period of the Terror and the guillotine, which has given rise to the popular image of the

KEY TERMS

Republic Government without a king.

Coup Overthrow of government (often violent).

revolutionaries. Certainly, once the revolution was underway, nothing was sacred any more.

So, the French Revolution showed the people of Europe that, with determination, change was possible and, in later decades, it inspired revolutionaries everywhere. What is often forgotten, however, is that in reality the victories were not easily obtained and were only secured by savagery at home and ruthlessness abroad. There were around 17,000 official victims of the terror and around 150,000 more killed in the fighting and reprisals of 1793–4. It is easy to stress the achievements and ignore the costs but, whatever view is adopted, there can be no denying the importance of the events of 1774–99.

CHAPTER 1

What were the origins of the French Revolution, 1774–88?

THE *ANCIEN RÉGIME*

The organisation of government and society in France before the revolution is commonly known as the '*ancien régime*' (the old system). This system had evolved over many years and was based on the medieval idea of a **hierarchical** society, with the king at the top and his subjects, each in their own place, according to their duties and birth, beneath.

The monarchy

The most important person in France was the king and, from 1774, the king was Louis XVI. He was the highest nobleman in the land, which placed him at the head of the social hierarchy, as well as giving him the position of head of government. It was his duty to ensure that his people were provided with law and order. To help him to run the government, he appointed ministers and he also chose the 36 *intendants*, who acted as his local officials and were responsible for rule in the different parts of France. The king of France is often described as an absolute ruler, meaning that his power was unlimited. His decisions were final and he had a right to imprison anyone by a *lettre de cachet*. Another way of describing his position is to say that he ruled by divine right. The king was anointed with sacred oils at his coronation, and it was believed that he became God's representative in France. This was a position that Louis XVI, like many kings before him, took very seriously.

However, although the French king was very powerful, he was not a **despot**. The king was expected to rule over a just (fair) régime and over the years many important rights and expectations had been established in France, which no king could ignore. For example, he was expected to pass only

KEY TERMS

Hierarchical means a structured system. Under the *ancien régime* in France, the hierarchy consisted of the king as the most important person in society and, below him, the clergy, the nobility and then everyone else.

Intendants were royal agents who were responsible for the administration in each of the generalities into which Louis XVI's kingdom was divided. They were also responsible for ensuring that tax collection was carried out effectively.

Lettre de cachet This was a royal order, signed by the king, by which a person could be arrested and imprisoned without trial.

Despot A ruler who could do just as he liked and rule as he saw fit, with no regard for his subjects.

Louis XVI was an absolute ruler, who ruled by 'divine right'. Contemporary portrait by Antoine Francois Callet.

KEY TERMS

Parlements There were 13 *parlements*, of which the most important was that of Paris. They acted as the supreme courts of appeal in legal cases and they also had political rights. Of these, the most important was the right to register, and if necessary challenge, royal edicts before they became law.

Lit de justice The name given to a formal session of *parlement* at which the king overrode objections and imposed a law by royal edict (announcement).

such laws as were necessary for the well-being of the whole kingdom and to preserve his subjects' freedom within the law. So, the normal pattern for law making involved his subjects too. The king consulted with his ministers and advisers, and an edict was drawn up. This was then sent to the ***parlements*** (law courts) to be approved, and they registered it as law. Although the king could enforce a new law by a system known as ***lit de justice***, he knew that to do this unwisely, or too often, would cause resentment and weaken his government.

The estates

France was a large country and, by the 1780s, had a population of not quite 27 million. Under the *ancien régime*, the French people were divided, according to their status, into 'estates' or social groups. These groups were very unequal in size and in power. It is difficult to give exact figures for this period, but it has been estimated that the First Estate, the clergy, had around 170,000 members, the Second Estate, the nobility, had 300,000–400,000 members, while the Third Estate, the commoners (or

everyone else), made up the rest of the population. Although the types of people within each estate varied considerably, each of these groups had a separate function.

- **The First Estate.** The clergy, clearly defined by its distinctive clothes and spiritual duties, occupied the highest position in society and its members were known collectively as the First Estate. These members, however, varied tremendously in type. There was a huge difference, in terms of wealth and power, between the humble parish priests, monks and nuns, and the bishops, archbishops and cardinals, who came from the ranks of the nobility. Although, as a whole, the Church was wealthy, deriving an income from the rents and dues attached to the **church land** that it owned, as well as the **tithes** that everyone was obliged to pay to the Church, not all members of the First Estate were rich. Indeed, many parish *curés* (priests) were far poorer than their parishioners.

KEY TERMS

Church land The Church owned c. 15 per cent of the land of the kingdom overall, however, its landed influence varied from 5 per cent in parts of the west, to 20 per cent in parts of the north and east.

Tithes A payment amounting to a tenth of a person's income. These were originally payable to the church in the form of produce.

KEY TERM

Religious observance
varied across France.
Although most Frenchmen
and women would have
claimed to be Catholic, with
Protestants making up only
2–3 per cent of the
population, figures for those
actually attending Mass (the
main Catholic service) have
shown that Catholicism was
strongest in parts of the west,
the north-east and south, but
weak in most large cities and
in the regions immediately
south of the capital, Paris.

KEY FACT

Ownership of land The
table below sets out the
approximate percentage of
land owned by each class in
late-eighteenth century
France. The total population
of France at that time was
nearly 27 million.

Nobles (3–400,000)	20 per cent
Church (170,000 clergy)	c. 15 per cent
Bourgeoisie (2.5 million)	c. 30 per cent
Peasants (24 million)	35 per cent

KEY POINT

Nobility of the robe/sword
The division between the
nobility of the robe and the
nobility of the sword is not
entirely clear cut. Most offices
became hereditary if retained
by a particular family for
several generations.
Distinctions of wealth also
varied tremendously across
the two groups.

Nevertheless, under the *ancien régime*, clerics were very influential in France. Although **religious observance** varied enormously between areas, the Catholic Church governed the daily lives of most of the men and women of France. Its spiritual role was regarded as essential to the well-being of the nation, and the Church controlled education and provided for the care of the sick. In return for their contribution to society, the clergy of the First Estate shared a number of privileges. They could, for example, only be prosecuted in their own, church courts. They could not be asked to perform military service or billet (house) troops, or provide money for the support of royal troops. They also had various financial privileges and were not required to pay the *taille* (the main French direct tax). Instead, the clergy had the right to hold their assemblies, at which they could make decisions about their own affairs and offer grants, known as *dons gratuits*, to the king.

- **The Second Estate** was made up of the nobility, which owned around a fifth of the **land** of France. Like the clergy, the nobility was also divided, and not all were exceptionally wealthy. The first group was the ancient nobility, including members of the king's own family, whose status came from their birth. They were known as the **nobility of the sword**, as they were originally the only men allowed to wear a sword. In some areas, however, where families had fallen on hard times, it was status rather then wealth that marked them out from their fellow Frenchmen. The other group was made up of those whose noble status derived from the work they did and was known as the **nobility of the robe**. Nobility might be acquired through the performance of a particular job, such as a judge, given in return for money, as a reward for outstanding military service or, more often, as a 'perk' accompanying a particular governmental office. Venal offices were those that could be purchased and proved a useful source of income for the crown during the eighteenth century. Consequently, the numbers of the Second Estate had grown quite considerably during the course of the century.

What the nobility had in common was a shared attitude to work and common privileges. 'Living nobly' generally meant living off the rents of **landed estates** (unearned income) and the attitude still persisted, particularly among the nobility of the sword, that a military career was the only suitable profession for a nobleman's son. When a man entered the ranks of the nobility, he normally abandoned business and trade although, by the end of the eighteenth century, there was a small group of 'business nobility' in France. Noblemen shared honorific privileges, such as the right to wear a sword, display a coat of arms or take precedence at public ceremonies, which helped reinforce their belief in a natural superiority. They also held a privileged position in law and had a right to be heard in a high court of law and to be beheaded rather than hanged if found guilty of a capital offence. They were exempt from the *corvée royale* (forced labour on the roads) and, perhaps most importantly, were exempt from the *taille* (the oldest form of direct taxation) and *gabelle* (salt tax) and had a lower rate of assessment in other direct taxes.

- **The Third Estate** was a very mixed group of those who were neither clerics nor nobility. By far the greatest proportion of this estate, comprising between 80 and 90 per cent of the population as a whole, was peasantry. The remainder was made up of the bourgeoisie and the urban workers. The bourgeoisie (middle classes) is a rather vague term, which is often divided in turn into

Landed estates The land held by the Second Estate was unequally dispersed, with 40 per cent in parts of the south-west, 33 per cent in Burgundy and less than 10 per cent in Flanders.

Caricature from the 1780s: 'The Third Estate under the tax burden'. On the rock is written 'Taille, Impots [Dues] and Corvées'.

Inflationary pressures on French wage-earners

Taxation The table below sets out the percentage of yield surrendered by peasant farmers in the form of taxes, tithes and feudal dues in late-18th century France. A farm of 5 hectares (12 acres) produced enough to support a peasant family, but 45 per cent had to be surrendered in taxes.

Taxes to king *taille* and *gabelle*	27 per cent
Feudal dues to lord of manor	10 per cent
Tithes to Church	8 per cent

the *haute bourgeoisie*, such as the wealthy merchants and tradesmen, and the *petite bourgeoisie*, such as small shopkeepers and craftsmen. The Third Estate also included those who were little more than beggars and lived on the borders of society.

Peasants worked on the land. By far the greatest number worked as labourers on the land of others but there were some better-off peasants who had managed to acquire land in their own right. Most peasant holdings were small but, collectively, the peasantry owned around a quarter of the land of France. Once again, this group was very varied. At the top, were the richer, land-owning peasantry and the tenant (renting) farmers of large estates and, at the bottom, the *journaliers* (day labourers) who could never be sure where the next day's work would come from.

The bourgeoisie relied on skill, rather than physical labour, for their income. They included professionals such as doctors, lawyers, non-noble office holders, financiers, traders, teachers, artists and master craftsmen. They were a mixed band, although they shared some education and 'relative' wealth. Their numbers had expanded during the eighteenth century, roughly trebling during the period 1660–1789, through the growth of commerce and overseas trade. At the top, the leading bourgeoisie identified more closely with the Second Estate, which many tried to join through the purchase of office, than with the peasantry, and they invested any surplus wealth in land and property. The lower bourgeoisie had fewer opportunities for advancement. The urban workers who lived in large towns were made up of small shopkeepers and skilled (artisans) or unskilled (manual) workers.

Few members of the Third Estate had privileges. They were required to pay direct taxes such as the *taille* and the *vingtième* (twentieth), and capitation and indirect taxes, such as the *gabelle*, the *aides* on drink, and taxes on tobacco, as well as their tithe to the church. The Third Estate was also required to do unpaid labour service to maintain the king's roads, a duty known as the *corvée royale*, although, in practice, wealthier citizens could buy their way out of this obligation. Peasants also had considerable feudal dues and were required to make money payments or provide labour for their masters. In parts of France, they were also obliged to use their lord's mill, oven and winepress, for which they paid a fee, but there was a good deal of regional variation. Nevertheless there is no denying that the demands, particularly for the peasantry, were heavy overall. The provincial assembly of upper Guyenne put it clearly when it stated, 'out of a dozen sheaves of corn, the seigneur takes three, the tithe owner one, while (government) taxes absorb two more'.

THE ENLIGHTENMENT

During the eighteenth century, France was regarded as the leader in fashion and styles of behaviour in Europe. French was considered the most civilised language and was used by the nobility everywhere. European nobles avidly followed French styles, in art, architecture and manners, as well as clothing and literature. Thus any new developments in France were rapidly absorbed and discussed by the educated elsewhere.

One influence that came from France during the course of the 18th century was that of the Enlightenment. This was a movement that emphasised the importance of human reason in guiding government and society. The writers of the Enlightenment were known as the *philosophes* and they believed that men could control their own destiny and that change was necessary to destroy the inequalities of the *ancien régime*.

The *philosophes* therefore questioned the power of the church. Traditionally, the church had taught its followers to regard life on earth as of little importance compared to the after-life, but the *philosophes* believed more could, and should, be done to improve the daily lives of ordinary people and they challenged the king's role, as God's representative. Although they did not, in the main, intend to undermine the power of kings, they did believe that rulers should use their power more effectively to benefit their subjects. They developed the idea that government was based on a 'contract' between the king and his subjects, with obligations on both sides. They wrote about the importance of using reason and common sense to promote human progress, wealth and happiness on earth.

The *philosophes* included many famous French writers, such as François-Marie Arouet, who assumed the pen name Voltaire (1694–1778), Charles-Louis de Secondat, Baron de Montesquieu (1689–1755) and Denis Diderot (1713–84), who edited a 35-volume encyclopaedia (1751–86), which summed up their beliefs. Jean-Jacques Rousseau (1712–78), although originally from Geneva, became an outstanding figure of the French Enlightenment. He was more outspoken than many others, and openly expressed his hostility to monarchy and support for **democracy**, although he was not a revolutionary.

By the last quarter of the eighteenth century, there were some signs that the ideas of the Enlightenment were beginning to take effect in France. The numbers taking up careers in the Church, and the number of religious books and pamphlets published declined, although there is little evidence that Frenchmen as a whole were any less devout than they had been. There were also growing complaints from some members of the Second Estate that the king relied too much on his personal favourites in government and that royal power needed to be more controlled. However, without the impetus of a financial crisis in France by the 1780s, it is extremely unlikely that these ideas would have brought about a revolution of the type France actually experienced after 1787.

KEY CONCEPT

Democracy When members of a country have a say in how they are governed and can influence the making of laws.

SUMMARY QUESTIONS

1 Describe the main features of the *ancien régime* in France.

2 How far was the king's position (a) strengthened, (b) weakened by the structure of the *ancien régime*?

3 How far did the ideas of the Enlightenment challenge existing ideas about absolute monarchy in France?

CHAPTER 2

What financial and political problems did Louis XVI face, 1776–89?

THE ECONOMIC CONDITION OF FRANCE

The revolution that began between 1787 and 1789 came about because King Louis XVI was facing bankruptcy. During the mid-eighteenth century, France would have appeared a prosperous country. It was a large nation, with plenty of fertile land and a growing population. Its agriculture was thriving and small-scale industry was growing. Internal trade had also expanded while overseas trade in wine and luxury goods was flourishing, with established colonial and European trading links. However, during the eighteenth century, France fought a number of financially ruinous wars. The wars of the Spanish (1701–13), Polish (1733–5) and Austrian (1740–8) Successions had occupied the first half of the century, while the Seven Years War (1756–63) against Great Britain in the colonies had proved expensive and disastrous. Nevertheless, the French went on to participate in the War of American Independence (1778–83), opting to support the American colonists in their fight against Britain. Although this war resulted in victory for their allies, it plunged France into an acute financial crisis.

The wars had been funded by massive borrowing and every time the crown took out a loan, it faced a future of mounting repayment debts. To try to meet costs, the king and his ministers had squeezed the maximum amount they could from France's established systems and had also been forced to resort to a number of temporary taxes, which they had imposed by ministerial decree. One that was particularly resented was the tax of the twentieth (the *vingtième*), which was a levy on income paid by all except the clergy. It was introduced in 1749 and was still being levied during the 1780s. Such demands encouraged opposition and increased the spread of enlightenment

> ### KEY FIGURES
>
> **French government finance, 1788** French revenue in 1788 totalled 503 million livres, against total annual expenditure of 629 million livres (a deficit of 126 million livres). Expenditure was accounted for as follows (figures are given in million livres):
>
> Interest on royal debt   318 (51 per cent)
>
> Defence   165 (26 per cent)
>
> Expenses of royal court   37 (6 per cent)
>
> Other   109 (17 per cent)

ideas. The real problem was that, although France was comparatively well off, its resources were locked up by the system of government, the organisation of society and the attitudes of the *ancien régime*.

Those in the First and Second Estates were largely exempt from taxation, while the overriding ambition of the most enterprising and successful traders and merchants of the Third Estate was to amass sufficient wealth to buy office, join the ranks of the Second Estate and then to abandon trade. This meant that those with the greatest wealth, or the potential to make the greatest sums of money, were failing to contribute to the country's economic welfare. Furthermore, the whole economic system in France was very precarious. The pattern of land distribution, for example, with the many small peasant holdings, meant that there was limited investment in land and that therefore improvement and productivity were both comparatively low. The largely rural economy was also dependent on the weather and a bad harvest could send prices rocketing and in turn hit industry and trade.

By 1786, the government's debts were far greater than any foreseeable income, and France's financial system was stretched to its limits. Thus, the government's desperate need for money became linked to the need for changes in the social and economic structure of the country. A failure to modernise the *ancien régime* to meet the costs of France's ambitious foreign policy, coupled with a run of poor harvests, help explain the timing of the revolution.

Jacques Turgot

When Louis XVI came to power in 1775, he appointed Jacques Turgot as his Controller-General of Finance. Turgot was interested in the writings of the French *physiocrats*, economic writers who believed in freeing agriculture from the restrictions of taxes and duties as a way of stimulating the wealth of the country. Although this approach had already been attempted unsuccessfully in the 1760s, Turgot nevertheless believed that this was the way forward, and he tried to introduce a number of financial and economic reforms. These improved accounting procedures, reduced the number of government officials, particularly those employed in tax collection, and restricted the **guilds** that controlled trade. He also tried to reintroduce free trade in grain but, unfortunately, this decision coincided with a particularly poor harvest and there was a good deal of hostility to the plan. The ensuing outbreaks of violence in northern France became known as the 'Flour War'. Turgot's other plan was to introduce a single tax on land, organised by representative assemblies of landowners, which would replace all existing taxes. This was a radical step and was opposed by rival ministers. Furthermore, the Paris Parlement refused (as it had done in the reign of Louis XV) to register the edicts. Consequently, Turgot was dismissed in 1776.

Jacques Necker

Turgot was succeeded by Jacques Necker, a Swiss banker, whose appointment coincided with the War of American Independence. Although he could not take the official title of Controller-General, as he was a Protestant, he acted as the leading financial adviser and tried to bring about a fundamental reform of the French taxation system at this time of acute financial strain. Necker continued Turgot's policies, cutting offices and introducing stricter methods of accounting. He even produced the first ever publication of royal accounts in 1781, the *Compte Rendu*. This was a carefully designed publicity measure. By omitting the costs of war, Necker made it appear as though there was a surplus in the royal finances of around 10 million livres. This provided sufficient reassurance to lenders to permit him to raise yet more loans without having to increase taxes, and also made him very popular with the Third Estate. They also liked the way he revealed the amounts spent on pensions to courtiers, something that did not endear him to other ministers at court.

The economic situation steadily worsened. The royal debt, which had stood at 50 million livres at the end of the Seven Years War in 1763 and had fallen to 40 million by the time of Louis XVI's accession in 1774, was to rise again, and reached 112 million by 1786. To make matters worse, the 1770s and 1780s were dominated by a series of poor harvests. Since the population was steadily rising, prices increased out of proportion to income. This, in

Guilds The organisations which controlled the different industries or trades. They regulated work practices, wage rates and apprenticeships. They were designed to protect the craftsmen but were often restrictive and old fashioned. They clung to the ancient privileges and could detract from, rather than encourage, economic development.

turn, diminished consumer purchasing power and so led to a decline in manufacturing industry and a further increase in urban unemployment. This made it harder than ever for the government to collect the taxes it needed. Necker vainly attempted to control the level of war expenditure and tried to use his popularity to force the king to admit him to his special councils, but he had too many ministerial opponents. In 1781, when he saw the hopelessness of the situation, he resigned. This in itself was significant. It was almost unprecedented for men to resign from the king's service and when he continued to publish comments on financial affairs and to criticise the policies of his successors it was a clear sign that Louis's regime was losing public confidence.

Charles de Calonne

Charles de Calonne became Controller-General of Finance in 1783. He faced an unenviable inheritance. Royal debts were mounting and interest payments taking up a large proportion of income but, while Louis and other ministers resisted change, there was little he could do, except seek yet more loans. However, during 1784–5 the credit began to dry up and the Paris Parlement refused to register any further loans. On 20 August 1786, Calonne informed Louis XVI that the state faced financial collapse. The total revenue for 1786, he claimed, would be 475 million livres, but expenditure was estimated at 587 million livres. He believed that the *Compte Rendu* had actually worsened France's situation by making it appear that the crown had a surplus whereas in reality the annual deficit was over 100 million livres.

Louis XVI was at first reluctant to agree to any radical change, but after several months of persuasion, amid the deteriorating financial situation of the autumn of 1786, a proposal was put forward. The 'temporary' tax of the twentieth would be replaced by a single land tax paid by all landowners (including the clergy), in goods, rather than in money. Since this meant that landowners would bear the brunt of taxation, the scheme involved them in the assessment and distribution of the new taxation through a network of local assemblies, elected by the landowners themselves. Other direct taxes were to remain, but would be reduced. Proposals were also made to stimulate the economy by removing internal customs barriers, abolishing the *corvée* and freeing trade in grain, internally and externally. Even under the *ancien régime*, a major change such as this required some consultation and appearance of support so, in order to gain assent for his radical programme of reform, Calonne decided to summon an Assembly of Notables. This appeared less daunting than a full meeting of the Estates-General which had last convened in 1614, although some leading nobles, such as **Lafayette**, were already arguing that only a 'truly national assembly' could assent to drastic new taxation.

The Assembly of Notables

The Assembly of Notables, which met at the Palace of Versailles in February 1787, was made up of 144 representatives of the nobility, including clerical nobility. They immediately attacked Calonne's proposals. They did not trust the man himself, particularly after the publication of the apparently favourable *Compte Rendu*, and believed that he must be at least partly to blame for the crisis. Most of the clergy was hostile to any encroachment upon its privileges and, although there were a fair number of nobles who were prepared to accept changes in taxation policy, they insisted that there must be a meeting of the Estates-General to discuss the matter. While the arguments raged, the financial crisis grew worse. The **Eden Treaty** on trade with Great Britain proved damaging to the fragile French economy and yet another poor harvest in 1786 reduced the income from taxation. In April 1787, Calonne tried to appeal to the public, behind the back of the assembly, claiming that its members had only considered their own interests and privileges. This merely provoked further criticism and led to Calonne's dismissal.

The king was placed in an impossible situation. The failure of his ministers to provide a solution to France's deep economic, social and governmental problems was tied up with the basic structure of the *ancien régime*. The king was duty bound to protect the 'laws and customs' of his kingdom and yet those very customs, which involved the unequal rights of his subjects, were preventing effective reform. Furthermore, the more complex government had

Marquis de Lafayette (1757–1834) A French aristocrat who had served in the armies in America during the War of Independence. He was greatly admired by the people of Paris. Appointed to the Assembly of Notables and the Estates General, he became the first commander of the National Guard. In 1792, he was forced to flee after his military failure against the Austrians. He returned to France during the Napoleonic period, became a Liberal spokesman in 1815 and supported Louis-Philippe in 1830.

Eden Treaty This trade treaty, signed in Paris in September 1786, provided for a mutual lowering of tariffs or import duties between Great Britain and France. Grain, wine and brandy from France would be able to enter Britain with lower tariffs than those charged on the same goods from elsewhere, while cottons, hardware and industrial products from Britain would similarly enter France on reduced tariffs. Unfortunately for the French, the growing economic crisis over the next few years meant that there was no surplus of food and drink to sell to Britain, while British textiles and industrial goods were able to swamp the French market, inflicting considerable damage on French industry.

A plan of the Assembly of Notables – feet marked on the plan show ceremonial positions.

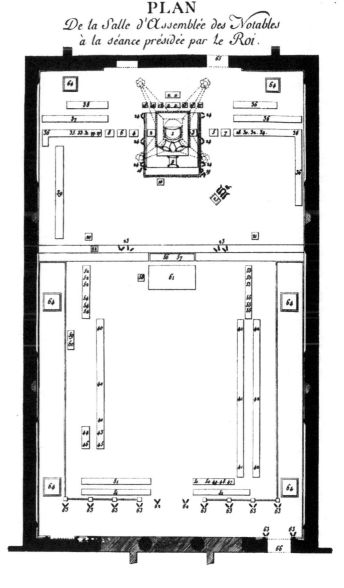

PLAN
De la Salle d'Assemblée des Notables
à la séance présidée par Le Roi.

become, the more he had been forced to rely on ministers and local officials. This in turn weakened his position and led to new criticism, particularly in the *parlements*, which were required to register his edicts. Such critics argued that the king was no longer fulfilling his role as a defender of laws and was allowing ministers to rule the country. The *parlements* were very hostile to the various experiments at raising tax and the failure of Calonne's efforts was partly associated with this fear of 'ministerial despotism'. After Calonne's dismissal, the *parlements*, led by that of Paris, emerged at the forefront of political opposition.

Archbishop Loménie de Brienne

Calonne was replaced by Loménie de Brienne, an archbishop and the leader of the assembly. However, he did nothing more than produce a slightly amended version of Calonne's plan, which was no more successful in winning support. The assembly was consequently dissolved in May. Brienne did, however, manage to stave off bankruptcy by taking out new loans at a very high rate of interest, and he attempted to force his proposals through by presenting them directly to the *parlements*. The Paris Parlement, which spoke for the provincial *parlements*, accepted the administrative reforms, but remained hostile to the land tax reform. It decreed that it lacked the authority to sanction this change and refused to register the necessary edicts. When crowds assembled on the streets calling for an Estates-General, the king made one last attempt to force acceptance of the proposals.

The Paris Parlement was sent to Troyes in August 1787 to take it away from the crowds, which were said to be influencing its deliberations. However, its attitude had hardened and little was achieved. The royal action merely brought renewed demonstrations of support for the *parlement* and, by September, the king was forced to give way and allow its members to return to the city. However, this did not end the **demonstrations**.

In such circumstances, Louis XVI was forced to abandon his new taxation schemes and instead promised to summon an Estates-General. Even this announcement failed to quell the opposition. When the king tried to force the approval of urgently needed 'loans' in November, at an emergency 'royal session' in which he surrounded the Paris Parlement with troops, there was widespread unrest. The king resorted to the exile of the **Duc d'Orléans** and arrested some of his critics. However, debate continued and, in May 1788, the Paris Parlement issued a document entitled 'the Fundamental Laws of the kingdom' in which it argued that only an Estates-General could sanction the levying of new taxes. This was countered by new royal decrees, the 'May Edicts', which deprived the *parlements* in Paris and elsewhere of their right to register and protest against royal decrees. This merely added fuel to the fire and increased the cries of 'ministerial despotism'.

The Revolt of the Nobles

Over the next few months the disturbances spread throughout France in a series of incidents known as the Revolt of the Nobles. Riots broke out in some of the provincial capitals where the *parlements* met, and one of the worst incidents occurred in Grenoble when, on the '**Day of Tiles**' (7 June), four were killed and thirty injured. Throughout the country assemblies of nobles were hastily convened to discuss how to take action in support of the *parlements*. It is interesting to note that, although members of the Third Estate participated in the rioting, so entrenched was the hierarchy of the *ancien régime* that it was the First and Second Estates which provided the leadership. An assembly of the clergy showed its support for the *parlements* by agreeing to provide, not its usual *don gratuit*, but a 'gift' of less than a quarter of the sum requested by the king.

However, the revolts were uncoordinated and would probably have petered out but for the collapse of the government's finances. The bankruptcy that had only just been kept at bay for so long, finally hit home at the beginning of August 1788. On 16 August, payments from the treasury were suspended and Brienne resigned, recommending the recall of Necker, the only man capable of winning public confidence. Necker returned in triumph proclaiming that the Estates-General would meet in May 1789. Apart from attempting to raise some temporary loans, he agreed to do nothing until the Estates-General had been summoned.

Day of Tiles Grenoble was a regional centre of industry which had suffered badly in the economic depression from 1788. As in Paris, the magistrates in it *parlement* had declared the May Edicts illegal. On 7 June the government sent in soldiers to exile the offending magistrates, but the workers came out in sympathy for the magistrates. When the soldiers tried to control the crowds, the latter took to the rooftops and began hurling tiles at them. There was a full-scale riot and some townsfolk were shot. It was the first large-scale urban rebellion of the revolution and showed the breakdown of royal authority and the helplessness of the military forces.

SUMMARY QUESTIONS

1 Why was there a crisis in the French economy by 1789?

2 Is it fair to blame Louis XVI for the government's failure to deal with the financial crises of the 1770s and 1780s?

3 Write a summary of the state of France in 1789, indicating the strengths and weaknesses. You should include: the royal family; society; the economy; the government.

CHAPTER 3

What led to the outbreak of revolution in 1789?

THE CALLING OF THE ESTATES-GENERAL, 1789

The Estates-General had last met in 1614. On this occasion, the representatives of the three estates had each met separately and decisions had been taken following one **vote per estate**. Clearly, in the circumstances of 1789, a procedure whereby the Third Estate would always be outvoted by the first and second was not favoured by the leaders of the Third Estate, or indeed by the more liberal-minded nobles. Instead, they argued for **voting by 'head'**, and wanted the Third Estate to receive double representation, as a token of its size. In this way the Third Estate would have as many representatives as the other two and would be able to determine decisions.

Discussions about procedure dominated the debates of the Paris Parlement from September 1788. Although it had previously been at the forefront of the opposition to the 'ministerial despotism' of the *ancien régime*, the *parlement* was essentially upper class and very wary of the power of the Third Estate. While it favoured an Estates-General, it did not want to see control passing from the Second Estate to the bourgeois leaders of the Third Estate. It therefore chose to support the traditional one vote per estate.

This, of course, provoked outrage among the Third Estate leaders, who whipped up support in a pamphlet war attacking their old ally. *Parlement* changed from being a friend, to an enemy out to gain more power for itself. No longer was it simply the actions of the king and his ministers that were in dispute, but the broader question of traditional society and leadership. In January 1789, **Abbé Sieyès** wrote a particularly influential pamphlet entitled *What is the Third Estate?*, which reflected the views of the more forward-looking thinkers. In it, he argued that the

KEY FIGURES

Voting by estates

First Estate (*c.* 300 clergy) = one vote
Second Estate (*c.* 300 nobles) = one vote
Third Estate (*c.* 600 commoners – double representation) = one vote
First Estate and Second Estate outvote Third Estate by 2 votes to 1

Voting by 'heads'

c. 600 Third Estate
+ some clergy
= outvote the rest

KEY PERSON

Emmanuel-Joseph Sieyès (1748–1836) Sieyès was an intellectual who had become a priest. During 1788–9, he settled in Paris and became a spokesman for the Third Estate. He wrote pamphlets and chose to represent the Third Estate in the Estates-General where he attacked royal and noble privileges. He was instrumental in the setting up of the National Assembly and he went on to gain power under the Directory in 1799. He was involved in the coup that brought Napoleon to power in 1799 and helped plan the consulate system. He became an imperial count and, after the restoration of the monarchy, spent the years 1814–30 in exile in Belgium.

Third Estate was 'everything'. It did the work and paid the taxes that made France a great nation, and yet it counted for nothing. It was not 'royal despotism', he claimed, that needed to be destroyed, but the power of the first two estates. The Third Estate needed to obtain a **constitution** to end the inequality of the *ancien régime* and should take control of affairs itself, if the upper estates refused to work with it in the Estates-General.

Louis XVI did not handle the situation well. His minister, Necker, encouraged him to show some willingness for reform and to support the demands of the Third Estate regarding procedure for the Estates-General. This, he felt, would help revive the popularity of the monarchy by showing that the king understood his subjects and was concerned to exercise his powers of leadership in their interests. However, although the king agreed to the doubling of the Third Estates' representatives in December 1788, he avoided making any pronouncement on voting procedure, which made the increased number of representatives meaningless.

There was, therefore, considerable confusion surrounding what would happen when the estates met, but expectations were high as the election procedure began. This was a cumbersome and unequal business in itself. While the first two estates had a one man, one vote procedure, the Third Estate had a system of indirect election, which was sufficiently prolonged to heighten the excitement further.

The *Cahiers de Doléances*

The royal announcement of the Estates-General had promised, 'not only that they (the Estates) might give their advice on everything we shall ask them to discuss, but also that they may tell us the wishes and grievances of our people so that every kind of abuse will be reformed'.

Consequently, in the ten months that elapsed between the announcement and convening of the meeting, it was not only the Parisians and the educated that were affected by the debates. All over France lists of grievances and suggestions for reform were being drawn up for each order. **The *cahiers de doléances* (notebooks) of the Third Estate** were originally produced by every village, urban guild and corporation, so even the humblest peasant would have been encouraged to question his position and become excited by the prospect of imminent change.

The French economy in 1789

The harvest of 1788 had been disastrous and the growing population put immense pressure on food supplies, which in turn forced up prices. By the spring of 1789, up to 88 per cent of a Parisian worker's wages was being spent on bread alone. The *intendants* tried to maintain grain supplies, but grain convoys were attacked and riots over food broke out as rumours spread that grain was deliberately being hoarded to force prices still higher. In these desperate circumstances, there was little surplus to spend on manufactured goods, and industry was in turn forced to lay off workers. Textile production was cut by 50 per cent in 1789. Popular protest was particularly marked in Paris where the Réveillon riots, which have been described as both the first great popular demonstration of the revolution in Paris, and the last of the *ancien régime*, broke out in April. Hundreds of workers took to the streets in a protest against some uncalled-for remarks about the high cost of wages by Réveillon, an otherwise respected wallpaper manufacturer. The scale of the riots, which lasted several days and resulted in a number of fatalities as troops opened fire, can only reflect the desperation of the workers concerned. They were well aware that the Estates-General was due to meet a week later and their cries of 'long live the king' and 'long live M. Necker' were proclaimed in the mistaken belief that both were champions of the Third Estate and would soon right their wrongs and provide cheap, plentiful bread.

The Estates-General

The assembly finally convened on 4 May 1789 in the great hall at the king's Palace of Versailles. There were 561 deputies for the first two estates and 578 deputies for the Third Estate. Of these, around 400 were lawyers and officials in government posts, another 100 or so were bankers, merchants and small-scale industrialists and there was also a scattering of 'intellectuals', some of them nobles and clergy, such as Sieyès and Mirabeau who preferred to

The Réveillon riots, April 1789.

KEY PERSON

Maximilien Robespierre (1758–94) Educated at a Jesuit college in Paris, Robespierre trained as a lawyer. He developed a burning desire to fight for freedom and equality and was elected as a Third Estate deputy. He soon made his mark as a speaker in the National Assembly and he became the leader of the Jacobins, who dominated the National Convention. He supported the execution of Louis XVI and the overthrow of the more moderate Girondins. He had a great following in Paris and he used this to eliminate his rivals and establish a virtual dictatorship.

represent the Third Estate despite their status. However, **Robespierre**, a lawyer in his early thirties, was the more typical representative.

A great deal of work has been done by historians in order to assess the views of those elected. Certainly, the deputies for the first two estates were not united in the defence of privilege, and when the *cahiers* were presented, those of the nobility were surprisingly liberal. They condemned the government of the *ancien régime* for its despotism and inefficiency. They even accepted that there was injustice, that merit rather than birth should qualify men for high office and that some privileges would have to go. It has been calculated that there were around ninety Second Estate deputies who were clearly in favour of some reform and there was a marked distinction between more conservative provincial nobles and those affected by enlightened ideas. Of the 291 clerical deputies, there were also around 200 in favour of change.

All *cahiers* emphasised the need for regular meetings of the Estates-General, no taxation without consent, freedom for the press and the abolition of the hated *lettres de cachet*.

However, the main demands for reform came from the Third Estate. The *cahiers* of the Third Estate reflected a desire for financial equality and the rights of individual citizens – particularly the abolition of feudal rights – as well as many other changes concerning agriculture and trade.

Even at this stage, after the many months of waiting and expectation, the king's government seemed unsure how to proceed. Various ministerial suggestions for reform had been discussed but nothing had been agreed to present to the deputies. Thus the king lost the opportunity to exert his authority. Instead, the first seven weeks of the meeting were wasted in endless wrangling about the meeting and voting procedure, while the king appeared aloof, probably more distracted than he might otherwise have been following the untimely death of his eldest son and heir. Finally, the patience of the Third Estate deputies ran out. Influenced by the arguments of men like Sieyès and **Mirabeau**, on 17 June, the Third Estate declared that it was the 'National Assembly', since it represented most of the nation. 'The National Assembly is the only title appropriate to the assembly as things are because the members have come at the wishes of practically the whole nation; there can only be one single body of representatives, and no deputy in whatever order or class, has any right to work apart from the present assembly, even if nobles or clergymen have elected him.' The National Assembly, they declared, would assume control over its own affairs and decide taxation. On 19 June, the clergy voted to join them, thus posing a direct challenge to the king.

The Tennis Court Oath

The king was clearly losing control of the situation and, in order to reassert his authority, he was prepared to accept Necker's suggestion that he should hold a royal session for all three estates on 23 June and offer the deputies a reform package. He was inclined to agree with Necker that he would have to allow voting by head on all important matters, if anything was to be achieved. However, before the meeting could take place, yet another development occurred. On 20 June, the Third Estate deputies found

KEY PERSON

Honoré Gabriel Riqueti, Comte de Mirabeau (1749–91) Although of noble birth, Mirabeau sympathised with the Third Estate and was elected as one of its deputies. He had already become famous before the revolution for his unprincipled behaviour, including an elopement with a married woman, for which he was originally sentenced to death. In the early years of the revolution he became a popular hero. He was a great speaker and a natural leader of the National Assembly, referred to as 'little mother' by the people. He worked within the Constituent Assembly to convince all parties that a limited monarchy was needed, but he was a natural intriguer, easily bribed and prone to changing position. Despite his prominence in the assembly, he enjoyed the confidence of the king, whom he secretly advised and on whose behalf he spoke. His death, in April 1791, was a setback to the progress of constitutional monarchy.

KEY PERSON

Jean Joseph Mounier (1758–1806) Son of a draper, Mounier had trained as a lawyer and bought a noble title becoming a *juge royal*. By 1789, he was already convinced of the need for change and became a natural representative of the Third Estate. His proposal for the Tennis Court Oath was partly to prevent Sieyès' more radical suggestion that the deputies should take themselves to Paris. He played an important part in drawing up the Declaration of Rights but he remained pro-monarchy and was subsequently discredited.

'The Tennis Court Oath' (1789). Painting by Jacques-Louis David.

that their meeting hall was closed, locked and guarded by royal troops, while preparations were made for the forthcoming royal session. They were understandably angry that they had not been informed of this, but it was more than the closure of the hall that led to their subsequent display of defiance. The presence of troops fuelled the fear that the king was preparing to use armed force against them and led them to assemble on a nearby, indoor, tennis court. Here, under the leadership of men such as **Mounier** and Mirabeau, they took the Tennis Court Oath: 'Nothing can prevent (the assembly) from continuing its discussions wherever it may be forced to meet; all members of this assembly shall here and now take a solemn oath never to abandon the assembly and to go on meeting wherever it has to until the constitution of the realm is set up'. In a wave of excitement, verging on hysteria, the deputies lined up to take the oath.

By the time the royal session took place, on 23 June, the attitudes of both sides had hardened. Regarding the Third Estate deputies' behaviour as a personal attack on his authority, Louis XVI chose to reject Necker's advice.

He was under a good deal of pressure from his wife, Marie Antoinette, and his brothers to stand firm so, while he did accept a good deal of reform – no taxation without consent, the abolition of *lettres de cachet*, the freedom of the press and the abolition of internal customs barriers, the *gabelle* and the *corvée*, he nevertheless declared that any resolutions made by the Third Estate acting on its own were void (worthless) and that the Estates-General should continue to meet in three separate assemblies. He then ordered the deputies to disperse to their different meeting places. The nobles and clergy followed the king out of the hall, but the National Assembly refused to go.

The following day, the Third Estate was joined by 151 clergy and, the day after, by 47 nobles, including a royal prince, the Duc d'Orléans. Popular demonstrations broke out in Paris and elsewhere. Rumours abounded of plots to withhold grain, destroy the National Assembly and starve Paris into submission. In the face of growing disorder, the king backed down. On 27 June he reversed his earlier decision and gave the pronouncement that should have come weeks earlier. The nobles and clergy were ordered to join the Third Estate and vote by head. By this stage, few Third Estate deputies trusted the king. From the beginning of June, there had been a large number of troops stationed in and around Paris. The king had claimed that they were there to preserve order, and this had seemed reasonable enough until 4800 extra troops were suddenly summoned on 26 June and 11,500 more on 1 July. By 4 July, there were just under 30,000 soldiers stationed around the capital. Rumour quickly spread that the king was planning to disperse the assembly by force.

SUMMARY QUESTIONS

1 Explain why the Third Estate set up a national assembly.

2 Did the events of 1789 in France demonstrate a conflict between the 'haves' and the 'have nots'?

CHAPTER 4

How did the revolution develop, 1789–90?

KEY EVENTS OF 1789

5 May	Estates-General opened (Versailles)
17 June	National Assembly proclaimed
20 June	Tennis Court Oath
23 June	Three estates ordered to separate
27 June	Union of three estates
11 July	Necker dismissed (again)
12–14 July	National Guard formed; Storming of Bastille
July/August	Great Fear
4 August	Feudalism 'abolished'
26 August	Declaration of Rights of Man
5 October	March of women to Versailles
2 November	Confiscation of Church estates

The Parisian crowd

By July 1789, the atmosphere in Paris was highly charged. The continuing rise in the price of bread (which reached its highest price since 1715 on 14 July 1789), the lack of employment and the presence of the army, in addition to the political events of May–June, ensured that the workers of the capital were ready to take to the streets at the least provocation. There was a ready band of men and women keen to listen to, and act on, the words of revolutionary speakers who gathered at the Palais Royal. The members of the crowd were known (from 1792) as the **Sans Culottes** since they wore long trousers. They consisted of a mixture of craftsmen, shopkeepers, traders, small-scale masters, clerks, wage earners, journeymen and labourers, along with

---

KEY TERM

Sans Culottes The Sans Culottes were so named because they went without knee breeches, the traditional dress of the upper classes. They addressed one another as '*citoyen*' (citizen) and regarded the term 'aristocrat' as one of abuse. They wore a red cap with a *tricolore* motif, which was the symbol of the revolution. They regarded themselves as defenders of the revolution and they became active at crucial points in risings or *journées*. They were also influential in the *sections* (voting districts) of Paris and in the National Guard. For more information, see A2 Section 2.

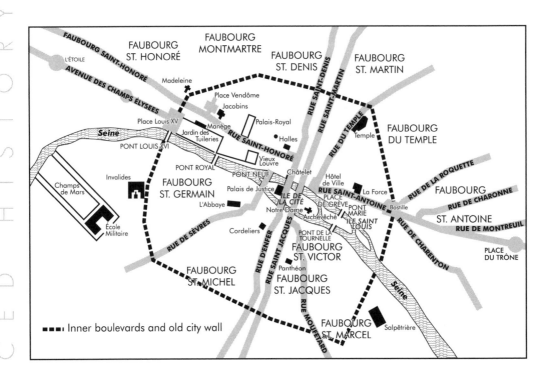

some middle-class factory owners, wine merchants and professionals. However, whatever their status, they shared the same militant outlook and a determination to rid the country of privilege and force change on a king whom they increasingly distrusted.

The spark which led to the first explosion of popular activity was the announcement of Necker's dismissal on 11 July. The king had grown tired of his lectures and advice and ordered his return to Switzerland, replacing him with the conservative Baron de Breteuil. It was a foolhardy decision. Necker had still been extremely popular with the crowds, who had a childlike belief in his ability to right their wrongs.

News of his dismissal, and the appearance of German cavalry troops to control disorder in the streets of Paris, led to panic and a conviction that Louis XVI was about to dissolve the assembly. Encouraged by the popular orators such as **Camille Desmoulins**, on 12–13 July the poorer citizens of Paris began raiding gun shops and swordsmiths in an attempt to provide themselves with weapons. Order broke down as some of the Gardes-français (French

KEY PERSON

Camille Desmoulins (1760–94) An impassioned speaker and the revolutionary responsible for rousing the mobs in Paris in 1789, Desmoulins nevertheless found himself a victim of the Terror and was guillotined in 1794.

Guards) began to listen to the speakers at the Palais Royal and other royal troops were forced from the streets. The king was informed that he could no longer rely on the loyalty of his troops, who stood by and took no action in the face of mounting disorder. There was an attack on the customs posts around the city, where the hated duties were collected on foodstuffs and other goods entering Paris, and 40 of the 54 posts were destroyed. Food stores and prisons were attacked, and the monastery of Saint-Lazare taken over.

This alarmed the wealthier citizens, mainly property owners, who held an emergency meeting of the Parisian **electors**. This met at the Hôtel de Ville (town hall). They voted to set up a committee, known as the *commune*, to run the city, as well as their own 'National Guard' (citizens' militia) to defend it. This had the dual purpose of protecting personal property from the attacks of the poor and protecting the city from attack by the king. Lafayette was appointed the first commander of the National Guard.

The fall of the Bastille

On 14 July, the Parisian crowds made for the Hôtel des Invalides – a retirement home for soldiers, which also acted as a weapon store. Here, a crowd of around 8000 seized 28,000 muskets and 20 cannon, but they could not find enough gunpowder or cartridges to use them. Rumour quickly spread that there might be stores of powder in the old fortress of the Bastille. This was a prison situated on the edge of the working-class district (the Faubourg Saint-Antoine), and its bleak outline was hated as a symbol of the *ancien régime*. The crowds, accompanied by some of the newly formed National Guard, made their way there and two representatives from the *commune* went to see the governor, the Marquis de Launay, to negotiate the handover of gunpowder and cannon. However, the crowd was kept waiting too long and grew impatient. Some pushed into the inner courtyard and firing began. In no time, a full-scale assault took place, in which de Launay was captured, decapitated and his head paraded on a pole around the streets of Paris. The significance of this event was tremendous. The Bastille had not been stormed, as later suggested, to release political prisoners. There were in

Painting of a Sans Culotte by Louis Boilly, 1792.

fact only seven inmates. It had been stormed for ammunition, and from this came the destruction of a symbol of the arbitrary power of the king. What is more, the royal troops had merely stood by – some defecting to the crowds and others waiting on events. There was now no denying that the king had lost control.

Royal troops were pulled out of Paris and it was clear that the action of the Parisians had saved the assembly, now known as the 'Constituent Assembly' in recognition of its new role, to draw up a constitution for France.

On 17 July, Louis XVI resigned himself to making an appearance in Paris and, as a symbol of his acceptance of the changes, wore the **revolutionary cockade** in his hat. In front of an armed crowd, on the steps of the Hôtel de Ville, he reinstated Necker and accepted the new Paris Commune, the National Guard and the National/Constituent Assembly. The crowds gave him a hostile reception. Any vestiges of support for the authority of the king were fast disappearing in Paris, and this change in attitude was soon to be mirrored in towns and cities all over France, where National Guards were set up, old-style town councils reformed or overthrown, royal *intendants* forced to flee and orders only obeyed if first approved by the Constituent Assembly.

KEY TERM

The revolutionary cockade
The red, white and blue cockade symbolised the revolution. Red and blue were the colours of Paris, and white that of the Bourbon royal family, of which the king was a member. The cockade was proudly worn by the Sans Culottes and was designed to show Paris and the king working together.

Peasant risings

Until early 1789, the peasants had played little part in the events leading to the revolution. They were more concerned with the land and their daily living, and were largely unaffected by the developments in Paris. However, the catastrophic harvest of 1788, the escalating bread prices and the lay-offs in the textile industry, on which many had relied for extra income, did affect them. Food riots were not new and those that occurred in early 1789 would probably have died out but for the events in Paris. However, the preparation of the *cahiers* encouraged the peasants to believe that the king was about to do something for them and news of the storming of the Bastille encouraged rioting against taxes, the *taille* and feudal dues.

By the summer of 1789, peasant risings were growing more widespread. Tithe barns were attacked to release the church's stores of grain and châteaux were pillaged or destroyed, as peasants began a desperate hunt for the *terriers* (legal documents) which documented each lord's rights over the peasantry. Rumours abounded, particularly one that claimed vagabonds in the pay of nobles were roaming the country, intending to destroy crops and wreak vengeance on the rebellious peasantry. Thus, the peasant

The spread of 'The Great Fear', 1789.

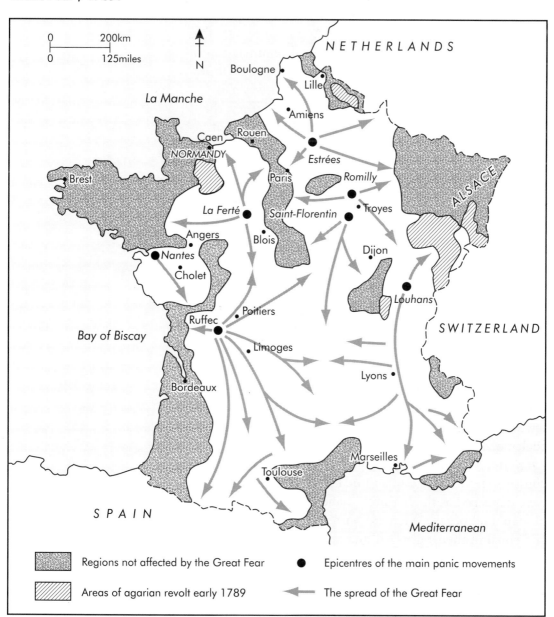

uprisings grew into what became known as 'The Great Fear', which spread through most of France between 20 July and 6 August. The development frightened the assembly, where the mainly bourgeois and liberal noble deputies grew concerned for their own property.

The August Decrees

The assembly was forced to respond to the peasants' demands. There was no question of using troops to crush the risings in the countryside. Had this been done, there would have been a risk of those same troops being used against the assembly itself. So, on 4 August, a remarkable debate took place, which ended in a total renunciation of feudal rights. In a surge of patriotic fervour, the deputies actually went far further than the original *cahiers* had proposed. The feudal system was abolished. Tithes, the purchase of office and special privileges were all swept away. The principle of fair taxation was established. All Frenchmen were guaranteed the same rights and duties and were to be able to enter any profession regardless of birth. The old structure, both of society and of government, was destroyed and the way made clear for a new, national system of administration. The *ancien régime* was at an end. The decrees gave the peasants most of what they wanted. Admittedly, they did not like the compensation payable to landlords for the loss of dues but, on the whole, these decrees committed most peasants to the new regime, and their debts were subsequently cancelled in 1793.

The Declaration of the Rights of Man

The excitement generated in the assembly by the renunciation of feudal dues was maintained over the next few weeks and, on 26 August, led to the Declaration of the Rights of Man and the Citizen, largely drawn up by Lafayette. This lay down the principles on which the new constitution of France was to be based. It contained what were described as the 'natural, inalienable and sacred rights of man' and began, 'Men are born free and remain free and equal in their rights'. It guaranteed freedom of expression, opinion, religion, fair trial, consent to taxation and the right to property. It stated that careers and offices should be open to all according to their talent – a principle known as meritocracy. It stressed the importance of an

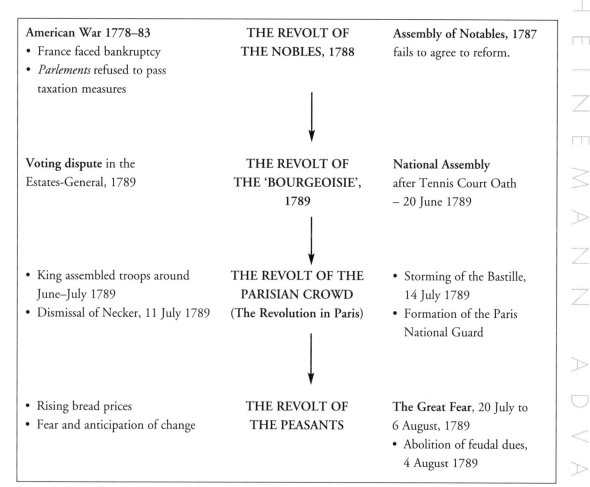

American War 1778–83	THE REVOLT OF	Assembly of Notables, 1787
• France faced bankruptcy	THE NOBLES, 1788	fails to agree to reform.
• *Parlements* refused to pass taxation measures		
	↓	
Voting dispute in the Estates-General, 1789	THE REVOLT OF THE 'BOURGEOISIE', 1789	**National Assembly** after Tennis Court Oath – 20 June 1789
	↓	
• King assembled troops around June–July 1789 • Dismissal of Necker, 11 July 1789	THE REVOLT OF THE PARISIAN CROWD (The Revolution in Paris)	• Storming of the Bastille, 14 July 1789 • Formation of the Paris National Guard
	↓	
• Rising bread prices • Fear and anticipation of change	THE REVOLT OF THE PEASANTS	**The Great Fear**, 20 July to 6 August, 1789 • Abolition of feudal dues, 4 August 1789

Stages of revolution.

elected assembly to express the view or 'general will' of the people and the need for laws to protect men's freedom. Such views were a clear break from those of the *ancien régime* and reflected the influence of the thinkers of the Enlightenment, particularly Rousseau. It was also a bourgeois document in its emphasis on the sanctity of property, but it would become a very important document for liberals in the nineteenth century. The universality of its pronouncements meant that it could be applied to any country or system of government.

The debate on the position of the king

Thanks to a good harvest in 1789, there was comparatively little unrest in 1790 and the Constituent Assembly was able to get on with its task of drawing up a constitution.

Perhaps not surprisingly, Louis XVI had hesitated to sanction the August Decrees, which he saw as a direct challenge to his power. There was, however, no question of abolishing the monarchy at this stage. The assembly was working on a scheme whereby France would become a constitutional monarchy, with restrictions on the power of king and ministers. Debate centred not on whether there should be a king, but on what position the king should have in the new constitution. The assembly considered, but rejected, the idea of a **second chamber**, since they wished to avoid any revival of aristocratic power. So they put forward a proposal for a single assembly, which would be elected every two years. This would decide the laws of the country and would determine taxation, but the king would be responsible for ensuring the laws were carried out. He would retain the right to appoint ministers, although they would be responsible to the assembly for their actions, and he would retain a 'suspensive veto'. This meant that he could delay legislation passed by the assembly for up to four years, but he could not entirely forbid (or veto) it. The king again withheld his approval.

The October Days

It was once more the actions of the Parisian crowds that pushed the revolution forward in the 'October Days'. A regiment of the King's Guard, which had been stationed in Flanders, returned to Versailles, where a banquet was held to celebrate its return. At this, the revolutionary cockade was mocked and trampled on and the white colour of the Bourbons was toasted. News of these activities was soon spread to a Parisian crowd that was once again facing an acute food shortage. It was too much for the women of the city, who stormed the *commune*'s headquarters, demanding bread – and then marched to Versailles to complain to the king and the assembly. Around 6000–7000 women, followed by 20,000 of the National Guard, invaded the assembly and sent a deputation to the king. Several of the royal bodyguard were killed before the National Guard managed to restore order. This *journée* had come about through a mixture of economic desperation and political fear, but its effect was enormous.

The march on Versailles by women of Paris, hungry for bread. Contemporary engraving.

à Versailles à Versailles 5 Octobre 1789

Louis was forced to give in. He approved the August Decrees and Declaration of the Rights of Man, promised to provide grain for Paris and agreed to return from Versailles to Paris with his wife and son. This was a defeat, not only for Louis XVI, but also for the assembly, which meekly followed him to the Tuileries palace. Many of the deputies felt just as much at the mercy of the Parisians as he did. Most had hoped to work out some sort of compromise with the king but, in the hostile atmosphere of Paris, this seemed much less likely.

The king lost all control of the situation as the *intendants* fled, members of the Third Estate seized control in the towns, and militias, rather like the Paris National Guard, were set up throughout France in defence of the revolution.

THE WORK OF THE CONSTITUENT ASSEMBLY

Between 1789 and 1791, the Constituent Assembly worked on the details of how to replace the governmental and administrative structure of the *ancien régime*. In many ways, it had proved easier to destroy the old system than create a new one. However, the Constituent Assembly eventually produced a system, which, despite later political changes, laid the foundations for subsequent French government.

A new constitution and electorate

- The new constitution, sometimes described as the Constitutional Monarchy, was based on the king, who retained 'supreme power' but only a four-year veto on law, and an elected National Assembly.
- The right to vote was restricted. Citizens were divided into two groups and only 'active citizens' received the vote. 'Active citizens' (who had the right to vote in the first stage of both local and national elections) were males over the age of 25 who had lived in one place for a year and paid the equivalent of three days' labour in taxes.
- To stand for office, or vote in the second stage of elections, an individual was required to pay the equivalent of ten days' labour in taxes.
- To become a deputy in the National Assembly, an individual had to pay the equivalent of 50 days' labour (known as a *marc d'argent* – a silver mark or 52 livres) in taxes.

This meant that, despite the Declaration of Rights, only 61 per cent of Frenchmen and no women had the right to take part in the first stage of elections, and far fewer at the higher levels, with only one in a hundred eligible to stand as a deputy. The system was a great leap forward from the *ancien régime*, but became a grievance of the Sans Culottes, since it favoured the wealthy and ensured bourgeois control of government at local and national levels. It left almost a quarter of adult males as 'passive citizens', unable to vote at all. Nevertheless, this was the widest franchise in Europe at the time.

Local administration

- French local government was reorganised and **decentralised** under a new three-tier system of *départements*, districts and *communes*. (There were to be 83 *départements*, which were in turn subdivided into 547 districts, which were further divided into 43,360 *communes*.)
- At each level, officials were elected to the ruling councils by active citizens.

- Councils were responsible for law and order within their localities and were given a range of specific duties, from the assessment and collection of taxes and the construction of public amenities, such as roads, to the maintenance of churches, and supervision of the local National Guard. (Later laws added to these duties, which came to include the registration of births, marriages and deaths, the requisition of grain and duties to root out opponents of revolution.)

Local government therefore fell largely into the hands of the educated bourgeoisie – men of some wealth, but selected on their merits. Problems occurred, however, where there were insufficient educated men to fill offices, and in some rural *communes*, there were just too few literate people.

The law
- In accordance with the principles of the Declaration of Rights, justice was to be free, fair and available to everyone.
- A single legal system was to be established (replacing the old muddle of different laws in different parts of France).
- Torture, branding and hanging were forbidden and fewer crimes were to be punishable by death – and that was to be by decapitation, formerly only available to the nobility.
- A new system of law courts based on the local *départements* was to replace the old *parlements* and feudal and church courts. Tribunals were established at each level of local government plus a central court of appeal and a high court for cases of treason. At the lowest level, justices of the peace would deal with minor civil cases, while more serious cases would go to the district courts.
- Judges and magistrates were to be elected, by active citizens, from a panel of suitably qualified candidates. The judges of the Court of Appeal would be elected by the *départements*.
- Criminal cases were to be tried in front of a jury of twelve citizens within each *département*.

The reforms brought a considerable improvement to the quality of justice. It became cheaper, fairer and one of the most enlightened systems in Europe.

Financial reform

Since financial crisis had been one of the causes of the revolution and had played a major role in the developments of 1788–9, it was essential to consider how to rebuild the economy, finance government and put France in a stronger economic position in the future. In this task the assembly largely failed. Too many (especially peasants) thought taxation had gone for good, and attempts to impose new taxes met with resistance, so that the assembly was forced to rely on short-term measures.

- The initial attempt to retain and collect the old taxes until 1791, in order to keep France financially solvent, met such opposition and avoidance that the *gabelle* (salt tax) was withdrawn in March 1790 and nearly all the other unpopular **indirect taxes** (except for external customs duties), within the next year. The **direct taxes** of the *taille* and twentieth were replaced by a new tax on land and property in 1791, similar to that proposed by Calonne in 1787.
- Free trade in grain was introduced (August 1789) and in other products (1790–1). Internal tariffs disappeared and a unified system of weights and measures was established.
- The old restrictive guilds (which controlled entry to trades) disappeared in 1791, but trade unions and strikes were declared illegal.
- In a bid to gain short-term finance, in November 1789 it was announced that church property would be sold for the benefit of the state. In return, the government undertook to pay the salaries of clergy directly, and to take over the Church's role in education and poor relief.
- Nobles who emigrated would have their property confiscated and sold.
- *Assignats* were issued to aid the purchase of land and these became a form of paper currency, which could be acquired by anyone and used for ordinary business transactions. However, too many were printed, which led to inflation and prompted later economic disorder and social unrest.

While there were still unfair variations in taxes in different parts of France, the peasants paid less overall, and since exemptions had been removed, a more just system had been created. However, poverty remained and French

KEY TERM

Biens nationaux is the term given to the sale of nobles' and Church land. Most land was sold in large lots and went to those with capital. It was predominantly bought by the middle classes, as well as some richer peasants. This boosted the number of landowners, determined to defend their purchases against any counter-revolution.

finances remained in crisis. The sale of Church (and nobles') land, however, provided income in the short term and had the additional benefit of binding those who bought these lands (the *biens nationaux*) in support of the revolution.

The Civil Constitution of the Clergy

The work of the Constituent Assembly also extended to church reform. While the Catholic Church remained the official, state church, some of the abuses or privileges of the church as highlighted in the *cahiers* were removed.

- Tithes, *annates* (payments to the Pope) and the *don gratuit* (the right of the clergy to decide its own taxation) were abolished.
- Pluralism (the holding of more than one Church office) was forbidden.
- Monastic orders that provided no education or charitable work for the community were abolished (February 1790).
- Civil rights and toleration were granted to Protestants (December 1789) and, later, Jews (1792).
- The sale of Church lands (November 1789) was countered by the state payment of clerical salaries. For many, this meant a higher regular clerical income.
- The Church was reorganised on the same pattern as local government (July 1790).
- Every *département* was given a bishop (this created 83 bishoprics, replacing the old 135).
- The Pope could no longer confirm (accept/reject) bishops who, along with other clergy, were elected to their positions by active citizens. Clergy were required to reside in their dioceses and new salary scales were established. This was known as the Civil Constitution of the Clergy.

The changes to the position of the Church and the clergy before July 1790 (with the possible exception of equal civil rights for Protestants), met with no particular hostility. However, the changes in the organisation of the Church turned into a struggle over authority. When the bishops and clergy proposed a National Synod (meeting of the French Church), to discuss the matter, the assembly refused, on the grounds that separate Church assemblies had just been abolished. Louis XVI was reluctantly forced to accept the Civil Constitution in August 1790, leaving the clergy with little choice but to appeal to Pope Pius VI. Unfortunately for them, he was not willing to make a pronouncement as he was, at that stage, involved in negotiations with the government over his right to **Avignon**.

The assembly, under pressure from the anticlerical people of Paris, then demanded, in November 1790, that the clergy take an oath to the new constitution. The results were catastrophic. Only 7 bishops (out of 160, and 3 of those 7 were non-believers) and 55 per cent of clergy (with variation by region), were prepared to do so and, after April 1791, when the Pope finally declared against the Civil Constitution, even some of these retracted.

The controversy split the country. Those who refused to take the oath were known as non-jurors (non-swearers) or refractories, and were deemed enemies of the revolution. They had the support of the Pope and a good following in the strongly Catholic parts of France – the west, north and north-east and south of the Massif-Central. Many peasants feared (wrongly) that the assembly was trying to change their religion and turned against the revolution for the first time. Their fear of eternal damnation was far greater than their commitment to the revolution. So this was the crucial turning point, which helped end the national unity and led to the beginning of civil war and counter-revolution. As the historian D.G. Wright has pointed out, 'a gaping breach over the Church augured badly for the operation of a constitution which demanded a good deal of national unity and goodwill on all sides'.

SUMMARY QUESTIONS

1 In what ways did (a) the people of Paris and (b) the peasants alter the course of the revolution in 1789?

2 Write a list of points showing how France had changed from the beginning of 1789 to the end of 1790.

CHAPTER 5

Why did France become a republic in 1792?

KEY INSTITUTIONS

The Jacobin Club This was so called because it met in premises rented from the Dominicans or Jacobins.

Cordeliers Club This was named after the monastery of the Cordeliers where its members originally met. It was founded in 1790. It did not restrict admission, and represented radical and Sans Culottes opinion. It was expanded in 1791, when other popular clubs joined with it. Eventually, some members found policies too extreme and withdrew, leaving the club in the hands of the extremists, Hébertistes and the Enragés. For further information, see Chapter 6.

KEY PERSON

Georges Jacques Danton, (1759–94) A lawyer and one of the bourgeois leaders of the Cordeliers Club, Danton was politically energetic and a brilliant speaker. He rose to prominence in 1792 and had immense prestige. He associated with the Sans Culottes and made patriotic speeches in Paris in 1792 to rouse support for the war. He became Minister of Justice in the Republic, but disliked the extremes of the Terror. His calls for moderation led him to the guillotine in April 1794.

POLITICAL CLUBS

From May 1789, when the Estates-General first met, political clubs had begun to spring up in Paris and elsewhere. Since there were no political parties, these clubs played an important role in keeping the public informed of events and acting as pressure groups to influence the assembly. One of the most prominent was the **Jacobin Club**, founded in 1789. It charged a high entrance fee and was well supported by wealthy liberal-constitutional monarchists. Robespierre led a minority group of more radical Jacobins. By early 1791, there were 90 such clubs.

The **Cordeliers Club**, founded in 1790, was more radical. It did not restrict admission and, although led by members of the bourgeoisie, such as **Danton** and Desmoulins, it had a widespread working-class following. It was hostile to the active/passive citizen distinction of the new constitution and its chief spokesman, **Marat**, edited a newspaper, *L'Ami du Peuple*, which attacked all those who had enjoyed privileges under the *ancien régime*. Another popular paper was **Hébert's** *Père Duchesne*.

The clubs, pamphlets and newspapers thrived on the discontent of the masses, linking economic protest to political demands.

THE FLIGHT TO VARENNES

Although the Constituent Assembly worked hard to bring the revolution to a close by providing a moderate constitution and sound administrative framework for France, their efforts were undermined in two ways. One was the increasing pressure they were placed under from the radicals within the political clubs, and the other was the unreliability of the king himself. Although Louis had accepted the various changes, he had done so with reluctance and often gave the impression that he was merely biding time until he could re-exert his authority.

The king's untrustworthiness was reinforced by his attempted flight on the night of 20/21 June 1791. His plans were shrouded in secrecy, but one suggestion is that he intended to travel to Montmédy in Lorraine (on the Luxembourg border). Here, he hoped to gain the protection of the royalist military commander and, from this much stronger position, renegotiate the terms of the new constitution with the Constituent Assembly. His brother, the Comte de Provence, on the other hand, claimed his intention was to leave France and return with the backing of his brother-in-law, Emperor Leopold II, and the Austrian armies, a move Marie Antoinette was known to favour. Certainly, the direction chosen allowed for both possibilities but whatever his intentions, he only reached Varennes (30 miles short of the border). He was brought back to Paris in disgrace and to the numbing silence of the hostile crowds. His action had destroyed his last vestiges of support and Parisians began to talk seriously, for the first time, of the idea of a republic.

The assembly faced a dilemma. Its mostly moderate members were not in favour of such a radical step and believed developments were going too far. To them a republic meant rule by the 'mob' and they feared civil (internal) war, and the opposition of hostile European monarchies. On the other hand, the king had shown his unreliability and the 'constitutional monarchy' which they had favoured looked unworkable.

On 16 July 1791, the assembly voted to suspend the authority of the king temporarily. This was followed by an intense debate over the king's fate, both inside and outside the assembly. Members of the Cordeliers Club argued that the king should be dethroned or put on trial. Some Jacobins, under Robespierre, also supported this view, but the majority of Jacobins, who were more moderate, broke

Jean-Paul Marat (1744–93) Trained as a doctor, Marat suffered from a painful skin disease and his unpleasant appearance was made worse by the way he deliberately wore dirty clothes as a sign of his position as *L'ami du peuple* (friend of the people). In his newspaper of the same name, he expressed his radical views. He believed in the power of the masses and was idolised by the Sans Culottes. He helped provoke the prison massacres of September 1792 and was an important force behind the Jacobin Terror, demanding 'blood and heads'. He was murdered in his bath by Charlotte Corday, a Girondin sympathiser, in July 1793.

Jacques René Hébert (1755–94) Hébert was the son of a goldsmith and his neat appearance and polite behaviour hid his talent for vulgarity and abuse. He was a prominent leader of the Sans Culottes and helped coordinate the *journée* of 5 September 1793. He supported the Terror and favoured the campaign for dechristianisation. He eventually grew too extreme even for Robespierre, who had him guillotined. He was the last great Sans Culottes leader and after his death their power began to wane.

KEY INSTITUTION

Feuillant Club This club was formed by a group of moderate revolutionaries who reacted against the more extreme republicans of the Jacobin Club. The members wanted to preserve a constitutional monarchy.

KEY TERM

Martial law is when normal rights are suspended and the people are subject to the law of the army. This meant that individuals could be arrested and held without trial, tried by a military court (without a jury) and condemned to death, without appeal, if found guilty.

away to form the new **Feuillant Club**. As the Cordeliers and Jacobins attracted more radical support, a stream of petitions was sent to the assembly, demanding the king be removed from power and put on trial.

THE DEMONSTRATION AT THE CHAMPS DE MARS, PARIS, 17 JULY 1791

The Champs de Mars meeting was organised by the Cordeliers Club to gain signatures for another petition. Fifty thousand Parisians attended, and disorder threatened, particularly after two suspected government 'spies' were discovered beneath the central platform. The Paris Commune feared trouble, declared **martial** (military) **law** and sent Lafayette and the National Guard to disperse the crowd. He opened fire and killed fifty, the first occasion the revolutionary movement had divided. Moderate revolutionaries fired on the more radical elements, and this division hardened over the next month as several popular leaders were arrested and others, such as Marat and Danton were forced into hiding. This was a victory for the moderates and the Feuillants, who subsequently controlled Paris and the assembly and who were determined that an agreement must be made with the king.

THE 1791 CONSTITUTION

The various changes brought about by the Constituent Assembly were finally put together in the new constitution of September 1791, which redefined the position of the king and the assembly. The king was to retain his hereditary position and appoint ministers, but his power was severely curtailed. He could no longer veto laws relating to the constitution or finance. He retained his suspensive veto in other matters but it was to be the assembly, not he, who determined foreign policy and assumed responsibility for the declaration of war.

The Constituent Assembly had finally completed the task it had set itself although, in the circumstances, this constitution looked extremely unlikely to work.

Nevertheless, it was time for the Constituent Assembly to disband and allow elections to take place under the new system it had created. Before it did so, however, a further resolution was passed, under the influence of Robespierre, that no member of the Constituent Assembly could be re-elected to the next assembly. This was known as the self-denying ordinance and Robespierre hoped to reduce the moderate influence through it.

THE LEGISLATIVE ASSEMBLY

The next assembly, which met on 1 October 1791, was known as the Legislative Assembly, as its job was to make laws.

Its deputies were almost entirely bourgeois. There were a few clergy, still fewer nobles and no peasants or artisans. The members of the Feuillant Club numbered some 264 deputies, while 136 belonged to the Jacobin Club and around 350 belonged to neither. The first two major laws discussed by the new assembly in November concerned the refractory priests and the *émigrés*.

The first declared all refractory clergy suspect. They were to lose their income and be treated as conspirators against the French nation. The second stated that any *émigrés* still out of France on 1 January 1792 would forfeit their property and be regarded as traitors. The king vetoed these laws in November, which only increased his unpopularity still further.

THE ORIGINS OF WAR

When the revolution broke out in France, the other powers of Europe had been happy to let events in France take their course. Some, such as the Prussians, were pleased to see the great power of France weakened by internal troubles. Others, such as the British, were sympathetic to the demands for greater liberty. However, the plight of the king and the growing radicalisation of the revolution changed this.

The revolution posed a challenge to monarchy and the Emperor Leopold II, brother of Marie Antoinette, felt obliged to provide Louis XVI with some appearance of support. In association with Frederick-William II of Prussia, he issued the Declaration of Pillnitz in August 1791, in which he expressed a readiness to join the other nations of Europe in helping to restore Louis XVI's powers. The declaration was, in reality, only a gesture. Leopold knew full well that countries such as Britain would never join an alliance to restore Louis XVI, and Russia was more concerned with Poland. However, Marie Antoinette had other ideas and maintained a secret correspondence with the Austrians. She believed war was the only way to defeat the hated revolutionaries, and thought the revolutionary armies would be easily overcome.

Within France there were differing attitudes to the prospect of war:

- Some army commanders, such as Lafayette, favoured war. Disillusioned by the development of the revolution, Lafayette now believed that the power of the monarchy should be strengthened, and he wanted a short, successful war to boost his own prestige and enable him to dictate new terms to the king and assembly.
- The Brissotins, deputies named after their leader Jacques Brissot, supported war for different reasons. They were hostile to the monarchy and believed a war would strengthen support for the revolution. It would expose those counter-revolutionaries within France – the refractory priests, 'unpatriotic' peasants, monarchists and nobles – and rouse support for the revolution. It would, they believed, lead to the defeat of the *émigrés* abroad and would help spread liberty to other oppressed nations of Europe. This group merged with some deputies from the Gironde in southern France and were also known as the **Girondins**.
- Outside the assembly, however, Robespierre (who could not be a member because he had sat in the Constituent Assembly) was one of the minority who were hostile to war. He believed Lafayette and other generals wanted war to overthrow the new constitution, and that war would destroy the revolution, but few heeded his words.

KEY TERM

Girondins This was the name given to the deputies from the Gironde *département*. Although they favoured the revolution, they disagreed with the Jacobins on a number of major issues. They spoke for federalism – giving more power to the localities – and disliked authority being centred on Paris. They grew increasingly hostile to Robespierre, whom they felt was leading the revolution along too radical a path, and was too reliant on the Sans Culottes, whose violence they disliked.

Louis was happy to go along with the clamour for war, hoping it would suit his own ends. In early 1792, he appointed a group of Girondin ministers, including the Foreign Minister, Dumouriez, who were intent on war. When, on 7 February 1792, Prussia and Austria joined forces with the aim of intimidating the French and, in March, Leopold of Austria died and was replaced by the young and more venturesome Francis II, the French decided the time was ripe to declare war on Austria (20 April). Prussia joined Austria the next month.

THE IMPACT OF WAR

The French armies were not prepared for war. They had been weakened by the many changes imposed by the revolution, in particular the loss of many noble generals. Organisation was confused, with muddles over recruitment, training and discipline, which made them no match for their enemies. By April, defeat in the Austrian Netherlands (Belgium) forced the French armies to retreat and left the French border open to invasion and, by May, Lafayette was begging the assembly to make peace.

The war and its failures divided the French nation further. The pro-war lobby blamed the failure of the troops on counter-revolutionaries at home. The court, nobles, refractory priests and other traitors were accused of passing secrets to the enemy. In May, the assembly passed laws to deport refractory priests, disband the King's Guard and set up a camp for 20,000 National Guards (*fédérés*) from the provinces to protect Paris, but Louis vetoed the laws. It looked as though Louis was trying to undermine the French efforts, particularly when he dismissed his pro-war Girondin ministers.

This led to another demonstration, or *journée*, in Paris, led by members of the radical Cordeliers Club. On 20 June, 8000 demonstrators, now calling themselves the Sans Culottes, stormed into the Tuileries, demanding that Louis XVI withdraw his veto and restore his Girondin ministers. Louis acted with dignity and did not give in, even though he was forced to wear a cap of liberty (the *bonnet rouge*) and drink the health of the nation.

The power of the king was diminishing as that of the radical masses was growing. In response to their demands, the assembly went ahead and established a *fédéré* camp, despite the king's opposition. It even issued a decree – '*la patrie en danger*' (the fatherland in danger) – on 11 July, which called on all men to support the war effort and added that, in view of the present troubles, its decrees would no longer require the sanction of the king. When the radicals responded to the call to arms by arguing that if all men were to be required to fight, then all should have the vote, 'passive citizenship' was abandoned.

When the commander in chief of the Austro-Prussian army issued the **Brunswick Manifesto** on 1 August, threatening death to those who opposed his advance and vengeance on Paris should any harm come to the king, this further increased the tension. The 'moderate' revolution of 1789 was at an end and as the largely republican *fédérés* from the provinces began to mass in Paris, bringing with them a new patriotic song – the **Marseillaise** – it seemed that the radicalism of the Sans Culottes had won the day.

THE BIRTH OF THE REPUBLIC

The transition from a constitutional monarchy to a republic was indeed brought about by the action of the Sans Culottes. Despairing of the assembly's failure to respond to the many petitions for the king's overthrow, on 9 August, the Sans Culottes took over the Hôtel de Ville and set up a new revolutionary *commune*. From here, on the morning of 10 August, a force of around 20,000 Sans Culottes and members of the National Guard, together with 2000 *fédérés*, marched to the king's palace of the Tuileries. Although the king and his family had already fled to the nearby assembly, the forces opened fire on the king's Swiss guards, killing around 600. In the fierce fighting that followed around 300 Sans Culottes and 90 *fédérés* were killed or wounded. The radicals invaded the assembly and demanded that the king be handed to them and imprisoned

KEY TERMS

Brunswick Manifesto This manifesto was intended to help Louis XVI. It declared that the Parisians were collectively responsible for the king's safety and that if he or his family were harmed in any way the Parisians would suffer 'an exemplary vengeance … delivering the city of Paris to a military execution'. Furthermore, it threatened any National Guards captured fighting with punishment 'as rebels to their king'. The effect of the declaration was to turn even more Frenchmen against the monarchy.

Marseillaise Five days after the declaration of war, a young army engineer, Rouget de Lisle, who had formerly earned a minor reputation as a composer in Paris, was asked to produce a marching song for the Strasbourg garrison. He produced what was to become known as 'La Marseillaise', a rousing anthem which expressed in words and music the great themes of the revolution – family, comradeship, blood and soil. It received its name when a group of *fédérés* brought it from Marseilles.

in **the Temple**. The assembly was forced to respond to the Sans Culottes' demands. By that evening, the king had been suspended from office and imprisoned. Furthermore, it had been agreed that elections would be held as soon as possible, with universal male suffrage, for a new assembly.

Various factors account for the failure of the constitutional monarchy:

- The king's own inflexibility – had Louis really been prepared to accept the changes and work towards a successful constitutional monarchy, he might have kept his throne.
- His willingness to listen to his wife and sister (Madame Elisabeth), his attempt at flight, his use of the veto and his untrustworthiness, particularly after the outbreak of war.
- The split among the revolutionaries themselves, divided between moderates and the radicals, with the latter winning increasing support in the atmosphere of war. Former supporters of the king, particularly liberal nobles, fled abroad as the mood grew more militant.
- The economic troubles and fear and hardship engendered by the war, which exacerbated existing tensions.

Until the new assembly – to be known as the National Convention – could be elected, the *commune* took control in Paris. Many moderates fled the old assembly, and those left, under Danton, largely obeyed the orders of the *commune*. They agreed that refractory priests should be deported and, in order to win over the peasantry, it was decreed that the remaining feudal dues should be abolished without further compensation and that *émigré* lands should be sold in small lots.

THE SEPTEMBER MASSACRES

During the month of August, the war situation grew steadily worse. Lafayette deserted to the Austrians and the Prussians crossed the French frontier. By September, they had reached Verdun, the last major fortress on the road to

The Temple Prison The Temple was a medieval castle in Paris which had formerly belonged to Louis's brother the Comte d'Artois. Louis and his family were imprisoned here, lodged on two floors together with a catering staff of 13 and a valet. The king was deprived of newspapers, but books were brought in on request from the king's libraries. However, he was made to suffer petty indignities. Men remained seated in his presence and no longer removed their hats.

'Departure of the Paris National Guard', September 1792. Painting by Leon Coginet, 1836.

Paris. Danton pleaded for volunteers and thousands of Parisians joined the fight to defend the capital. Their departure, however, only added to the fears of those left behind.

On 11 August, the assembly had granted powers to local authorities to arrest those suspected of 'counter-revolution', such as refractory priests and noblemen. Rumours began to spread that the priests and nobles in the Parisian jails were planning to escape and hand Paris to the Prussians. Jean-Paul Marat, one of the *commune*'s leaders, called for the conspirators to be killed.

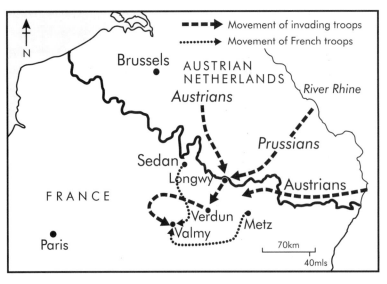

With the fall of Longwy and Verdun to Austrian and Prussian troops, the roads to Paris lay open. They were met by combined French troops at Valmy and defeated (September 1792).

From 2 to 6 September, the Sans Culottes began 'visiting' the prisons and massacring their inmates. Probably around 1400, and possibly as many as 2000, of the 2600 prisoners held in Paris were murdered even though most of them were only common criminals.

Elections for the new Convention were taking place during this atmosphere of crisis and fear, and many Girondin deputies from the provinces were shocked by the massacres. They turned against the Jacobins and their Sans Culottes supporters, describing them as *buveurs du sang* (drinkers of blood). However, the massacres came to an end with news of the French victory over the Prussians at Valmy on 20 September 1792 – the same day that the new Convention opened. This reversed the tide of war, removed the threat to Paris and appeared to justify the revolution. The future began to look brighter. The fight for 'liberty, equality, fraternity' appeared to be succeeding.

THE NATIONAL CONVENTION

There was a good deal of intimidation during the elections to the Convention, with many royalist sympathisers disenfranchised (their vote was taken away), so it was not surprising that all those elected for Paris (24 members) were Jacobins and republicans. Robespierre headed the poll there. They were supported by the Jacobins from the French provinces and soon won the nickname the **Montagnards** (the Mountaineers) because they occupied the high seats on the left of the assembly hall. On the other side of the hall were the Girondins from the provinces, and in the (flat) centre, a moderate, middle group who became known as 'the Plain'.

The 782 deputies were predominantly bourgeois and they actually agreed on most policies. They favoured a republic, wanted to win the war and sought enlightened reform in France. However, they differed in their sources of support and were deeply suspicious of one another's motives. Whereas the Jacobins were supported by the Sans Culottes and the popular clubs of Paris, the Girondin following was stronger in the provinces, and their hostility to the *journée* of 10 August lost them the support of the more militant elements of the community. The Jacobins suspected the Girondins of seeking conservative compromise, while the Girondins feared the Jacobins would stop at nothing, including bloodshed, to serve their purposes. While the Girondins favoured decentralisation – in accordance with the ideas of the Constituent Assembly – the Jacobins believed Paris was the heart of the revolution and favoured greater centralisation for the duration of the war emergency. They vied with one another for the support of the Plain.

The first decree of the Convention, on 21 September, was to abolish the monarchy and proclaim a republic. There was great excitement that this was the dawn of a new era, and this spirit was picked up in the birth of a **new calendar**, in which subsequent years were to be dated from the first day of the Republic.

The French republican calendar

Revolutionary month	Reference	Gregorian calendar
Vendémiaire	*Vintage*	22 Sept–21 Oct
Brumaire	*Fog*	22 Oct–20 Nov
Frimaire	*Frost*	21 Nov–20 Dec
Nivôse	*Snow*	21 Dec–19 Jan
Pluviôse	*Rain*	20 Jan–18 Feb
Ventôse	*Wind*	19 Feb–20 Mar
Germinal	*Buds*	21 Mar–19 Apr
Floréal	*Flowers*	20 Apr–19 May
Prairial	*Meadows*	20 May–18 Jun
Messidor	*Reaping*	19 Jun–18 Jul
Thermidor	*Heat*	19 Jul–17 Aug
Fructidor	*Fruit*	18 Aug–16 Sep
Sans-culottides	*National holidays*	17 Sep–21 Sep

SUMMARY QUESTIONS

1 Why did it prove impossible to establish a constitutional monarchy (one with limited power) in France?

2 Why did France go to war in April 1792 and what effect did this have on the revolution?

CHAPTER 6

What effect did the war and the Terror have on France, 1793–4?

The execution of the king

The biggest problem facing the new Convention was the fate of the king. Robespierre, Danton and Marat, supported by the Montagnards, favoured trial and execution, in response to the demands of the Sans Culottes. Brissot and other Girondins accepted a trial but were reluctant to kill the king.

For several months, the Girondins were able to hold off the Jacobin arguments. They benefited from the continued **French success in war**, as the armies went on the offensive and successfully advanced to the left bank of the Rhine. On 19 November 1792, the Convention issued the 'Edict of Fraternity' (brotherhood), promising aid to all oppressed people. By January 1793, the military success looked set to restore France's 'natural' frontiers – the Rhine, the Alps and the Pyrenees.

Meanwhile, however, the discovery of a chest containing papers that seemed to prove that the king had corresponded with the revolution's enemies, had proved sufficient to force a trial. This began on 10 December and Marat insisted that each deputy announced his decision publicly, claiming this was the only way to root out traitors. In such circumstances, no one dared declare him innocent. Of 721 deputies, 693 declared him guilty, 361 voted unconditionally for the death penalty and 319 for imprisonment. When the Girondins proposed a reprieve, the Convention rejected this by 387 votes to 334.

Louis XVI was publicly executed by **guillotine** on 21 January 1793. This was a victory for the Montagnards and the Sans Culottes, whose suspicions of the Girondins had grown even greater over the preceding months. The Montagnards were now able to dominate the Convention,

KEY POINTS

French success in war The Girondin General Dumouriez occupied Belgium, after defeating the Austrians at Jemappes (Belgium) in November, and in the south, Savoy (Nov 1792) and Nice (Jan 1793) were annexed.

The guillotine Compared to earlier methods of execution, this was more humane. Its name (but not its existence) came from Dr Joseph Guillotin, who campaigned to have the privilege of a more humane execution extended to all social classes, not just the aristocracy. It was new to France, but it had been used in other countries, including Scotland during Elizabethan times. French guillotines were made to order in Germany and constructed under the supervision of the Academy of Surgeons.

even though a good number of Girondins had voted for the death penalty.

The spread of war

Encouraged by the successes of the French armies during 1792, the Convention declared war on Britain and the **United Provinces** in February 1793 and, a month later, on Spain. The declaration against Britain was undertaken in the mistaken belief that Britain was ripe for revolution too. In any case, Britain, like most other powers of Europe, had been alarmed by the French Edict of Fraternity and talk of natural frontiers. The British were particularly opposed to French plans to extend the northern border to the 'natural' frontier of the Rhine. This involved the annexation of all of the Austrian Netherlands (Belgium) as well as a large part of the United Provinces and was regarded as a potential threat to British trade and security.

France found that it had undertaken more than it could cope with. The French Girondin General Dumouriez was defeated by the Austrians at Neerwinden in March and deserted to the enemy, together with the Duc de Chartres, the son of the 'liberal' Duc d'Orléans (Philippe Egalité), who would become the future King Louis-Philippe. This weakened the Girondins' position in the Convention, as the French were once again placed on the defensive. They lost Belgium and the left bank of the Rhine and, by the summer, were once again threatened with invasion by Austrian and Spanish forces.

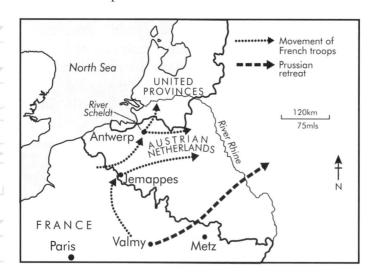

With the victory of Jemappes, the invasion of the Austrian Netherlands (Belgium) and the reopening of the River Scheldt to trade by all, Britain was brought into the war in 1793.

Internal difficulties and the rising in the Vendée

The situation in France was grim during the first half of 1793. The expansion of the war was accompanied by growing economic difficulties. War forced up prices and the Convention tried to pay for the war by printing more *assignats*. Although the 1792 harvest was good, farmers were reluctant to sell their grain for what was becoming the worthless paper money, so bread was again in short supply.

In these circumstances, the Convention faced several risings within France. These were partly a protest against the *levées*, partly a reaction to economic hardship and fear, and partly a genuine protest against the way the revolution had developed, in particular the measures against refractory priests and nobles.

The **rising in the Vendée**, a rural region in western France, which began in February 1793, reflected all these causes. It broke out among peasants who found themselves paying a large amount of land tax (more than under the *ancien régime*). Led by local nobles, whose royalist views were added to the peasants' resentment, the frustration of the people was directed at the new local officials, constitutional priests and National Guards, who were rooted out and massacred. The situation became so serious that the Convention had to order 30,000 to leave the front to deal with the rebels.

Control in wartime

The Convention faced a very difficult situation. There was a call for more radical measures to ensure the Convention maintained control of the country and prevented a political and economic collapse in the face of external and internal threats. For this purpose, a number of 'emergency' measures were taken between March and May:

- *The Revolutionary Tribunal* was set up in Paris (10 March) to try those accused of counter-revolutionary activities.
- *Representatives-on-mission* were appointed from among the deputies to go out into the provinces to speed up conscription and to check up on the conduct of army generals. They had wide powers to take over local government and enforce decrees.

KEY TERM

Levées The enforced conscription of men to serve in the army.

KEY EVENT

Rising in the Vendée The area was strongly Catholic and there had been much hostility to the Church 'reforms' and the sale of church lands. The final straw was a demand for troops from the area.

- *Comités de surveillance* (watch or revolutionary committees) were set up in each *commune* and in each *section* of major towns to watch foreigners and suspected traitors. They also received extensive power under a decree that allowed them to try (without jury or appeal), and execute, armed rebels within 24 hours of capture.
- *The Committee of Public Safety* (CPS) was set up (6 April, but reformed in July) with authority over ministers to coordinate the war effort inside and outside France. Its duty was to supervise and speed up activities during the crisis. It was still responsible to the Convention, which renewed its powers each month, but it soon became a powerful instrument of government.
- *The Committee of General Security* (CGS) was a 12-man committee responsible for rooting out counter-revolutionaries and dealing with matters of internal security. It controlled an extensive spy network and ran a secret revolutionary police force.
- *The Armées révolutionnaires* (added in September) were groups of Sans-Culotte volunteers who acted on behalf of the authorities, seizing grain, attacking anyone found to be hoarding and helping destroy counter-revolutionaries.
- *The Maximum* (4 May) was the name given to a law that established the maximum price that could be charged for grain. (In September, prices of other goods too were fixed at the 1790 level plus one third, and wages at the 1790 level plus a half.)
- *A compulsory loan* (May) was imposed on the wealthy and it was also decreed that the property of all *émigrés* was to be confiscated and they would be executed if they returned to France.
- *Rationing cards* were issued to ensure the fair distribution of bread and meat.
- *The death penalty* was established for hoarding.

Although these measures helped establish control and went some way towards alleviating the lot of the poor and preventing bread riots, the use of restrictive controls did undermine some of the very principles that the early revolutionaries had fought for. They also reversed the Girondin and revolutionary idea of decentralisation.

Maximilien Robespierre, 1758–94. Portrait by Joseph Boze.

The fall of the Girondins

This legislation was another blow to the Girondins who had never been popular with the Sans Culottes. The Girondins feared the radicalism of the Sans Culottes and tried to pass laws to limit the powers of the Paris Commune. In turn, the Sans Culottes believed the Girondins were too moderate and blamed them for the failures of war. A group of extremists, known as the Enragés (madmen), and journalists such as Marat and Hébert led the attack on them as 'the enemy of the revolution'. On 2 June, 80,000 National Guards surrounded the Convention. Encouraged by Robespierre, the Jacobin leader, they demanded the expulsion of the Girondins. Twenty-nine Girondin deputies and two ministers were arrested. It was once more a display of the power of the Parisian masses and, in June, two decrees, a new declaration of rights and a new constitution were declared, in response to popular pressure. The declaration included the right of people to work, to have assistance when in need and to be educated. It gave the vote to all adult males and asserted that rebellion was acceptable in the interests of the revolution. It was a reflection of just how influential the Sans Culottes had become, but it was suspended for the duration of the war.

The control of France in war

Control was now in the hands of the Jacobin Montagnards who dominated the new Committee of Public Safety. **Robespierre**, who joined the CPS at the end of July, was a dominant personality throughout this period, and was known as the 'incorruptible', for his insistence on putting the good of the country (as he understood it) above all other considerations. Under his influence, the committee was prepared to take decisive and radical steps.

However, there was no clear dividing line between the various 'emergency' bodies that had been set up. The watch committees, the representatives-on-mission and the revolutionary armies, as well as the central committees, all tended to act as they saw fit, which has led to the period of July–December 1793 being labelled 'the **anarchic** terror'.

Food riots broke out in Paris and, on 13 July Marat, the hero of the Sans Culottes, was murdered by a young Girondin, Charlotte Corday. His martyrdom led to an outburst of indignation in Paris.

The federalist revolt

Worse still was the anti-Jacobin activity in the provinces. There was resentment of the new central controls. Sixty *départements* protested against the expulsion of the Girondins and there were serious conflicts in eight *départements* and the cities of Lyons, Marseilles and Bordeaux, as well as some smaller towns. This is sometimes known as the federalist revolt, and was not anti-revolutionary, but anti-Jacobin and anti-Paris.

However, in places it became serious. Troops had to be sent to Marseilles to retake the city after its Jacobin officials were executed. Lyons was besieged for two months before it gave in, in October 1793. In Toulon, the Convention resorted to cutting off food supplies in an attempt to halt opposition, but this led the town authorities to appeal to the British enemy, who occupied the city on 28 August. It was not until the young general Napoleon Bonaparte led the attack against the Jacobins and British in December that order was restored. However, since there was little cooperation between the various provincial revolts, the revolutionary armies were gradually able to retake most areas in the autumn and, by the end of 1793, the worst of the revolt had passed.

The war effort

As well as internal revolt, France also faced difficulties as the war continued to go badly for France throughout the summer of 1793. France itself was invaded by the Austrians in the north and the Spaniards in the south. The British had troops on the Netherlands border. Recriminations flew. 'Suspect' army generals were blamed for failures, and General Custine, for example, was brought to trial and guillotined on suspicion of passing secrets to the enemy.

The spread and threat of war called for a major overhaul of military and economic planning.

In August 1793, **Carnot** ordered a *levée en masse* to
provide soldiers for the armies and set up state factories for
arms and ammunition. Church bells and religious vessels
were melted down to provide raw materials and the
government assumed control of foreign trade and shipping.
The efforts of every citizen were deemed important.
Women and children were required to make uniforms and
other necessary items, and even the elderly were told to
lend their voices in encouraging the young to fight.

This massive war effort, and the failure of the allied
commanders to coordinate their plans, was eventually to
turn the war in France's favour again but, for most of
1793, the situation remained uncertain, and was not
helped by the continuing economic problems. In Paris,
faced with grain shortages, starvation and unemployment,
the Sans Culottes marched on the Convention in another
journée, on 4–5 September 1793. Trouble was only averted
by the proclamation of a series of radical measures, which
ominously announced 'Terror is the order of the Day'.

The Terror

Between September and December 1793, the Convention
went into overdrive in its attempt to maintain food
supplies, round up 'enemies', and harness the nation's
energies for war. The *armée révolutionnaires*, beginning
with that in Paris, and then those in the provinces, were
ordered to track down deserters, hoarders, refractory priests
and other political enemies.

By the new Law of Suspects (17 September 1793), anyone
believed to be a danger to the Republic, whether through
royalist or Catholic sympathies, or simply by hoarding or
evading state laws, could be arrested, imprisoned
indefinitely without trial, or brought before the
Revolutionary Tribunal. Harsh justice and violence was
not a new feature of French life, but until this point it had
mainly come from the crowds rather than the authorities.
'What was new after September 1793,' writes D.G.
Wright, 'was that the **terror was organised** and became for
the first time a deliberate policy of government.'

In October, in response to Sans Culottes pressure, there
was a series of show trials, which led to the guillotining of

Marie Antoinette (16 October), 31 Girondin deputies (31 October), Philippe Egalité, Duc d'Orléans (6 November) and Mme Roland, wife of a Girondin ex-minister (9 November). As well as the showpieces in Paris, local watch committees, the revolutionary armies and the representatives-on-mission all pursued the course of 'revolutionary justice', with horrifying results.

Activity in the provinces was frequently more extreme than that in the capital. Moderates were replaced by militants in local government and, where there was rebellion, protestors

The spread of war, 1792–4.

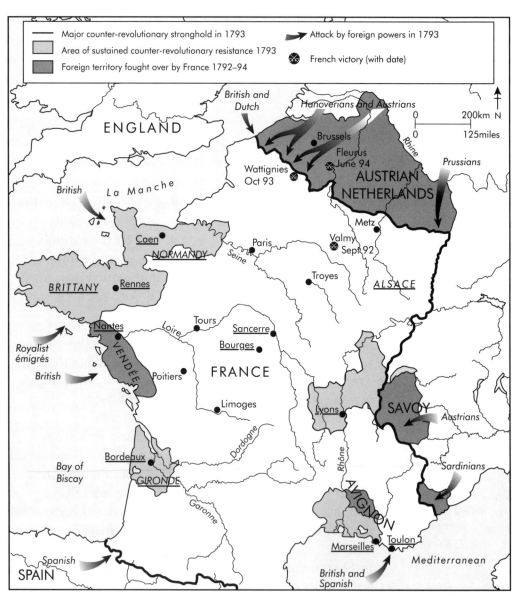

were crushed with terrific atrocities – massacres, mutilations and the burnings of farms and crops. Men and women were shot without trial and it was said that, by the time the rising in the Vendée had been crushed, the countryside was like a desert, with farms destroyed and famine forcing those left to flee.

Many acts of savagery were committed. In Nantes, the local representative-on-mission, Carrier, killed hundreds of prisoners by tying them up, naked, in sealed barges, which were then sunk in the River Loire. In deliberate mockery of the Catholic faith, these included monks and nuns, tied together in an underwater marriage (*noyade*). In Toulon, 800 were shot and a further 282 sent to the guillotine. Lyons, France's second city, was torched by its zealous representatives-on-mission, and suspect citizens were shot by cannon into previously dug mass graves.

Estimates of those killed in the Terror are unreliable and it must be remembered that, while some areas suffered huge losses, others were relatively unscathed.

Dechristianisation

The Terror was also a period of dechristianisation, when the Catholic Church came once more under attack. There was a campaign to close all churches by the spring of 1794, to destroy religious signs and symbols and force priests to marry or adopt orphans. The Paris Commune led the way and destroyed religious and royal statues, changed street names with religious connections and banned the wearing of clerical dress. The *commune* stopped paying clerical salaries in May 1793 and, in November, ordered the closure of all Parisian churches. **Notre Dame** became the 'Temple of Reason'.

The Convention seemed to encourage dechristianisation by sanctioning the deportation of any priest denounced by six citizens and supporting the new revolutionary calendar. However, despite its popularity among the Parisian Sans Culottes, dechristianisation met only with anger and suspicion among the more conservative rural peasantry. Robespierre was well aware of the dangers of too fierce a persecution and tried to get the Convention to end the

KEY FIGURES

Estimates of killings One study has cited 17,000 official executions (16 per cent in Paris and the rest in areas of revolt – 52 per cent in the Vendée and 19 per cent in the south-east). Of the victims, 28 per cent were peasants and around 31 per cent urban workers. If the number executed without trial or who died in prison is added the figure is probably around 50,000 and possibly as high as 60,000, of which probably around 15 per cent were nobility and clergy.

KEY PLACE

Notre Dame During the 'Festival of Reason' (November 1793), this towering gothic cathedral in Paris was renamed the Temple of Reason. A mountain made of papier-mâché and painted linen was built at the end of the nave and Liberty (an opera singer) dressed in white and holding a pike performed a ritual to visitors, bowing to the flame of reason and sitting on a bank of flowers and plants. The Jacobins were divided over such displays and when the Convention was invited to visit the Festival as a body, they refused.

attacks and, in the decree on 'the liberty of cults', religious toleration was confirmed. However, this had little effect in practice.

The role of Robespierre

The part of Robespierre in these years has been the subject of enquiry by a number of historians. He has been accused of betraying revolutionary principles by turning the Committee of Public Safety into a dictatorship. He spoke of a 'Republic of Virtue', in which men would be free and equal, and yet he seemed to believe the Terror was necessary to attain this goal. The real problem was that he believed he knew what was best for the people of France and, in his mind at least, this justified the means. He was, of course, only one of the Committee of Public Safety and he may have regarded the Terror as only a temporary stage, but it was his name that became most associated with its excesses.

Furthermore, although he disliked the crowds and more easily identified with the bourgeoisie, Robespierre was not afraid to use the Sans Culottes for his own ends. He was consequently very popular with the people of Paris, who referred to him as the 'incorruptible'.

The Committee of Public Safety

By the end of 1793, the federal revolt had been largely brought under control and **the war situation** seemed to be improving for France. Furthermore, there was some improvement in the economy, thanks to the price controls and the enforced loan on the rich. It might, therefore, have seemed an appropriate time to relax the controls and end the Terror.

However, by a law of 4 December (the Law of 14 Frimaire) it was decreed that the CGS and the CPS should have still greater powers. It was argued that there had been too many conflicting bodies, all supposedly acting in the interests of France, and that a more centralised system would provide more effective government. This was, in some ways, a step back to the system of the *ancien régime*. The CPS, supported by the CGS, was to assume responsibility for foreign policy and local government.

The war situation The Spanish and Piedmontese armies had been driven from the south in the autumn, and the British from Toulon. After the battle of Wattignies in October, the British and Austrians had left the north and, by December, moved east from Alsace also.

The revolutionary armies, except that of Paris, representatives-on-mission and all unofficial bodies, were disbanded and, in May 1794, the provincial revolutionary tribunals were abolished.

This was a blow to the Sans Culottes, whose anger was channelled into attacks on the CPS and Robespierre by their leader, Hébert. Robespierre soon countered this. In March 1794 he accused the Hébertistes of planning a military dictatorship, so sowing seeds of doubt among their followers and weakening the popular support that they had previously enjoyed. He sent their leader and 18 supporters to the guillotine without provoking the crowds and was then able to disband the Parisian revolutionary army and close potential places of opposition, the Cordeliers Club and other popular societies. He also turned on those who argued in favour of an end to the Terror, in particular Danton and Desmoulins. A **financial scandal** provided an excuse for Danton's execution in April 1794, followed by that of Desmoulins and other followers. Such examples stifled all criticism of the CPS.

Instead of ending the Terror, therefore, Robespierre merely led it forward to an even more intensive phase, centred on Paris. This is sometimes known as the Great Terror, to distinguish it from the earlier Anarchic Terror. Since all enemies of the revolution now had to be brought to Paris, a law was passed to speed up the work of the Revolutionary Tribunal. By the law of 10 June 1794 (22 Prairial), 'enemies of the people' were defined as those who had sought to 'mislead opinion … and corrupt the public conscience'. Trials were simply to determine liberty or death and the defendants had no rights. Such terms could include anyone. The result was another sudden increase in the number of executions. In the summer of 1794, over a thousand a month were being executed and virtually everyone brought before the Revolutionary Tribunal was condemned to death.

The end of Robespierre

For a while, Robespierre appeared supreme, but **his enemies were growing**. He also annoyed the CPS when he attempted to set up a police bureau under his own

KEY EVENT

Danton's financial scandal
Some of Danton's friends in the Convention had abused their position, winning financial advantages from the directors of the Company of the Indies in return for changes in favour of greater leniency in the law. Danton was not personally involved, although he was not averse to the idea of using favours to make government work, and he was hostile to the self-righteousness displayed by Robespierre and his followers. Nevertheless, he was accused, along with the crooks of the fraud, for, among other equally feeble charges, laughing whenever the word *vertu* (virtue) was mentioned.

KEY THEME

Robespierre's loss of support Robespierre had already lost many of his supporters among the Sans Culottes, with the execution of the Hébertistes, the dissolution of the popular societies, and the Maximum on wages. His vision, to unite all Frenchmen in the 'Cult of the Supreme Being', launched in May 1794, pleased no one, Catholics or non-Catholics.

authority to prosecute dishonest officials, so encroaching on their power.

After a brief disappearance from public life between 18 and 26 July, Robespierre returned to give the Convention a rambling speech, as of an exhausted man, which ended with an accusation that members of both the CGS and the CPS itself were turning against the revolution. He refused to give names, but those with whom he had quarrelled feared for their lives. On 27 July Robespierre was shouted down and arrested in the Convention, with his brother Augustin and his allies, Couthon and Saint-Just. Robespierre and 21 others were executed on 28 July. This was known as the Coup of Thermidor and those responsible, the Thermidorians (after the date 10 Thermidor). They were a mixture of men from the two committees, ex-supporters of the Terror and deputies of the moderate Plain. This event marked the end of revolutionary extremism. The Plain now emerged as the most dominant group and was joined by many Montagnards. The few remaining radical Jacobins were no more than a silent minority.

The Thermidorian Reaction

Even Robespierre's death failed to bring the Terror to a quick end, although the French armies were now doing well in war. The Austrians were defeated at Fleurus on 26 June 1794, permitting the recapture of the Austrian Netherlands (Belgium), and armies advanced to the north, south and east. However, the Terror was about to pass into its final phase.

The structures of the Great Terror did gradually disappear:

- The Revolutionary Tribunal was abolished on 31 May 1795, after a year with the comparatively small number of 63 executions.
- The Law of Prairial (June 1794) was repealed and most of those still held under its terms released from prison.
- The Jacobin Club was closed (November 1794).
- The powers of the great committees were curbed. The CPS lost its say in domestic affairs and a decree said that

25 per cent of the members of the two committees had to be changed each month.

- The Paris Commune was abolished.
- Moderates were restored to power in local government.
- Work began on a new constitution.
- The state stopped paying clerical salaries (September 1794) which formally separated the church from the state. Freedom for all religions was guaranteed (February 1795) although clerical dress and the use of church bells remained forbidden.
- The Law of Maximum was abandoned (December 1794) and public workshops restored to private ownership.

However, the country was in a bad state, economically. Massive inflation occurred as *assignats*, printed in excess to pay for the war, fell to less than 10 per cent of their original value. This was made worse by another poor harvest in 1794, and a severe winter of 1794–5 in which rivers froze and factories closed down. By the spring of 1795, the prospect of famine led to more trouble from the Sans Culottes.

The rising of Germinal (1 April 1795) was peaceful, although 10,000 people poured into the Convention to demand bread, but that of Prairial (20 May 1795) was rather more serious. **Women** and National Guards invaded the Convention and forced it to agree to a food commission. The next day, around 20,000 National Guards, joined by some gunners from the regular army, surrounded the building and aimed their cannons at the Convention. However, no one was prepared to open fire and the Convention soon regained control and was able to rely on sufficient forces to force the rebels' surrender. Six thousand were arrested and 42 National Guards and some Montagnard deputies executed. This was the Sans Culottes' final display. They had become divided. They no longer had the power of the revolutionary army and sections of the National Guard had remained loyal to the Convention. Without the Paris Commune to coordinate their activities, their days were numbered.

KEY THEME

Women, hunger and revolt Through the winter of 1794–5 a combination of economic collapse and freezing weather produced an increase in suicides, deaths and poverty. Farmers refused to sell for paper money and this hit hard at those who relied on fixed incomes, particularly the workers of Paris. It is little wonder, therefore, that housewives, desperate to feed their hungry families, were prominent among those that invaded the Convention.

Revolutionary governments 1789–95

(May–July) 1789 **National Assembly**	**Monarchy** King has right to veto (forbid) laws		Fall of Bastille (14 July) Great Fear in countryside (July)
1789–91 **Constituent Assembly**	**Constitutional Monarchy** Law-making assembly elected every 2 years King to appoint ministers and have 4-year suspensive veto	Abolition of feudalism (4 August) Administrative reform: Local administration Law Finance Church reform: Civil Constitution of the Clergy, 1790	October Days (1789) Flight to Varennes (June 1791) Growth of political clubs Massacre of the Champs de Mars (17 July 1791) War and fear of counter-revolution
1791–2 **Legislative Assembly**	**Constitutional Monarchy** But king's veto no longer applied to laws on the constitution or finance	Attempted deportation of refractory priests Establishment of *fédérés* camp in Paris	Defeat in war (April 1791) Threat of invasion King's dismissal of Girondin ministers (April 1792) Invasion of Tuileries (20 June 1792) Attack on Tuileries (10 August 1792) King imprisoned and suspended September Massacre (1792)
1792–5 **National Convention**	**Republic** Committee of Public Safety from April 1793 assumed dictatorship December 1793–July 1794	Execution of Louis XVI (January 1793) Continuation of and elimination of counter-revolution Establishment of institutions of Terror Dechristianisation	Rifts in Convention – fall of Girondins in *journée* (31 May–June 1793) Civil war in the Vendée (February–December 1793) Federal revolt The Anarchic Terror (September 1793–June 1794) The Great Terror (June 1794–5) Thermidorian Reaction (July 1794) Risings of 1795 Germinal (1 April) Prairial (20/21 May) Vendémiaire (October) White Terror

What can we learn from this contemporary illustration?
Anonymous cartoon titled 'The Last Victim'.

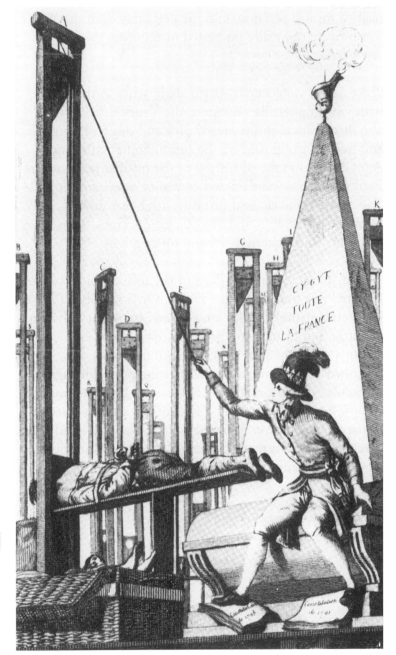

The White Terror This was a reaction against the revolution. Those who had improved their personal lot in the revolution now had the tables turned on them and were the subject of reprisals. A similar right-wing (or pro-monarchist) reaction took place after the defeat of Napoleon and was also known as the White Terror (see page 128). In both cases the 'white' refers to an association with the Bourbon monarchy.

The White Terror

Those who had formerly been persecuted now turned their vengeance on those who had done well out of the revolution. The purchasers of land (the *biens nationaux*), the constitutional clergy and government officials, as well as the Parisian Sans Culottes all came under attack in the so-called **White Terror**. But the Terror of 1795 was not really a royalist reaction, and the perpetrators of the White Terror were not really interested in restoring the *ancien régime.*

Once again, violence was particularly acute in the west with violent guerrilla warfare in the Vendée. There were also disturbances in the areas north and south of Lyons and murder gangs roamed the south. Some returning *émigrés* tried to take advantage of the **royalist reaction**. In Paris the *jeunesse doré* (gilded youth) or *muscadins* (middle-class youths who dressed extravagantly) beat up and intimidated Jacobins and Sans Culottes. The killings continued throughout 1796 and for much of 1797.

The final armed rising in Paris of the revolutionary period reflected this time of White Terror. On 5 October 1795, (13 Vendémiaire) 25,000 armed Parisians – not only Sans Culottes, but factory and property owners and even civil servants – marched on the Convention in what was described at the time as a royalist rising protesting against the new constitution. They were resisted by government troops. A promising young officer of the artillery, General Bonaparte killed over 300 with what he later referred to as 'a few shells'. This marked the last attempt to intimidate an elected assembly until 1830.

SUMMARY QUESTIONS

1 Why was Louis XVI executed?

2 List the reasons for the fall of the Girondins.

3 Outline the main reasons for the development of the Terror in France.

4 Explain Robespierre's role in the government of France.

Royalist reaction In Nîmes, 'Companies of the Sun' were formed by royalists to attack their oppressors and in Brittany, the Chouan movement (named after its leader Cottereau, known as Chouan) was supported by around 3000 *émigré* troops who were landed at Quiberon Bay by the British and proceeded to attack grain convoys and to murder local officials. Thousands of former Jacobin terrorists were murdered by the combined forces of the Chouans and *émigrés*, but General Hoche led the government troops against them and forced them to surrender. Six thousand prisoners were taken and around 750 of these rebels were shot.

CHAPTER 7

What problems did the Directory face, 1795–9?

The Directory This was the name given to the body responsible for carrying out the laws made in France between August 1795 and November 1799. There were five directors jointly responsible for the conduct of affairs. They formed the executive part of government and were assisted by a complex legislature (comprising the councils of the Ancients and of the 500) which made the laws.

The work of the Convention to create a new and better constitution for France led to the creation of **the Directory**, in 1795. The aim was to produce a system that would avoid both the extremism of the Jacobins and Sans Culottes, and the conservatism of the royalists and the *ancien régime*.

THE NEW CONSTITUTION (CONSTITUTION OF YEAR III)

The Constitution of Year III provided a new basis for government in France:

- Elections would be in three stages. At the first stage, all males over 21 who paid direct taxes could vote. They chose the electors, and the electors, the deputies. To become an elector, a man had to pay taxes equivalent to 150–200 days' labour – a very high amount so restricting this office to the very rich (around 30,000 were eligible).
- There were to be two government chambers. The first, the Council of 500, composed of deputies over the age of 30, would draw up legislation. The second, the Council of Ancients, 250 deputies over the age of 40, would examine and approve or reject (but could not change) bills.
- A third of the members would be retired every year.
- There would be annual elections.
- There would be a Directory, or council of five, chosen by the Ancients from a list drawn up by the 500. It would enforce the laws and run all government affairs.
- The Directory would hold office for five years, but one member would drop out each year (chosen by lot).
- Members of the Directory would not be able to sit in either of the two large councils and their powers were limited (they could not introduce or veto laws, declare war or peace and had no control over finance).

- The Directory appointed ministers (who also could not be in the councils) and government commissioners.

The Convention also decreed that two-thirds of the deputies in the first councils were to be chosen from existing deputies in the Convention. This was to prevent a royalist reaction.

The original directors were Carnot, **Barras**, Reubell, Letourneur, and La Revellière-Lépeaux, all of whom had voted for the king's death.

THE PROBLEMS OF THE DIRECTORY

The constitution was designed to prevent any one group from exerting too much power, yet its elaborate system of checks and balances, which relied on cooperation between the groups, made government difficult. The arrangements, intended to prevent dictatorship, meant there was no single person or body in overall control, which led to political stalemate. The directors proposed laws, but could not vote on them. They could not insist that the Council of Ancients pass these, and any attempt to change the constitution was slow. The task faced by the Directory was not an easy one.

War, continuing economic crisis, threats from both sides of the political spectrum and the legacy of the Terror did not help:

- Financially, the Directory survived through short-term measures and the restoration of some indirect taxation, which was very unpopular. It also relied on the plundering of foreign states (particularly in Italy and Germany), occupied by French armies. *Assignats*, which had grown so worthless that even beggars refused them, were discontinued in February 1796 and a new currency was introduced, although that also soon lost value as did *rentes* (government investments). Those bourgeois investors and property owners who had gained by the revolution now found themselves losing out.
- Politically, they faced a groundswell of royalist support – probably a reaction to the developments of the last two years. The royalists did well in elections, but were unable

KEY PERSON

Paul-François Barras (1755–1829) Barras was an ex-representative-on-mission whose extremism had brought him into conflict with Robespierre. He had commanded the Convention's forces in the events of Thermidor and this had made him very influential. He was a dissolute and unprincipled character and his inclusion among the new Directors showed the decline in revolutionary leadership. He was more concerned with power than with the needs of the people, but did much to promote the career of Napoleon.

KEY PERSON

François Noel 'Gracchus' Babeuf Babeuf believed in a primitive form of communism based on the distribution, rather than production, of goods. His ideas had considerable influence on radicals and socialists in the 19th century. He wrote, 'the Revolution is not yet complete because all the good things of life are taken by the rich who rule as dictators while the poor toil in misery like slaves and are considered of no account by the state'.

to form a majority under the terms of the constitution, which prevented them dominating the councils.

- The threat of the left-wing extremists had not passed either and, in 1796, **Gracchus Babeuf** plotted to overthrow the Directory. Babeuf favoured the abolition of private property and has been regarded by some as the first communist. However, he had little popular support, his plot was easily put down and he was guillotined in 1797.

The end of the Directory

By 1797, the numbers of those favouring constitutional monarchy had grown considerably and there was the possibility that, by 1798, the royalists might have a majority in the councils. Of those forming the Directory, only two were now devout republicans. This posed a dilemma. The directors' powers included control of the army and the republicans began to use this to force change from 1797.

The fall of Robespierre and the problems of the Directory.

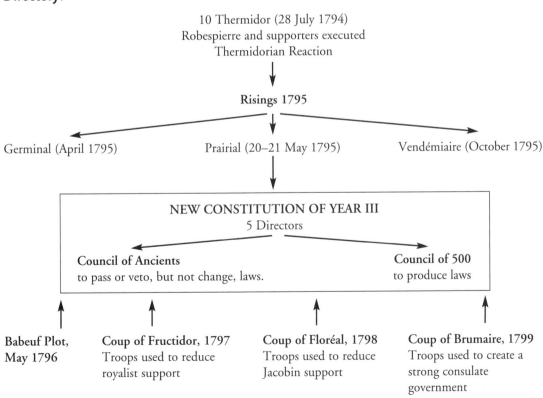

10 Thermidor (28 July 1794)
Robespierre and supporters executed
Thermidorian Reaction

↓

Risings 1795

Germinal (April 1795)   Prairial (20–21 May 1795)   Vendémiaire (October 1795)

↓

NEW CONSTITUTION OF YEAR III
5 Directors

Council of Ancients
to pass or veto, but not change, laws.

Council of 500
to produce laws

Babeuf Plot,
May 1796

Coup of Fructidor, 1797
Troops used to reduce royalist support

Coup of Floréal, 1798
Troops used to reduce Jacobin support

Coup of Brumaire, 1799
Troops used to create a strong consulate government

To prevent a royalist restoration, they brought troops to Paris. On the night of 3–4 September (the coup of Fructidor, Year V) the army seized strong points in the city and surrounded the councils. They ordered the arrest of two directors and 53 deputies. The remaining deputies were so frightened, they agreed to laws cancelling the election results in 49 *départements* (and so removing 177 deputies). The arrested directors, deputies and leading royalists and *émigrés*, together with hundreds of refractory priests, were then exiled. (Furthermore, by the 1799 law of hostages, the property of the relatives of those who fled could be seized in areas resisting the new laws.)

The constitution had been severely undermined and when, in May 1798 (Floréal), the Jacobins did well in the elections, the Directors again overturned the results. By 1799, the **Directory had lost all support**. On 10 November 1799 (19 Brumaire), the Directory came to an end in a coup led by Napoleon Bonaparte.

THE ACHIEVEMENTS OF THE REVOLUTIONARY ARMIES

The main achievements of the period of the Directory were not at home, but in **military campaigns** abroad. By the autumn of 1795, France remained at war only with Great Britain and Austria.

In 1796, a pincer attack was mounted against Austria. The campaign involved moving two French armies, one from Bavaria and one from Italy, where the young General Napoleon Bonaparte was in command, in a joint campaign. Napoleon rose to the challenge and, in a swift and successful campaign, swept through Piedmont and Mantua in Northern Italy, defeating the Austrian armies there, and was set to cross the Alps and head for Vienna. However, the attack from Bavaria had been less successful and Napoleon realised he could go no further. Napoleon therefore concluded a very favourable **peace treaty with Austria**, whereby he created the new Cisalpine Republic from his conquests and obtained Austrian acceptance of the Batavian Republic in return for allowing Austrian control of Venice and part of the Venetian Republic.

KEY THEMES

The Directory's loss of support It had acted unconstitutionally and failed to maintain order. Its tax demands were resisted, forced loans unpopular and the return of conscription following failure in war, 1799, widely resented. Government administration in the provinces virtually collapsed and, by November 1799, there was civil war in the Ardèche. The Directors Sieyès and Roger-Ducos plotted to use the army again and force the councils to abolish the Directory.

Military campaigns By the time the Directory was established, the French had taken the Austrian Netherlands (1794) and the United Provinces (1795), and these had been merged to form the new Batavian Republic. France had also conquered the Rhineland and by the Treaty of Basle (6 April 1795), Prussia made peace with France, agreeing to French control over the left bank of the Rhine. In July 1795, France had entered Spain and signed a peace treaty, which led to an alliance between the two countries in October 1796.

Peace treaty with Austria The significance of this peace deal, which was confirmed by the Peace of Campio Formio (October 1797), was less in what it said, than in the way Napoleon had himself negotiated it, without reference to the Directory.

The French plan to defeat Britain had centred on an invasion with the help of the Dutch and Spanish fleets. However, after British victories at Cape St Vincent against the Spanish fleet, and Camperdown, against the Dutch in 1797, such hopes were dashed. The Directory could not afford to dwell on failure. It needed conquests to retain support and occupy the army, so French attention was again turned to mainland Europe.

The year 1798 proved a successful one in this respect. In January 1798, French troops seized Switzerland and created the Helvetic Republic, annexing Geneva to France. In Italy, a Roman Republic was set up in the Papal States, forcing the Pope to flee to Tuscany. The Ligurian Republic replaced the Genoese Republic in June 1797. In March 1798, the left bank of the Rhine officially passed to France following a Congress of the Holy Roman Empire and, by the spring of 1798, the French looked extremely powerful.

However, Britain remained an undefeated enemy. After Britain's naval victories, Napoleon, who had been put in command of the army to prepare for an invasion of England, decided to strike at Britain through Egypt (vital for British trade to India). He sailed in May 1798, with a vast fleet of 38,000 troops, capturing Malta (9 June), and advancing into Egypt, capturing Alexandria (July), defeating the Mamluks at the Battle of the Pyramids (21 July) and taking Cairo. However, on 1 August, **Nelson** destroyed most of the French fleet at Aboukir Bay in the Battle of the Nile. This left the French armies cut off from their home base, and was a major defeat. It led to the formation of the second Coalition against France, which included Russia, which had taken the protectorship of Malta in 1797, and was therefore provoked by Napoleon's audacity. War resumed in 1799 and, although France occupied the rest of Italy, annexed Piedmont to France and turned Naples into another republic – the Parthenopean – early successes were followed by defeats along the Rhine and in northern Italy and Switzerland. When the Directory fell, the future looked far less promising.

KEY PERSON

Horatio, Viscount Nelson (1758–1805) Nelson, the son of a Norfolk parson, was to become Britain's greatest naval captain during the French wars. He first distinguished himself against the Spanish fleet at Cape St Vincent in 1797. He had an excellent understanding of strategy and tactics at sea and, although he failed to prevent the French expedition to Egypt in 1798, he put his knowledge to good effect in trapping the French fleet in Aboukir Bay at the mouth of the Nile and placing it between the two lines of British vessels. Only two of Napoleon's 13 ships escaped in this impressive British victory. Nelson went on to become Commander in the Mediterranean (1803), blockading Toulon, and finally lost his life defeating the combined Spanish/French fleets at Cape Trafalgar in 1805.

The achievement of the revolutionary armies to 1799.

SUMMARY QUESTIONS

1 How did the constitution of 1795 differ from that which had gone before?

2 Would you judge the Directory to have been a success or a failure? Give reasons for your answer.

AS ASSESSMENT: THE FRENCH REVOLUTION

STRUCTURED QUESTIONS IN THE STYLE OF OCR

1 (a) Assess the aims of the revolutionaries in France in 1789. (30)
  (b) Assess the relative importance of economic distress, the outbreak of war and religious divisions as reasons for instability in France from 1789 to 1795. (60)

Reading
Before answering these questions you should reread the first part of this book. You will need to look specifically at Chapters 1, 2 and 3 for question (a) but for question (b) you will need to select relevant material from all the first six chapters. You may also find it useful to refer to Sections 1, 2 and 3 of the A2 section.

How to answer the question
Question (a) specifically asks for aims 'in 1789', so you should focus on the ideas and arguments of key individuals and groups at the outbreak of revolution. You will certainly need to think about 'who' the revolutionaries were, and this should lead you on to appreciate that they were a mixed bunch, not all sharing the same aims. You will need to make a brief list of revolutionaries and aims before you begin – and you will need to arrange these carefully so that your written answer is orderly.

Examples:

- Intellectuals – to carry forward the ideas of the Enlightenment, such as a constitution, limited monarchy, greater toleration and freedom from oppression.
- Peasants – to be freed from the burden of feudal dues and taxation, food and land.
- Sans Culottes – to improve employment, food supplies and standard of living.
- Bourgeoisie – to obtain more say in government, access to office and freedom from legal and financial restraints.
- Liberal nobles – to reduce the king's power, solve the economic crisis and strengthen France.
- Poorer clergy – to reform the Church, increase their income and status and help the poor.

You might choose to divide these categories still further. You could, for example, look at the different attitudes of those in towns and rural areas, in Paris and the provinces or within the bourgeoisie as a group. You could use certain key figures as representatives of the different groups, or as particularly influential in 1789. A good answer might, for example, contrast the views of men like Robespierre, Mirabeau, Lafayette, Danton and Marat, although it would need to make clear who these men represented, and look at the wider picture too.

So there are many possible approaches, but the important point is that answers should be **structured**. In responding to the question, try to look for points on which the revolutionaries agreed, and those on which they differed. In this way, you will show that you understand the links between the varying groups and are able to draw some conclusions. One factor worth emphasising, for example, is that in 1789, all the revolutionaries looked to a future that would incorporate the king in the scheme of government.

Question (b) is a comparative question. You are asked to assess the relative importance of three key developments to the growing instability in France. You will again need to plan your answer carefully. Start by looking at each factor in turn and noting the key connections with growing instability. Remember the answer must cover the whole of the period 1789–95, so it is not enough, for example, to note the connection between economic distress and the outbreak of revolution in 1789, you will also need to be aware of the interaction of each of these factors with developments down to the fall of the Jacobins in 1795.

For example, religious division was not a major issue in 1789, except in relation to tax privileges and the debates over voting by order in the Estates-General. However, it became a major source of dissension after the Civil Constitution of the Clergy in 1790 and helped deepen the split in French society. It then provided the counter-revolutionaries with a large base of support (particularly from the peasants) and was therefore instrumental in the development of unrest in 1793 and the Terror.

As well as looking at each of the three factors you will need to balance them against one another and reach some sort of conclusion about their importance. Were they all equally important? Was one clearly more important? Do they interrelate, so that one leads to another? Whatever conclusion you intend to reach, you should try to make your judgement clear throughout your answer. Although it might seem easier to approach this question chronologically, adding a conclusion to summarise your views, the most effective responses will be based on the factors under consideration and will make comparative comments throughout.

You might choose, for example, to stress the importance of economic factors as being of overwhelming importance. In this case, you might deal with the religious divisions first, the outbreak of war second and then begin a paragraph with 'Despite the clear importance of religious divisions and the outbreak of war to the instability of France during these years, by far the most important cause of trouble was economic distress …'. You will, of course, need to give reasons for your views. *Never* assert without proof.

STRUCTURED QUESTIONS IN THE STYLE OF EDEXCEL

(a) What measures were taken to meet the demands for reform in France between 1789 and 1792? (15)

(b) Why was the monarchy later abolished and Louis XVI executed in 1793? (15)

Reading
Before answering these questions you should reread Chapters 3, 4 and 5 for question (a) and Chapter 6 for question (b).

How to answer the question
Question (a). This is a reasonably straightforward 'recall' question, but the best answers will still need to be carefully **planned**. You will need to ask yourself what the demands for reform were, and it would be more appropriate to group the measures taken by category, rather than launching into a chronological list. For example:

- Demands for political reform – the calling of the Estates-General, establishment of the National Assembly, declaration of rights, reform of local administration, establishment of a republic.
- Demands for legal reform – the work of the Constituent Assembly, new courts, elected judges.
- Demands for financial reform – the abolition of the old taxes, sale of church and nobles' property, removal of privilege.
- Demands for social equality – the moves to the National Assembly, August Decrees, confiscation of property.
- Demands for Church reform – the reform of abuses and the Civil Constitution.

By looking at each of these groups in turn, and showing links between the factors where appropriate, your answer should show qualities of sustained **organisation**, **coherence** and **direction** – all features of a top-level response. Try to end with a brief summarising conclusion that shows you have thought about the relationship between the demands, the reforms and their implications.

Question (b) contains two parts and it is important to separate these in your mind. Why the monarchy was abolished refers to the events leading to the establishment of the republic in September 1792. Why the king was executed in January 1793 demands reference to the controversy over the fate of the king, the influence of the war and the growing power of the Jacobins from 1792 to 1793.

Simple statements about Louis XVI and his failure as a monarch are unlikely to score well. A good answer will provide both long- and short-term reasons for the abolition of the monarchy. Take care not to spend too long describing the failures of the *ancien régime*. The main focus of the question should be on the years 1792–3.

You might spend one paragraph discussing the underlying problems of the monarchy – the failure of absolutist rule, demands for reform and inadequacy of Louis XVI and his family. Your second paragraph might consider the deterioration of the relationship between the king and the assembly. This would bring in the attitude of the Sans Culottes and the political clubs and the king's reluctance to accept political change until placed under pressure.

The third paragraph might deal with the immediate causes of the abolition of the monarchy –the effect of war and the flight to Varennes in particular. The fourth could then consider the execution – noting the change in attitude of the deputies and in particular the influence of the Jacobins, together with the impact of war. Some discussion of the king's own contribution to his fate could also be included here. Make sure you allow time for a concluding paragraph, which should summarise your arguments, make it clear what the most important factors were and show how the interaction of various factors contributed to the events concerned.

STRUCTURED SOURCE-BASED QUESTIONS IN THE STYLE OF AQA

Study the following source material and then answer the questions that follow.

Source A
The Constituent Assembly wanted to create a Church that was free from abuses, free from foreign (papal) control, democratic and linked to the new system of local government. The deputies simply wanted to extend to religion the principles applied elsewhere. They also wanted to tie the Catholic Church in France more closely to the state as this would strengthen the Revolution. There was no serious conflict with the Church, however, until the Civil Constitution of the Clergy in July 1790.
   Adapted from *France in Revolution*, by D. Townson, Hodder and Stoughton (1990).

Source B

The French Revolution had many turning points, but the oath of the clergy was unquestionably one of them. It was certainly the Constituent Assembly's most serious mistake. For the fist time the revolutionaries forced fellow citizens to choose; to declare themselves publicly for or against the new order. It was found that around half the clergy of France felt unable to agree [and] many clerics in the country at large became refractories*.

Adapted from *The Oxford History of the French Revolution*, by W. Doyle, Oxford University Press (1990).

(*refractories = those rejecting the Civil Constitution)

Source C

The Civil Constitution of the Clergy was a sensible settlement: parishes [were] reorganised according to a more logical pattern, the aristocratic monopoly of high Church office was eliminated and reasonable salaries guaranteed to priests. Bishops and priests were to be elected by active citizens; even if some clerics stood to lose, the clergy did not rush to reject the Civil Constitution.

Adapted from *Revolution and Terror in France 1789–95*, by D. G. Wright, Longman (1974).

> (a) Use Source B and your own knowledge. Explain briefly the importance of the Civil Constitution of the Clergy in the context of the French Revolution in 1790. (3)
>
> (b) Use Sources B and C and your own knowledge. Explain how the view of the Civil Constitution of the Clergy in Source B differs from the view in Source C. (7)
>
> (c) Use Sources A, B, and C and your own knowledge. Explain the importance, in relation to other factors, of the issue of religion in promoting counter-revolution in France in the period 1790 to 1794. (15)

Reading

Before answering these questions you should re-read Chapters 4, 5 and 6.

How to answer the questions

First, take note of the mark allocations and ensure you **divide your time** appropriately. Obviously, you will need to read the sources carefully before you begin, and you also need to allow time for planning answers to (b) and (c).

Sub-question (a) asks you to explain the importance of a key term, and this should be done **briefly** but **clearly**. It also requires you to place that term in context. There would not be enough time for much development here, but a high mark would be achieved by the inclusion of key factors that reveal a clear understanding.

The answer might mention the issue of the Church in the revolution, the clerical opposition to the election of clergy and the oath, the part of the Pope, the strength of support for refractory priests within France (perhaps referring to specific regions) and the link to counter-revolution.

Sub-question (b) requires source analysis. Do not fall into the trap of writing what each source says in turn, and only answering the question in a conclusion. It is far better to base the answer on one or two points on which the given sources differ, for example pointing out that while Source B says the oath/Constitution of the Clergy was a serious mistake, Source C refers to it as a sensible settlement. Furthermore, while Source B claims around half the clergy of France disagreed with it, Source C says the clergy 'did not rush to reject' it.

A good answer also needs to provide some explanation for the disagreement and should reveal your own knowledge of the issue. You might comment, for example that Source B is specifically referring to the oath whereas Source C refers to the constitution in general, and this had proved reasonably acceptable before the introduction of the oath. Source C also focuses on the change as an administrative reform rather than looking at the political context.

Sub-question (c) is a mini-essay. It requires reference to all three sources, but these should be used in support of an argument, not merely addressed at the beginning of the answer. The importance of the issue of religion in counter-revolution would include:

- The part of the Church in the *ancien régime* and the way this was changed by the revolution (Sources A/C).
- The effect of the Church/state connection brought by the revolution (Sources A/B).
- The attitude of different groups – for example, the clergy (Sources A/B/C), peasants, nobility, king, Sans Culottes, Jacobin revolutionaries – and how this exacerbated the split.

A good answer also needs to refer to other factors and to balance the importance of religion against these. The danger of military defeat, the impact of conscription, the execution of the king, the Terror and its instruments, economic problems, rural and Sans Culottes discontent, as well as both right-wing (noble) and left-wing (radical) political opposition, could all be included here.

AS SECTION: NAPOLEONIC AND BOURBON FRANCE 1799–1830

INTRODUCTION

Between 1804 and 1814, France was an empire, ruled by the former army general, Napoleon Bonaparte. Having first accumulated power as a consul, from 1799 he took the title Emperor Napoleon I, by crowning himself at a grand ceremony in Notre Dame Cathedral in Paris. Napoleonic rule resolved some of the conflicts that had torn the country apart after the revolution. He negotiated a concordat with the Pope, which recognised the Catholic Church in France once again and healed the rifts brought by the Civil Constitution of the Clergy. The price of the concordat was the church's acceptance that the lands of the church and *émigrés* would never be restored. This was essential to Napoleonic stability, satisfying the property owners and winning their support for the regime.

Napoleonic rule also brought glory in war – at least to 1808 and, in some areas, for longer. It extended French rule, through annexations and **satellite states** to an extent never dreamed of before. Napoleon liked to think of himself as being like one of the great Roman emperors, spreading civilised values to the lands he conquered. However, the imperial dream was not to last and, after two disastrous campaigns in Spain and Russia, Napoleon was driven to abdicate. He made one more bid for power during the period known as the '100 Days' in 1815 but, after his defeat at Waterloo, was banished to a remote Atlantic island, although his name and **legend** were to live on.

From 1814/15 to 1830, France was once again ruled by the **Bourbons** – Louis XVIII and Charles X, brothers of the guillotined Louis XVI. Although this period is known as the 'Restoration', the France that they ruled was very

KEY TERMS

Satellite states These were states that retained their own rulers but were subject to overall French control. For more information, see Chapter 10.

Napoleonic legend A legend soon grew in France that Napoleon had been a great ruler who had brought nothing but glory to France. He had freed Europe from the oppression of the *ancien régime* and defended peoples' rights and liberties.

The Bourbon succession The former Dauphin, son of Louis XVI, who had been called Louis XVII by the monarchists after the execution of his father, died in a cell in a Parisian jail in 1795.

HEINEMANN ADVANCED HISTORY

different from that before the revolution. Louis XVIII's return had been conditional on the acceptance of a charter that created a **constitutional monarchy**. It also confirmed the revolutionary land settlement and, although Charles X arranged compensation for the original owners, this actually finalised the change. Although the more extreme or 'ultra' supporters of the Bourbons would have liked to turn the clock back, particularly with regard to the power of the nobles and the Church, all the basic changes brought by the revolution survived. What is more, power was no longer sacred and, when Charles X tried to go too far in his restoration of royal authority, the liberal deputies in government combined with the radical republicans of Paris to oust him from the throne. It is significant that, in 1830, the so-called 'middle-class monarch', Louis-Philippe, came to power as the 'the King of the French' (the choice of the French people) and not the King of France.

CHAPTER 8

How did Napoleon come to power in France, 1796–1804?

BACKGROUND AND MILITARY CAMPAIGNS

Napoleon's origins hardly marked him out as a likely future French emperor. He was born in 1769, twenty years before the revolution. He came from the island of Corsica, which had been acquired by France from Genoa (Italy) just a year earlier, in 1768. He was therefore more Corsican than French and, although his family were minor nobles, they were not persecuted during the revolution like the true French nobility. Nevertheless, Napoleon's father had been able to take advantage of an edict of 1776 that allowed noblemen to send their sons to be educated at one of the royal military academies, at state expense. He had sent Napoleon to Brienne, 1779–84, where he learnt to speak French, and the École Militaire in Paris, 1784–5, where he became an artillery officer at the age of 16. He was therefore a new and ambitious young officer at the time of the revolutionary events of 1789 and, although he played no direct part in what went on, he supported the revolution, like many others of his kind. When the king was overthrown and many officers of noble rank began to emigrate, Napoleon took advantage of his Corsican background to rise quickly through the ranks and he played a part in driving the British from Toulon in December 1793. For this, he was promoted to the rank of Brigadier-General, although he was still only 24.

He helped crush the rising of Vendémiaire in Paris in 1795 and, in March 1796, he married Josephine de Beauharnais and was appointed commander of the French army in Italy in the offensive against the Austrians. His success in a number of battles against the Austrians 1796–7 (see Chapter 7), won him a great reputation as a military leader. His personal confidence, ambition and scornful attitude towards the Directory, which was ruling France, were also revealed in his decision to make the Peace of

Campio Formio (October 1797) without their authority. It may have been fear of his ambitions that persuaded the Directory to send him off on the Egyptian campaign (1788–9), but his successes there only enhanced his reputation. By 1799, he was ready to come to power in the Revolt of 19 Brumaire.

The Revolt of 19 Brumaire

In 1799, while campaigning in Egypt, Napoleon learned of what seemed like France's imminent defeat at the hands of the Second Coalition (Britain, Austria and Russia). Fearing an invasion of France, he decided to return. By the time he did so, that danger had passed, but another was around the corner. The directors had decided that the only way they could retain control and provide stronger government was to force a change in the system of elections, by using the army. To do this they needed the cooperation of a powerful general and this fitted well with Napoleon's own ambitions. He hurried to Paris to meet with **Abbé Sieyès**, now one of the directors, and the plot was hatched. Careful preparations were made. A number of deputies in the Council of 500 and members of the Council of Ancients were bribed (see Chapter 7 for details of the constitution of the Directory). It was important that they were willing to move from the centre of Paris, where the radical crowds might rise in rebellion, and out to the suburbs. Furthermore, it was arranged that Lucien, Napoleon's brother, would be elected as President of the Council of 500. This placed him in the prime position to control events.

Rumours were spread of a foreign-inspired plot to destroy the Republic and the two councils obediently moved 'for safety' to the Palace of St Cloud on the outskirts of Paris. Napoleon had control of the Paris garrison, numbering about 100,000 men, but he needed to tread carefully if the coup was to succeed. Had the armed mobs risen against him, he would have been in a very difficult position. Napoleon addressed each of the councils and informed them of the need to set up a new provisional government in the name of the revolution. Despite all the preparations, things did not quite go to plan and, in the Council of 500, Napoleon was greeted with cries of 'outlaw the dictator'.

KEY PERSON

Abbé Emmanuel Sieyès (1748–1836) Sieyès was a Catholic priest who had supported, and stood for, the Third Estate at the time of the Estates-General in 1789. He wrote the very influential book, *What is the Third Estate?*, which was much discussed at the outbreak of revolution, and it was his proposal that led to the setting up of the National Assembly. He survived the Terror, helped draw up the constitution of 1791 and became an important member of the Directory in 1799. However, he was frustrated by its weakness and consequently supported the coup of November 1799, although its results were not as he intended. He played a part in drawing up the constitution of the Consulate but was unable to prevent Napoleon's ambition to be sole ruler. He was created a count under the Empire but, on Napoleon's defeat in 1814, he was exiled to Brussels. He returned to die in Paris in 1830.

Law of Brumaire
Napoleon's coup took place in Brumaire. The Law of Brumaire was the new constitution or system of government established after the coup.

Authoritarian means that power is concentrated in the hands of whoever is at the top. Those in 'authority' have the means to force their will on others. Under the Law of Brumaire, Napoleon had such power, and used it.

Tribunate and Legislature
Although they had theoretical powers, neither of these councils was allowed to exert much influence. The former was eventually abolished in 1808 and the latter was reduced to no more than a 'yes' body.

Indirect elections by universal suffrage The new constitution gave the vote to around 6 million Frenchmen over 21, but the system of indirect voting was so complex that the ordinary man had very little say in government. Within each *commune*, voters chose 10 per cent of their number to form a communal list, from which local officials were drawn. These 600,000 in turn chose 10 per cent of their number to form a departmental list and these chose 6000 of their number for a national list of persons fit for public service. From this list, the senate chose the 400 members of the two councils, which discussed and passed the laws.

Although Lucien did his best to maintain order, there was some fighting and Napoleon claimed that he was nearly assassinated.

On Lucien's orders, a contingent of soldiers had to be used to calm the 500. The councils were then forced to agree to the abolition of the Directory and the creation of a new government. Napoleon's coup had worked – but only just. Napoleon had acted in a rather hesitant and indecisive manner in his dealings with the councils but, fortunately for him, there was no trouble from Paris and the army remained loyal. Although he later claimed to have undertaken the coup to defend liberty and the revolution and rescue France from instability and weakness, there was little evidence of this at the time.

The Consulate

By the **Law of Brumaire**, a new government was established, under the direction of three consuls: Sieyès, Ducos (another former director) and Napoleon. Originally, Sieyès had envisaged that each of the three consuls would share political authority, but Napoleon argued that a 'First Consul' was necessary for stability and that the two remaining consuls should have only an advisory role. The strength of his position meant that there was little room to argue, and the constitution that was finally approved was an **authoritarian** one, dependent on Napoleon himself. Although there was a Council of State and a Senate to advise the consuls, these were packed with Napoleon's supporters. There were also two further councils to help with law making – known as the **Tribunate and Legislature**. These were **indirectly elected by universal suffrage** but, in practice, their views could be largely ignored. Napoleon could introduce legislation, appoint and dismiss ministers and direct foreign policy. Although the three consuls were to hold office for ten years, it was clear who would direct government. Sieyès was won over with the gift of a large country estate by way of compensation.

In February 1800, a **plebiscite** was held to demonstrate support for the new constitution. Officially, just over 3 million were in favour, as opposed to 1500 against but, since voting was in public, local officials were under pressure to record supportive votes and there was every incentive anyway to accept a system that was already in place, the results can hardly be trusted. It is likely that many eligible persons did not in fact vote at all.

In 1802, there were further changes. Napoleon was anxious to win over the buyers of *biens nationaux* and prevent any support for a royalist restoration. Consequently, he made the right to vote dependent on taxation, giving them more political influence, and reassured them with pronouncements that there would be no attempt to restore *émigré* or church lands. In gratitude, so it would seem, huge numbers voted in Napoleon's favour in his next plebiscite. This asked for approval of his move to become Consul for life, with the right to nominate his own successor. Secure in his new position, Napoleon ensured that the councils were packed with 'safemen' and that the Senate was filled by his own nominees – men well provided with generous gifts of land and money.

THE ESTABLISHMENT OF NAPOLEON'S EMPIRE

The emperor

It was not long before Napoleon began to assume some of the trappings of a king. He enjoyed ceremonial and began holding grand state occasions, showing himself to be quite at home in a 'royal' role. From here, it was not a very large step to his becoming emperor. Napoleon still faced some opposition from royalists and *émigrés* and, in 1804, there was an assassination scare. The **Duc d'Enghien** was accused of trying to arrange the murder of Napoleon. Although the details were hazy, it was just the excuse Napoleon needed. His loyal followers in the Senate decreed that Napoleon should be declared Emperor of the French, with an **hereditary title**. This change was also subsequently approved by plebiscite.

Napoleon did not want to be called a king, given the pre-revolutionary associations that this had. He did, however, want to found a dynasty. Napoleon envisaged the

HEINEMANN ADVANCED HISTORY

Bonaparte dynasty as one, and perhaps the grandest, of the ruling houses of Europe.

A magnificent ceremony was held in Notre Dame Cathedral in Paris, attended by the Pope. However, it was Napoleon who placed the crown upon his own head, as well as placing that of his wife, the empress, Josephine, upon hers. Now all that was needed to fulfil Napoleon's ambition of creating a lasting imperial dynasty was an heir. When Josephine failed to provide a son and passed childbearing age, he secured an annulment to the marriage. In 1810, at the age of 40, he married Marie-Louise of Austria (Marie Antoinette's niece) and, a year later, Napoleon junior, King of Rome, was born.

Securing his position

Despite the apparently overwhelming approval given by the various plebiscites, Napoleon still had plenty of opponents in the early years of his rule. They fall into three broad categories:

- The left-wing extremists or radicals who had inherited the ideas of the Jacobins (see Chapters 5–6) and wanted a **democratic** republic were horrified by Napoleon's

KEY CONCEPT

Democratic Democratic in this context means a system of government in which the ordinary people had a real say in how their country was run, probably through direct elections to an assembly.

Napoleon crowning Josephine as empress at his coronation in 1804. Painting by Jacques-Louis David, 1806–7.

accumulation of power, which they regarded as a betrayal of revolutionary principles. They had a good deal of support in the lower ranks of the army and among the lower classes in the towns, particularly Paris.

- The right-wing royalists, who were helped by the *émigrés* abroad and occasionally by foreign powers, felt it was time to reverse the changes of the revolution (which they felt Napoleon was maintaining) and favoured a return to the Bourbon monarchy. They were particularly strong in the west of France.
- Moderate republicans/liberals, who believed that Napoleon was creating a dictatorship to the detriment of the people, did not believe in 'rule by the mob' and feared the power of the lower classes. They did, however, want a fair constitution guaranteeing rights such as freedom of speech and freedom of the press. **Benjamin Constant** and **Madame de Staël** were among this group.

Between 1800 and 1804, in order to establish his position, Napoleon used a mixture of repression and reform although, once his power was secure, he more often resorted to the former.

He showed no toleration for the left-wing republicans. He used the excuse of an assassination attempt to weaken the threat they posed. On 24 December 1800, an attempt to blow up Napoleon with a bomb, on his way to the Opéra, failed. Although it had been inspired by royalist rather than left-wing opponents, Napoleon took the opportunity to deport 129 Jacobin leaders and arrest others. This did not stop the radical opposition, but it did make it easier for Napoleon to infiltrate clubs and associations with his informers. In time, radical political opposition became extremely difficult and dangerous.

To win over the royalists, Napoleon made some minor concessions. In January 1800, he offered amnesties to all those who laid down their arms. He also made **religious concessions** and promised an end to the laws attacking the *émigrés*. However, repression was his normal reaction to trouble and, when the armistice ran out, he ordered General Brune to use the utmost severity to crush **royalist rebellions**. His measures were effective and, after April

KEY PEOPLE

Benjamin Constant (1767–1830) was a moderate republican. He went into exile in 1803 when he saw how Napoleon was advancing his own position. He returned in 1814, during the period of the '100 Days', to advise Napoleon on the drawing up of the Acte Additionnel (see Chapter 11) which provided the basis for a liberal scheme of government. After 1815, he became a liberal spokesman in Louis XVIII's chamber of deputies.

Madame de Staël (1766–1817) was Constant's mistress and Necker's daughter. She escaped from France during the Terror but returned to set up a 'salon' for the discussion of liberal political ideas during the Directory. Her criticisms of Napoleon led to her exile 1804–14.

KEY POINTS

Religious concessions Napoleon allowed Christian worship on a Sunday. The position of the Catholic Church was enhanced by the Concordat of 1801 (see pages 93–4).

Royalist rebellions The biggest rising that Brune crushed was that of the Chouan rebels in Brittany in 1800. The Chouan movement stemmed from the period of the White Terror of 1796–7 (see Chapter 6).

1800, there were no further large-scale uprisings during the Napoleonic period. Other royalists were forced into exile and any potential troublemakers were harshly dealt with, as in the kidnap and murder of the Duc d'Enghien, after rumours of a plot in 1804 (see page 84).

The moderate liberal opposition was easily controlled by censorship and the changes made to the constitution. Without means to influence government or communicate their ideas it was difficult for them to coordinate support. Napoleon's wooing of the buyers of *biens nationaux* paid off as property owners rallied to support the regime. Napoleon made a Concordat with the Church, whereby the Pope accepted the loss of Church lands (see Chapter 9, pages 93–4) and promised social and economic stability. Since most property owners feared both a royalist restoration and a Jacobin revival, Napoleon won them over without difficulty.

By 1804, Napoleon's position was reasonably secure. His government was based around a Senate and Council of State, which were both packed with supporters and firmly under his control. Government posts had been used as a means of reward through which he could ensure loyalty and reduce the potential for any future opposition. He was now able to consolidate his rule without hindrance.

SUMMARY QUESTIONS

1 Explain the steps by which Napoleon rose to power in France.

2 Would it be fair to describe Napoleon as a dictator by 1804? Give reasons for your answer.

CHAPTER 9

What changes did Napoleon make in France, 1804–15?

SOCIAL CHANGE

The Legion of Honour and other titles

In 1802, Napoleon established the Legion of Honour to reward those who had served him well and shown their loyalty. Most selected for this award were chosen for their outstanding military service, but of the 38,000 awards made in the years up to 1814, 4000 went to civilians, for their contribution to government. The Legion of Honour conferred no financial advantages on its recipients, but a good deal of prestige was attached to the status it brought.

Of greater financial worth were the *sénatoreries* awarded to old Members of the Senate, from 1804. These were a reward for support and provided large country estates, a palatial residence and an annual income of 25,000 francs to those so favoured. No wonder few senators were prepared to speak against Napoleon's policies.

There were also new titles for members of **the Imperial Court**, after 1804, and positions such as 'Marshal of France' for 18 outstanding generals. These also carried rewards, usually in the form of estates. From 1808, the Imperial Court developed into a great hierarchy of imperial nobility, with princes, counts, barons and chevaliers. Furthermore, when a title was conferred on someone with a sufficiently large income it became hereditary. Around 3500 titles were granted in this way between 1808 and 1814. With the higher ranks came gifts of land in the newly conquered territories of Europe, while lesser 'nobles' received smaller gifts of property or money.

Through this elaborate system, Napoleon was able to ensure that the fate of his supporters was closely linked to

> **KEY TERM**
>
> **The Imperial Court** Titles followed a hierarchy. From 1804 to 1808, the titles given ranged from the lower dignitaries, such as the prefects of the palace, through the grand officers, to the grand dignitaries such as arch-chancellor. Four-fifths of the new titles awarded in this period went to the military who became marshals or Grand Officers of the Empire and received estates, mostly in Poland, Germany and Italy. From 1808, the titles were reclassified. Grand dignitaries became princes; senators and archbishops became counts; bishops and mayors of large towns became barons; members of the Legion of Honour became known as chevaliers.

his own. The imperial nobility needed the empire not only for their honorary position, but also for their income and land.

Education

Despite his talk of creating a society in which all careers would be open to 'talent' – in other words, determined by ability rather than birth – in practice, Napoleon's educational policies favoured those from the property-owning classes and, in particular, from the military elite. It was almost impossible for those of lower birth to obtain the education needed for better careers and few were able to rise above primary level, where the emphasis was on teaching the value of obedience and good morals.

KEY TERM

Notables was another name given to the bourgeois and noble property owners. Some of these were the purchasers of the *biens nationaux*, who had benefited from the revolution; others were recipients of titles, gifts and property under Napoleon's new honours system.

Secondary education was largely restricted to the sons of *notables*. There was no provision for girls, as Napoleon believed too much education would actually prejudice them in a society in which their role was to marry and bear children. So it was only for favoured boys, whose fathers were army officers, that free education was offered. They could attend one of the 37 selective state *lycées* introduced in 1802 to provide a military based training. For those that could afford them, there were other, less prestigious, secondary schools introduced in 1805.

At both, the curriculum was closely controlled and consisted of history, maths, French, science and geography, along with ensuring military values and loyalty. To coordinate the various schools, Napoleon founded the Imperial University, a kind of Ministry of Education in 1808. It controlled the curriculum, not only in the state schools, but also in private schools. All lessons were standardised. It appointed teachers to secondary schools, inspected schools and demanded an oath of loyalty and obedience from all staff.

As a result of Napoleon's changes, education became very restrictive and yet another means of enforcing loyalty and control. Naturally there were those, even among the bourgeois property owners whom Napoleon favoured, who were not happy with these changes. Indeed, those that could afford to often sent their sons to the more expensive church secondary schools, which were more easily available after Napoleon made peace with the church in 1801.

Censorship and propaganda

Napoleon was well aware of the political value of censorship and propaganda and he maintained a tight control over newspapers, books, plays and artists. He regarded freedom of the press as dangerous and likely to weaken a state, so he took measures to control reporting and reduce the number of newspapers in France. He cut the number of Parisian journals from 73 to 13, in January 1800, and again to nine by the end of the year. By 1801, only four remained and they were subject to police supervision with censors appointed to each paper from 1809. In 1810, provincial papers were reduced to one per *département*. No paper was allowed to discuss controversial subjects, and only official news, as reported in military bulletins and the government journal, *Le Moniteur* (written by Napoleon or his ministers), could be included.

To control the spread of politically unacceptable ideas, official reports were made on all books, plays, lectures and posters appearing in Paris until 1810. This system was then replaced by a regular system of censors and half of the Parisian printing presses were closed down. Publishers, who already had to send two copies of every book to the police before publication, now had to take out a licence and swear an oath of loyalty before they were allowed to print. Booksellers were also controlled and could be punished by death if found selling unsuitable material. Some authors and playwrights were forced to flee abroad, while theatres could only operate under licence and many were closed.

On the other hand, books, plays and the arts were encouraged for propaganda purposes, where the subject matter emphasised and honoured Napoleon's achievements. Through *Le Moniteur*, reports of great military victories were spread. Architects, sculptors and painters were commissioned to produce works of art praising Napoleon's achievements and giving him heroic status. Statues, arches (such as the Arc de Triomphe, begun in 1809), and paintings were all used to glorify the

Napoleonic regime. Jacques-Louis David, Napoleon's official portrait artist, was made responsible for paintings and was required to judge the suitability of all subject matter. The most favoured paintings portrayed Napoleon as a statesman, military hero or even a Roman emperor.

RELIGIOUS CHANGE

Frenchmen had been divided over the issue of religion ever since 1791, when the Civil Constitution of the Clergy (see Chapter 4) and Papal condemnation of the revolution had forced Frenchmen to choose sides. This was a situation that Napoleon wanted to change, partly in the interests of stability, but also to win prestige and gratitude. His reasons were certainly not spiritual, although he did enjoy religious ceremonial. He understood the power of the Church to bind his people together, to heal the rifts, win over the nobility and ensure the support of a loyal band of priests. During the time of the Directory, Catholic worship had, in any case, gradually become more open. It was not, therefore, difficult for Napoleon to recognise and legalise what was already happening in the country.

The election of Pope Pius VII in 1800 provided Napoleon with an opportunity to make a Concordat (agreement) with the Catholic Church. In 1801, the Pope's position as 'head of the Catholic Church' was accepted. Catholicism would be recognised as the 'religion of the majority' and Catholic worship would become freely available, although still subject to police regulation. In return, the Church accepted the changes brought by the revolution and promised to make no attempt to recover church lands. State control over the Church in France was confirmed, which meant that the clergy were still appointed by the government, paid as civil servants, and under an oath of loyalty to the state.

The agreement was made at a time when the French army was in effective control in Italy, so it is hardly surprising that the Pope was prepared to accept its rather ungenerous terms, and was even persuaded to attend Napoleon's coronation as emperor in December 1804. The Concordat was regarded as a great triumph by Napoleon and his supporters, and it did indeed succeed in winning the loyalty of those who, if not actively in opposition to the revolutionary changes, had been upset by them. Napoleon had successfully retained the support of the property owners, who were reassured that the Church had no intention of reclaiming its former lands, and had also acquired another means of exerting state control in the provinces. His authority over the appointment of bishops, in particular, provided him with useful agents, through whom he could spread state propaganda and curb subversive behaviour. In April 1802 the Concordat was confirmed in the **Organic Articles**. To the Pope's dismay these also guaranteed religious toleration to Jews and Protestants. Both Catholic priests and Protestant ministers were to be regarded as salaried state officials and no papal legislation could be published in France without government approval.

Relations became strained, as Napoleon was not content to leave the Church alone. He regarded the Church as another instrument through which he could assert state control and, in 1806, standardised the church **catechisms** and created a new one, to be taught in all schools. Clergy were carefully watched by the local prefects and police and he also interfered with the Church calendar when he ordered that 16 August (the day after his own birthday) be celebrated as 'St Napoleon Day', replacing the traditional religious festival on that day. Napoleon was on dangerous ground. Propaganda stressed that it was a Christian's duty to obey Napoleon and that he should be honoured like God. To flout his policies, such as conscription, men were told, was to ignore the will of God. This sort of behaviour, together with Napoleon's liberal treatment of Protestants and Jews, turned Pius VII increasingly against the emperor. Relations reached their lowest point during war in 1808 when Napoleon imprisoned the Pope and annexed the Papal States to his new kingdom of Italy.

It could not, therefore, be said that Napoleon's religious policy was a complete success. Indeed, despite the state control, many clergy remained royalist and the Church continued as an independent force, gaining ground with

KEY TERMS

Organic Articles These were a series of articles published in April 1802 which defined all aspects of ecclesiastical law. In particular they emphasised the state's control over the activities of the clergy. They were told to 'see that this religion attaches you to the interests of the country'. They were to teach citizens that 'the God of peace is also the God of war, and that he fights on the side of those who defend the independence and liberty of France'.

Catechism A catechism is a statement of belief, usually consisting of a series of questions and answers which believers memorise.

the increasing popularity of church schools. After 1808, some of the underlying concerns began to surface and it became a focus for opposition during the final years of Napoleon's rule.

LEGAL CHANGE

There were two aspects to the legal change that took place under Napoleon.

- French law, a huge and mixed collection of legal pronouncements dating from the time of the *ancien régime*, was rewritten, simplified and clarified, in order to establish a single code, or set of laws, for the whole of France. Napoleon took a personal interest in this work and presided over nearly half the Senate sessions during which it was discussed, although professional lawyers were employed to draw it up.
  A new Civil Code, sometimes known as the Code Napoléon, was published in 1804. It was based on **Roman law**, which had been in use in parts, but not all, of France before the revolution and was, in many ways, quite illiberal. It restated some of the legal changes of the 1790s, including the abolition of feudalism, a guarantee of civil rights and confirmed the legal titles to the *biens nationaux*, former church, crown or *émigré* property. It also reinforced the practice of *partage*, meaning the division of lands between male heirs rather than *primogéniture* where they went to the firstborn son. However, the emphasis throughout was on male rights. These went beyond the ownership of landed property to a man's relationship with his wife and his family. A wife or disobedient child could be sent to prison by the husband and divorce was made difficult and expensive. Furthermore, the code allowed slavery to be reintroduced in the French colonies while, at home, all workmen were to be issued with a *livret*, without which no man could gain employment, but with which, workmen were no longer free agents. They had their movements watched and their work and any misdemeanours recorded. Other codes followed, such as the Code on Civil Procedure (1806), the Commercial Code (1807), the

KEY TERMS

Roman law was derived from the system of law used in the Roman Empire. This had been the basis for law in the south of France before the revolution. It emphasised male authority and the rights of fathers.

Livret This was a cross between a work permit and an employment record. It had to be presented to an employer before work could be given. Details of the worker's performance, and any police record, went on the card. Should the employee wish to change jobs, he had the dual problem of getting the card returned and explaining his record to any new employer.

Code on Criminal Procedure (1808) and the Penal Code (1810). In the Criminal and Penal codes, hard labour, the loss of the right hand and branding were all accepted as punishments, which was certainly a step backwards from the heyday of the revolution.

- The second aspect of legal change was administrative. Judges were no longer elected, but appointed by the government. Appointments were made for life, but all judges were kept under close supervision. New courts were set up, including military courts for armed rebels and special tribunals, from 1801, for political crimes. These courts consisted of army officers and magistrates, without a jury, and defendants had no right of appeal against their judgments. In 1810, a system of arbitrary imprisonment without trial (like the old *lettres de cachet*) was established. This was another step back to the *ancien régime*, although it was not much used and, in 1814, there were only 640 such prisoners. However, house arrest was commonly imposed on anyone who did not warrant imprisonment, but was deemed a danger to state security. It is an indication of the nature of Napoleon's legal system that a number of extra prisons had to be built in the years 1800–14 to accommodate the growing number of inmates. It has been estimated that the number of prisoners tripled in this period to approximately 16,000 ordinary convicts.

ADMINISTRATIVE CHANGE

The prefects

Local administration was based on the work of the prefects. One was appointed to each *département* and worked under the control of the Ministries of Police and the Interior. Prefects had wide-ranging duties including the collection of taxes, the control of prices and food supplies and the appointment of mayors and town councils. They also supervised the work of the sub-prefects and magistrates who were responsible for the day-to-day operation of local government. Prefects took charge of conscription, tracked down deserters and reported on **subversive** behaviour. Indeed, they are sometimes referred to as the government's 'eyes and ears', as they worked to

> ### KEY TERM
>
> **Subversive** This refers to political activity that was not acceptable to the regime. Many so-called political subversives were radical republicans.

ensure loyalty, disseminate propaganda and carry out all government orders. Clearly such work demanded absolute loyalty and Napoleon took a personal interest in all appointments. He chose men from the ranks of the military, middle classes and nobility, according to their trustworthiness and talent for the job.

The police

The police were another important part of Napoleon's centralised administration system. **Joseph Fouché** was made Minister of Police until 1810, when he was replaced by Savary. The police were responsible for national security and the minister reported daily to Napoleon. They had spying duties and were also responsible for censorship, prison surveillance and monitoring food prices.

There were various branches:

- **The Sûreté** (special branch) in Paris reported daily on food prices and provided reports on, and if necessary stamped out, any rumours or inappropriate views. They spied on those believed to be politically dubious and searched for army deserters.
- **The *gendarmes*** were responsible for everyday law enforcement. There were around 18,000–20,000 throughout France by 1810.
- **The secret police** were independent from Fouché and checked up on his agents. They collected specific information for Napoleon.

As well as the police, the prefects, sub-prefects, mayors and members of provincial councils were also expected to act as spies. Senators too were required to report once a week from their *sénatoreries*, so there was no shortage of information.

Overall, the prefects and police did an effective job in maintaining order and preventing trouble. On the whole, opponents of the regime found it extremely difficult to organise any kind of protest. However, some problems did remain. The authorities never succeeded in removing the gangs of wandering labourers, or destroying the urban unemployed, who were ready to cause trouble in times of

KEY PERSON

Joseph Fouché (1759–1820) Fouché was elected to the National Convention and became an important Jacobin leader during the Terror. He organised the conspiracy that overthrew Robespierre. He became Minister of Police during the Directory, and retained this post under Napoleon. However, Napoleon never entirely trusted him and employed spies to watch his movements. He was suspected of intrigue with the British in 1810, and dismissed, but he came back to hold a position as Louis XVIII's Minister of Police.

KEY TERM

Sénatoreries As part of their gift, recipients of *sénatoreries* (see page 90) were appointed as *préfets* (prefects) of a whole region. They were told, 'Your most important duty will be to supply Us with trustworthy and positive information on any point which may interest the government, and to this end you will send Us a direct report once a week'.

economic depression, as occurred during the later years of Napoleon's rule. Furthermore, they were not entirely successful in their drive for recruitment into the army. Although harsh punishments, such as forced labour and lengthy prison sentences, could be handed out, desertion and avoidance of conscription was never brought under control, particularly after 1813.

TAXATION AND THE ECONOMY

As in other areas, Napoleon's financial and economic policies involved a tightening of central control. The revolutionary governments had never succeeded in stabilising French finances and Napoleon was determined to remedy this.

First, Napoleon tried to improve government revenue from taxation. In 1800, the Central Treasury was reorganised and a more complete tax register was introduced. The collection of direct taxes was then improved, with the establishment of a panel of tax collectors, supervised by the prefects and under the control of the treasury. (So as to retain bourgeois support, however, land taxes were not raised.)

Accounting procedures were improved and expenditure and income carefully recorded. New indirect taxes (*droits réunis*) were also introduced on consumer goods and customs duties were increased. Taxes on salt, tobacco and alcohol quadrupled and these all helped increase treasury finances.

Secondly, Napoleon improved the circulation of money. In January 1800, the Bank of France was founded, and this was brought under state control in 1806. The bank took responsibility for money supply and **government bonds**, whereby Napoleon ensured that he could raise loans at reasonable interest. Since the *assignats* had made people wary of paper money, which had contributed to inflation, Napoleon introduced a new metal coinage in 1803, based on a silver franc. This helped provide a more stable currency.

KEY TERM

Government bonds were documents promising repayment with interest on loans made to the government.

Napoleon's policies were helped by an economic upturn, including a series of good harvests during the early years of his rule. This, along with the plunder he was able to gain through success in war and the purchase of foreign grain stocks, helped keep bread prices stable. War also provided employment and, by 1802, the budget balanced and the financial situation remained good.

However, after 1806, taxes started rising again as military expenditure began to outstrip income. By 1810, France was once more in severe debt, with inflation, rising unemployment and the collapse of banks and businesses. A bad harvest in 1811 sent bread prices soaring and contributed to the growing loss of confidence in Napoleon.

KEY TERM

The Continental System
This was the name given to the attempt to exclude all British trade from Europe in order to weaken Britain, expand the European market for French goods and increase the cohesion of the Napoleonic Empire (see Chapter 11 for its military implications).

Napoleon also tried to stimulate the French economy through his **Continental System** (see Chapter 11). This was designed both as a means of defeating Britain, whose money gained in trade was helping to keep the armies of his enemies at war, and a measure to help French industrialists, by providing them with a huge market.

From 1793, British goods had been prohibited from entering French territories but, under Napoleon, this ban was extended by the Berlin and Milan decrees of November 1806 and 1807 to all territories controlled by or allied to France. Even neutral shipping that had called at a British port could have its goods confiscated. Napoleon thus tried to prevent continental trade with Britain, while demanding that conquered and allied Europe bought French goods. It failed because the French navy were in no position to enforce the ban, smuggling undermined it, the French Atlantic trading areas were themselves badly hit as the colonial and wine trade virtually stopped in the west, and the French manufacturers suffered from British retaliation. France and the continent desperately needed certain products supplied by the British, especially sugar and coffee, but even extending to coats and shoes.

Admittedly, some parts of France benefited. Strasbourg and Marseilles developed their trade with Germany, Italy and eastern Europe, and Alsace and Belgium did well, but there was no significant increase in demand elsewhere.

So the system was more a liability than an aid and since, to enforce the system, Napoleon had to annex Spain and Portugal, it directly led to the Peninsular War of 1807, which was a major feature in his downfall.

Thus, despite Napoleon's measures, the French economy experienced limited growth during this period. Money for investment was limited, communications poor, technology backward and population growth limited, partly because of the ever-growing loss of men in war. Although warfare stimulated the iron industry, techniques in France were far behind those used in Great Britain. The disappearance of colonial markets and the protection of industry encouraged by Napoleon removed any incentive to change or adapt to new technology. As a result, Napoleonic France remained pre-industrial.

SUMMARY QUESTIONS

1 How successful were the measures taken by Napoleon to establish firm, centralised control in France?

2 Who benefited from Napoleon's rule in France?

CHAPTER 10

How did the Napoleonic Empire in Europe develop, 1804–11?

THE ARMY UNDER NAPOLEON

By the time of Napoleon, France already had the best army in Europe. With its population now over 30 million, the largest in Europe, France was well placed to maintain the huge fighting forces needed for continental war at that time. The *levée en masse* (see Chapter 6) had harnessed the nation's resources and conscription ensured a plentiful supply of fresh young men. Furthermore, the patriotism roused by the revolution, which gave these men a cause to fight and die for, filled the ranks of the army with a strong determination and fighting spirit. As the empire expanded, potential resources of men and war materials grew and, by 1805–6, Napoleon had an army of 500,000–600,000, plus auxiliaries from conquered states.

The revolutionary armies had been reorganised during the republican period by Lazare Carnot (see Chapter 6 and A2 Section 5), who also worked as a minister under Napoleon. Carnot encouraged the use of **mixed order tactics** (as recommended by Count Guibert) and forces had been trained to move quickly around the battlefield, with a bayonet charge rapidly followed by a cavalry attack, giving the enemy no time to regroup.

During the years of comparative peace, 1800–4, Napoleon used his experience as an army commander, as well as the ideas of the eighteenth-century military writer **Jacques, Comte de Guibert**, to build on Carnot's work and reorganise the French forces:

- Napoleon knew from experience that the division of the army into completely separate units, each under independent command, had made it difficult to

KEY TERM

Mixed order tactics involved employing a mixture of columns (files) and lines of soldiers. Napoleon developed this tactic both on the battlefield and in marching, which made his troops less vulnerable and predictable.

KEY PERSON

Jacques, Comte de Guibert An eighteenth-century military writer, who inspired Napoleon and provided many of the ideas that helped the French armies win against the more old-fashioned tactics of their enemies to 1808. He recommended living off the land and fast cavalry charges aimed at the rear or flanks (sides) of the enemy to create surprise and confusion.

coordinate strategy. He therefore rearranged the army into separate corps (groups) of around 25,000–30,000 men each, plus some special groups, such as the Imperial Guard. The whole structure was put under Napoleon's sole control. He was the Commander in Chief.

- These corps were expected to carry a minimum of supplies so that they could cover 12–15 miles a day. They were encouraged to '**live off the land**' rather than waiting on supply wagons, which were slow and prevented a rapid advance.

- Napoleon believed speed and flexibility was the key to success. Each corps was given its own role in a campaign, but had to be prepared for sudden changes of plan to confuse the enemy.

- On the battlefield, Napoleon avoided forming his troops into clear battle lines, but would move them around so as to encourage the enemy to take up a disadvantageous position. His favourite trick was to launch a surprise attack from the flank (side) or rear. The traditional armies of his opponents drawn up in lines would be slow to respond, and Napoleon could then add to their confusion by mounting massed and rapid attacks from all directions. The French army would pursue any retreating forces relentlessly, inflicting heavy casualties.

This mixture of mobility, speed and surprise ensured the success of the French armies against the old-fashioned armies of their opponents in Napoleon's campaigns up to 1808. Weaponry was still rather primitive, although there had been some improvements in light artillery, and training was minimal. However, as veterans fought alongside raw recruits, the latter learnt from their seniors and the fighting force was moulded in action.

How much of his army's success should be credited to Napoleon himself is a matter of some debate and is discussed in A2 Section 5. He was not an innovator. Indeed, he was uninterested in new military inventions that were brought to his notice, such as a primitive submarine, incendiaries or telegraph, and he introduced no new training methods. He has been criticised for his reluctance to delegate or share views with other commanders, which did prove a hindrance in later campaigns. Others have questioned whether he really had 'grand strategies' and battles carefully planned in advance, as he later claimed.

However, he certainly won battles and commanded the loyalty and respect of his troops. It took Napoleon to put the ideas expressed years earlier into practice. His personal leadership, military understanding, daring and **opportunism** seemed to be a winning combination. These, combined with superior numbers, brought much success, at least until 1808.

KEY CONCEPT

Opportunism Although Napoleon claimed to plan battles in advance it was more often his flexibility that won the day. He was not frightened to adjust plans according to changing circumstances.

WARFARE AND CONQUEST TO 1808

The early campaigns

Napoleon's early campaigns, in Italy (1796–7) and Egypt (1798–9), had already shown some of his strengths as a military leader (see Chapter 7). Putting his military strategies to good effect, he mounted a bold and daring campaign in Italy, outmanoeuvring the Austrians and revitalising the demoralised troops which he inherited. He also showed an understanding of the needs of his men when he ensured that they were paid in silver, and not

Napoleon's military strategies.

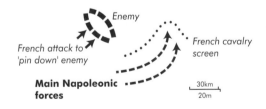

a) 'Manoeuvre on the rear'

The enemy was pinned down by a frontal attack by part of the French Army. However, the main French forces, concealed by a cavalry screen, moved rapidly towards the enemy's rear and attacked from behind.

Enemy

French attack to 'pin down' enemy

French cavalry screen

Main Napoleonic forces

30km
20m

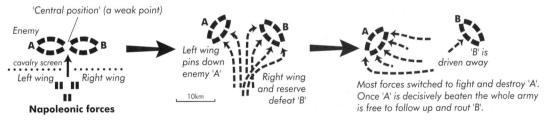

b) 'Manoeuvre on the central position' (employed when facing more than one army)

'Central position' (a weak point)

Enemy

A   B

cavalry screen
Left wing   Right wing

Napoleonic forces

A   B

Left wing pins down enemy 'A'

Right wing and reserve defeat 'B'

10km

A   B

'B' is driven away

Most forces switched to fight and destroy 'A'. Once 'A' is decisively beaten the whole army is free to follow up and rout 'B'.

paper, money. This won their loyalty, and his disregard for orders from the Directory in France only increased their admiration.

Although he liked to exaggerate his personal achievements, the Italian campaign was a resounding success, although that in Egypt was less well managed. Napoleon's forces again fought well but he could also be criticised for allowing his fleet to be taken by Nelson and abandoning his army in order to seize political power in France in 1799. Napoleon believed that political power was essential for him to fulfil his destiny. From the very outset of his career he seems to have had visions of being a modern-day **Charlemagne, Julius Caesar or Alexander the Great** who would found a new empire, not only spreading French power, but also extending liberal culture and civilised values to the rest of Europe, if not beyond.

Napoleon crossing the Alps. This painting by Jacques-Louis David is typical of the adulatory art which Napoleon inspired.

The Second Coalition, 1798–1802

When Napoleon seized power in 1799, France was at war with Austria, the Ottoman Empire (Turks) and Britain. Russia had dropped out of the Second Coalition in September 1799, but Napoleon still needed peace with his remaining enemies in order to consolidate his position. Negotiations began, but the fighting continued as Napoleon secretly hoped that there would be an opportunity for a quick victory to add to his prestige.

Napoleon consequently decided to attack the Austrian army which was besieging the French in Genoa, Northern Italy, by crossing the Alps and cutting off their line of communication with their capital, Vienna. It was a risky campaign and, although he crossed the Alps with his troops successfully, by the time he met the main Austrian army at Marengo (June 1800), his forces were divided. However, he was saved by the arrival of reinforcements under General Desaix and Napoleon could therefore claim a great success. This was followed by another French victory at Hohenlinden in Bavaria (December 1800) and led to the peace of Lunéville (February 1801). The Austrians recognised the French possession of the Austrian Netherlands (Belgium) and the left bank of the Rhine and accepted the French gains in Italy. Austria lost control of the whole of northern Italy (except Venetia) and had its influence in Germany reduced.

Britain had lost its fighting partner and, after nine years of warfare, was also keen for peace. Consequently, it suited both sides to make the Peace of Amiens (March 1802). France agreed to the independence of Naples and Portugal, and Egypt (then in British hands) was returned to the Ottoman Empire. This 'honourable peace' was also hailed as a victory in the Napoleonic propaganda. Peace helped stabilise French finances and was popular at home, but it had not solved the differences between the countries, and provided more of a breathing space than a lasting peace.

The Third Coalition, 1805–8

The British were still suspicious of Napoleon's plans, both in Egypt and Europe and, while the British involved

England and France divide the world between them, 1802. Cartoon by James Gillray. William Pitt, Prime Minister of Great Britain (left), takes the ocean, while Napoleon carves off Europe.

themselves in conspiracies against Napoleon, Napoleon used the 'breathing space' to begin a massive shipbuilding programme and plan a British invasion. By 1804, the peace had entirely broken down and Napoleon had an army of 150,000 waiting to cross the Channel. However, his **invasion plans** came to nothing, even though the fleet remained in waiting for another year.

The nearest the French came to success was when Villeneuve managed to break out from Toulon and gather a large Franco–Spanish fleet at Cadiz with the intention of luring British ships away from the Channel. However, when Villeneuve attempted to sail from Cadiz, he was attacked by the British under Nelson (October 1805), leading to the great British victory off Cape Trafalgar. Even before this, Napoleon had decided to abandon the invasion. Britain had managed to persuade Austria and Russia to join a third coalition against him and he chose to march his army to face the Austrian forces south of the Danube. (Napoleon had managed to keep Prussia out of this coalition by hinting that **British Hanover** might be theirs.)

During the wars against the Third Coalition (1805–8), Napoleon was at the height of his military success. He forced an Austrian surrender at Ulm (under General Mack)

KEY FACT

Failure of Napoleon's naval plans Napoleon had little understanding of naval matters and was defeated by the wind, the weather and the difficulties of breaking free from the watch of the superior British navy that kept guard in the Channel. He actually damaged his own fleet by insisting they put to sea for a review on a day when a storm was brewing.

KEY PLACE

British Hanover Hanover was one of the states which made up Germany. The elector (ruler) of Hanover had become king of Great Britain in 1714 and subsequent British kings had retained this title, although Hanover was never formally incorporated into the British Empire.

in October 1805 and defeated a larger combined force of the Austro–Russian army at Austerlitz in December. His brilliant strategies ensured great victories with limited French losses, and Napoleon's prestige rose. Austria was forced to accept the humiliating Treaty of Pressburg. This recognised the loss of all Austrian lands and authority in Italy and Germany and, in 1806, Austria had to accept the territorial reorganisation of Germany, including the creation of the Kingdom of Westphalia and the Confederation of the Rhine, which destroyed the old Holy Roman Empire that Austria had dominated.

Prussia, which had sat on the sidelines, now joined the Third Coalition. Prussia did not like being forced into Napoleon's Continental System, was uneasy about the new Confederation of the Rhine and felt betrayed after complicated discussions over Hanover broke down. However, their intervention did not go as they planned. Although Prussia had a huge army and formidable reputation as a strong military power, in a one-week campaign Napoleon destroyed the Prussian armies at the battles of Jena-Auerstadt (October 1806) and was able to march in triumph into Berlin.

As stories of Napoleon's invincibility spread, the great emperor turned to the last of his continental enemies, Russia. In February 1807, he marched through Poland to attack Russia, won an indecisive victory at the Battle of Eylau (which took place in a blizzard) and rounded off his success at Friedland in June. Russia sought peace and, at a dramatic meeting on a raft in the middle of the river Niemen (the Russian border) in July 1807, Russia and France made the Peace of Tilsit. The young Tsar Alexander I was rapidly charmed by Napoleon and, in a complete turnaround, France and Russia became allies. Russia agreed to the French creation of the Duchy of Warsaw out of Poland and accepted Napoleon's territorial changes in the rest of Europe. This left Prussia powerless and a further treaty forced it to pay an indemnity, accept a French army of occupation and limit the size of its own army to 42,000.

By 1808, Napoleon had achieved some outstanding success. Only Britain remained at war and he was relying on the Continental System, to be strengthened by his advance into Spain in 1807, to strangle his final rival.

THE NAPOLEONIC EMPIRE IN EUROPE

What was the extent of the empire?

Napoleon's continental empire was vast. Napoleon had gone far beyond France's original aim of extending its territory to its 'natural frontiers' of the Rhine, the Alps and the Pyrenees. Under Napoleon, the Grand Empire, referring to French controlled lands and its associated states, was made up of many different parts:

The expansion of the Napoleonic territories.

1804   108 departments
1805   Ligurian Republic annexed.
      Kingdom of Italy created from Republic of Italy: Napoleon is made king; Eugène de Beauharnais, Napoleon's stepson, is viceroy.
1806   Venetia incorporated into Kingdom of Italy.
      Kingdom of Naples created; Napoleon's brother, Joseph, is king.
      Kingdom of Holland is created from Batavian Republic; Napoleon's brother, Louis, is king until it is annexed in 1810.
      Confederation of the Rhine formed with Napoleon as 'Protector'; Holy Roman Empire is abolished.
1807   Kingdom of Westphalia created, partly from Prussian and Hanoverian territory; Napoleon's brother, Jérôme, is king.
      Portugal subjugated; French general made governor (1808).
      Duchy of Warsaw created from conquered Polish lands given to the king of Saxony.
1808   Kingdom of Spain created; Napoleon's brother, Joseph, moved from Naples to be king. Joachim Murat (husband of Napoleon's sister, Caroline) now becomes king of Naples.

KEY PLACES

The Hansa towns From the fourteenth century, the prosperous trading towns of the north coast of Germany had grouped themselves together in the Hanseatic League. By the eighteenth century, the most important of these towns – Bremen, Hamburg and Lübeck – were known as free cities (not under a prince or similar ruler). They were very wealthy and keen to preserve their independence. Napoleon had left them untouched when he reorganised Germany in 1803, but by 1811 he felt strong enough to force their annexation.

Parma and Kingdom of Etruria annexed (Grand Duchy of Tuscany created for Napoleon's sister Elise, 1809).

Papal States (part) incorporated into the Kingdom of Italy.

1809 Papal States annexed (part not already included 1808 in satellite Kingdom of Italy).

Trentino and South Tyrol incorporated into the Kingdom of Italy.

Illyrian Provinces annexed.

1810 Remainder of Hanover ceded to Kingdom of Westphalia.

Kingdom of Holland annexed (Napoleon thought Louis was too lenient with the Dutch to remain king of a satellite Holland).

Appointment of Napoleonic marshal Bernadotte as Crown Prince of Sweden and heir to the throne; Scandinavian involvement in continental blockade.

1811 The **Hansa towns** of Hamburg, Bremen and Lübeck, and the Duchy of Oldenburg, are annexed.

Napoleon at the height of his powers, *c.* 1810.

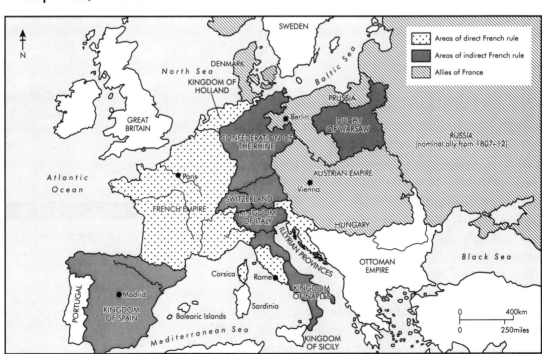

- The *pays réunis* (annexed territories) was the name given to the additional territories directly annexed to France by Napoleon. By 1811, these included the north of Italy and the Papal States, the Illyrian Provinces on the Adriatic coast, Holland and the Hansa towns of North Germany (Hamburg, Bremen, Lübeck and the Duchy of Oldenburg, 1811).
- The *pays conquis* (satellite states) protected the French borders and provided France with men for its armies. They included, at various points, Switzerland, Spain, Naples, parts of Italy, the Germanic Confederation of the Rhine and, until 1810, Holland. In eastern Europe there was the Duchy of Warsaw (from conquered Polish lands), which acted as a barrier against any future Russian ambitions. Prussia's west German lands were also incorporated into a satellite state, Westphalia. These states were often put in the hands of one of **Napoleon's relatives**.
- The *pays alliés* (allied states) were ruled by their own sovereigns, but owing allegiance to Napoleon. Saxony, a member of the Confederation of the Rhine, was one such state. The king of Saxony was also made ruler of the Duchy of Warsaw as a reward for his loyalty. At various points, each of the great powers, Prussia, Russia and Austria, became allied to France and others, such as Sweden, which was forced to accept a Napoleonic marshal as heir to the throne in 1810, were also brought into the French orbit.

Why did Napoleon build an empire?

It is difficult to determine whether the Napoleonic Empire was actually planned or whether it developed by chance as a result of Napoleon's various military campaigns. When Napoleon dictated his memoirs in later years, he claimed to have been inspired by the desire to create a 'universal empire', rather in the manner of his great hero, Charlemagne. He wrote of his ambition to create **national states** under French rule. He said that he dreamt of uniting the Poles, who for many years had been divided and ruled by neighbouring states, into a single country of their own. He wanted the new states to share the enlightened ideas of liberty and equality, which the revolution had brought about in France and to see the end of feudalism and the

KEY FACTS

Lands allocated to Napoleon's relatives

Holland	Louis (brother), up to 1810
Italy	Eugène (stepson) made viceroy
Naples	Joseph (brother) up to 1808; then Marshal Murat (brother-in-law)
Westphalia	Jérôme (brother)
Spain	Joseph (brother)

KEY TERM

National states were made up of peoples with the same racial and cultural origins. Nationalism became a powerful force in nineteenth-century Europe.

KEY TERM

Liberal After 1815, liberalism also grew as a movement in Europe. It encouraged people to fight against oppression and to demand a say in the way their country was run. The legend that grew around Napoleon, and was added to by his own writings and records of his conversations in exile, suggested he had helped the people he conquered achieve liberty.

ancien régime. We shall never know how much Napoleon had genuinely believed all he said and it is worth bearing in mind that some of his claims may have been little more than wishful thinking. There was obviously a strong incentive for Napoleon to create a **liberal** image in the light of what happened after 1815.

Whether we believe his intentions or not, it is generally felt by modern historians that Napoleon did little directly to further the cause of nationalism. His rearrangement of states seems to have been done without much consideration for national groupings. It is likely that his arrangements, for example in Germany and Italy, were nothing more to him than convenient administrative units. The nationalism he aroused was less due to the way conquered territories were treated by the French, than because of the sense of solidarity that grew among people in resistance to French rule.

Even if Napoleon did not specifically set out to create an empire, it seems likely that he soon recognised its value. It provided plunder, which helped increase French resources and income. It offered protection to the mother country. It helped feed his ever-growing need for men for his armies. In short, the empire brought a number of valuable benefits to France and his later attempts to expand the empire, particularly into Spain and Portugal, were fired by his desire to strengthen France by completing the stranglehold of the Continental System.

Last but not least, there is no doubt that imperial conquest suited Napoleon's own personal ambition. Napoleon certainly displayed a liking for power, and the creation of the empire helped to strengthen his position. It also proved a useful propaganda tool, diverting attention from possible trouble at home, provided for his own family and gave him new resources of land and titles in the conquered territories with which to reward his supporters.

The control of the empire

The administration of the imperial territories varied according to their status:

- The *pays réunis* were brought under French law and the French system of government. Territories were divided into *départements*, a French administrative structure was established, the Code Napoléon introduced and the courts reorganised. The Concordat and Imperial University were extended to these territories and the taxation system and liability for conscription standardised with that of France. Feudalism was abolished, subjects were given the same civil rights and property and lands belonging to the nobility or church were confiscated and sold.

  The changes were not all welcomed. While some aspects of the French administration and law were more enlightened than had been previously enjoyed in these territories, some states, such as Piedmont in Italy, where feudalism had been abolished before the French arrived, were already quite forward-looking, and French taxation and conscription policies were universally resented. If anyone benefited from French rule, it was the urban and bourgeois classes, but recent research suggests that the period of French control did not change social structures a great deal. Obviously, those areas annexed by France during the revolutionary period had longer to absorb the French influence than those annexed later, and degrees of change varied.

- In the *pays conquis*, traditional administrative structures were left in place, but feudalism was, in principle, abolished. In practice, change was not enforced and, in places such as the Duchy of Warsaw, noble privileges, feudal dues, labour services and serfdom continued. Much depended on the attitude of the ruler, and even Napoleon's own relatives were not entirely committed to French direction. Under the rule of Louis Bonaparte in Holland (up to 1810), conscription was never introduced and the Continental System not fully enforced. In Naples, under Joseph Bonaparte up to 1808, and then Napoleon's brother-in-law Murat, the government failed to establish the Code Napoléon (which had been introduced elsewhere in Italy), and to enforce the continental blockade. When he moved to Spain, Joseph Bonaparte introduced hardly any significant reform. In Westphalia, Jérôme Bonaparte did produce a more enlightened regime, abolishing feudalism, introducing the Code Napoléon and permitting religious toleration. However, even here, there was a reluctance to enforce the Continental System, which was damaging to the state's trade.

So Napoleon treated the empire, and in particular the satellite states, as a French resource from which he would extract the maximum advantage. The satellites provided around a third of the strength of the **Grande Armée** and had to provide substantial **'tribute' money** to France. Napoleon's financial exactions and economic policies did indeed prove damaging to a number of areas. Italy, for example, had to pay a crippling annual tribute to France, from 1806, as well as providing other specific cash contributions. It was also required to provide an army of 55,000 to serve France and to accept the workings of the continental blockade. Such heavy demands ruined the Italian economy. In the Duchy of Warsaw, also, the financial demands, coupled with the amount of land seized and given as gifts to French marshals and generals, bankrupted the Duchy.

SUMMARY QUESTIONS

1 Why was Napoleon so successful against his enemies up to 1808?

2 What were (a) the strengths and (b) the weaknesses of Napoleon's Empire in 1808?

KEY TERMS

Grande Armée The revolutionary armies were turned into Napoleon's 'great' army. The army, a mixture of veterans and new recruits was, at its peak, unswervingly loyal and bolstered by its special status in the Napoleonic regime. In the later years, the increasing reliance on newly conscripted soldiers from the empire weakened its morale.

Tribute money was levied, rather like a fine, as the price of defeat for satellite states. It served to remind them of their relationship with France and Napoleon. To the latter, they were servant or vassal states: they owed allegiance to him, rather like in medieval times when states and peoples had owed allegiance to their overlord. They existed to serve the interests of France.

How did the Napoleonic Empire in Europe develop, 1804–11?   113

CHAPTER 11

What challenges did Napoleon face, 1808–15?

The continental blockade

Napoleon's fortunes began to turn in 1808. Some of this can be linked to his obsession with the continental blockade against Great Britain (see page 101). Napoleon had made two serious miscalculations when he set up the blockade. First he had underestimated the resilience of Britain in resisting its effects and secondly he had failed to recognise the difficulty of maintaining a blockade that involved controlling the whole European coastline. British trade was never destroyed, and Britain's economy was strong enough to take the strain. Britain found new markets, especially in South America. In any case, its continental trade never entirely ceased, particularly with satellite states, which were as anxious as Britain to maintain trading links. This was the essential flaw in the system. It relied on the cooperation of France's satellites and allies, and Napoleon could never be sure of their support. Furthermore, to enforce the system he needed to control Spain and Portugal, and his decision to undertake the Peninsular War in 1807 was a major feature in his downfall.

The Peninsular War

Spain had been a French satellite state since its defeat in 1795. In 1807, Napoleon secured Spanish agreement to move a small French army across its territory and into Portugal. He wanted to defeat Portugal, a British ally and trading partner, and impose the Continental System along that stretch of coastline. Following a reasonably successful campaign there, Napoleon decided to bring Spain itself more closely under French rule. He used the excuse of divisions in the Spanish royal family to send an army under **Joachim Murat** into the north of Spain and, in March 1808, Murat entered Madrid. However, there was strong resistance to the French domination, particularly after Murat repressed a revolt by the people of Madrid

KEY PERSON

Joachim Murat (1767–1815) Murat was an innkeeper's son who had served under Napoleon in the first Italian campaign and the Egyptian expedition. He earned a reputation as the finest cavalry commander of his day and he led the troops in Napoleon's coup of Brumaire. In 1800, he married Napoleon's youngest sister, Caroline, and he was made a marshal in 1804. He went on to become a prince, and then King of Naples in 1808. He served the French army in Spain, Russia and at Leipzig, 1813. In 1815, he tried to raise support for Napoleon's return but was caught and executed in October 1815.

with great severity in May 1808. Napoleon therefore forced the abdication of the Spanish king, Charles IV (and his heir) in June and installed his brother Joseph on the throne.

Joseph had been a popular king in Naples, but the Spanish people resented the imposition of this French outsider. Catholic clergy helped stir up opposition and Spanish property owners joined local resistance committees, known as *juntas*, and began to arm. **Guerrilla bands** and regular soldiers combined to defeat the French army at Baylen on 20 July. This was the first time a French army had been defeated and it stimulated further resistance not only in Spain, but in Austria and Portugal as well. Joseph abandoned Madrid and the French retreated to the north while, in Portugal, a British force under Sir Arthur Wellesley (later Duke of Wellington), defeated the French at Vimiero in August.

With the French collapse in both Spain and Portugal, Napoleon himself went to Spain with 100,000 veterans of the Grande Armée. He defeated the Spaniards and retook Madrid in December. However, further British forces under Sir John Moore were despatched to Portugal and, to meet this threat, Napoleon had to abandon his Spanish offensives. He was also facing trouble from the Austrian army at the beginning of 1809, so he left Spain in the hands of marshals and never returned.

The campaigns dragged on and, although the British had smaller forces, they proved superior in a number of other ways:

- They were well supplied by the British navy, from their Portuguese bases, which they could also use for the evacuation of troops if necessary.
- They possessed well-trained musketeers.
- They had the support of local 'hit and run' guerrilla forces.
- They had the tactical advantage of being able to assault the over-extended French communication lines.
- The old French game of living off the land was thwarted by the burning of crops and shelter as local opponents used a 'scorched earth' policy.

KEY TERM

Guerrilla bands

Throughout the Peninsular War, the French army faced two types of opponents – the military forces of the Spanish, Portuguese and British, and the roaming bands of armed peasants who waged guerrilla, or 'little', war. The attacks mounted by the peasant bands were particularly vicious and involved ambushes, night raids and surprise raids on isolated outposts. Subsequently, the word guerrilla has entered our language to describe similar warfare elsewhere. The guerrilla bands not only inflicted material damage but also discredited the French by provoking them into reprisals on civilians. They showed how small bands of determined fighters could resist much larger trained forces.

- The British command was effective, under Wellesley, after Moore's death, and contrasted with that of the French marshals, who quarrelled among themselves.

So, despite several French victories in 1809, the British maintained constant pressure on the French troops creating an 'ulcer' that wastefully consumed French time, troops and resources down to 1814.

By 1813, Wellington was strong enough to leave the British defences of Torres Vedras around Lisbon and advance into Spain. He drove the French back in 1813 and defeated them at Salamanca, forcing a retreat. In June 1813, the French army (depleted because of the Russian campaign) was decisively beaten at Vittoria and Joseph fled as Wellington entered Madrid. During the winter of 1813–14 Wellington was at last able to cross the Pyrenees into France. Here he defeated the French at Toulouse on 10 April 1814, just before news of Napoleon's abdication on 6 April reached that city.

The Spanish campaign had proved disastrous. The long campaign cost around 3 billion francs and, of the 600,000 French troops that served in the peninsula, around half were killed. The image of French invincibility was shattered. Napoleon's failures can partly be credited to the weakness of the French armies and their tactics in comparison with those of the British and their Spanish–Portuguese supporters. However, Napoleon himself must also be held, at least partly, to blame.

It could be argued that Napoleon had grown overconfident and undertook the campaign without sufficient forethought. His commitments were too great. Possibly, if he had stayed longer in the peninsula himself, he might have been able to turn events around. However, he judged, rightly or wrongly, that the Austrian campaign was more important. The need to divert experienced troops from Spain to fight Austria and then Russia, in and after 1812, weakened his chances in Spain. Having extended himself so far, he could never muster a large enough army for a decisive blow.

The Austrian campaign, 1809

Austria chose to go to war with France again in February 1809. It had never been satisfied with the harsh peace terms Napoleon had imposed at Pressburg and wanted to restore its influence in Germany and Italy. The Austrian army, now under the much more able commander Archduke Charles, had been strengthened since its earlier defeats. The Austrians had copied the French 'corps' system and, following the French defeats in Spain, there was hope of greater success, even though they failed to win over Prussian or Russian support.

Leaving Spain in 1809, Napoleon hastened to fight the Austrians. The armies met in Bavaria, where there were some indecisive clashes, and Napoleon continued his advance towards Vienna. However, at Aspern-Essling, he was checked in May and lost 20,000 men. He called up his reserves and went to battle again in July. This time, Napoleon was successful in a two-day battle at Wagram. This was to be his last great victory and, even here, the losses were heavy and at least 32,000 of his men were killed.

KEY PLACE

Illyrian Provinces These ran along the coast of the Adriatic, opposite Italy and adjacent to the rest of the Austrian Empire. They provided Austria with an outlet to the sea. (See map on page 109.)

In October, Austria signed the Treaty of Schönbrunn, agreeing to give up the **Illyrian Provinces** on the Adriatic coast and to reduce its army to 150,000. It also had a £4 million (sterling) indemnity imposed on it.

Napoleon's marriage to the Austrian princess, Marie-Louise (daughter of the emperor), in 1810 was meant to seal a new Franco–Austrian alliance and, in 1811, Napoleon's son was born. Napoleon believed that the future was bright. However, with hindsight it is clear that a turning point had been reached. Despite the French victory, the Austrian campaign had not been easily won. Napoleon's strategies had failed to work as well as in the past. The problem was that the Austrian armies had begun to show some of the qualities that had previously enabled the French to win: above all, greater mobility. In comparison, Napoleon's own army had been weakened by the division of his troops and the need to rely on more new recruits and foreigners from his satellite states. These had proved less disciplined than his veteran soldiers and some had even deserted at Wagram. Napoleon too had shown that he could make mistakes. He had underestimated the strength of the opposition at Aspern-Essling and found himself outnumbered.

The Russian campaign, 1812

Although the treaty made between Tsar Alexander I and Napoleon at Tilsit in 1807 continued to 1812, the relationship had soured over the years. There were a number of disagreements:

- Neither side really trusted the other. The French were wary of Russian ambitions in the Ottoman Empire, while the Russians feared French ones in Poland.
- There was also friction over Napoleon's annexation of the Duchy of Oldenburg, which had been in the hands of the tsar's brother-in-law to 1810.
- Napoleon was annoyed at Russia's lack of support in the Austrian war of 1809, while the tsar was angered by **Napoleon's decision, in 1810, to marry** an Austrian princess. A marriage to the tsar's sister had previously been considered.
- The main cause of disagreement was over the tsar's disregard for the Continental System. At the end of 1810, he had introduced a new trade tariff discriminating against France in favour of Britain. Napoleon therefore determined to force the tsar to toe the line.

Napoleon made careful preparations. He already had the support of Austria, and he persuaded the Prussians that it was also in their interests to help him. He built up a huge army. It consisted of 450,000 men (of whom less than half were French), 150,000 auxiliary troops and over 1000 guns. In June 1812, without any declaration of war, he began his advance, crossing the river Niemen and entering Russia.

He hoped to make a quick attack and force a decisive battle, but his problem was finding an enemy to fight. Without any particular prearranged plan, the smaller Russian armies constantly retreated and refused to turn and fight even when ordered to do so by the tsar. So it was that

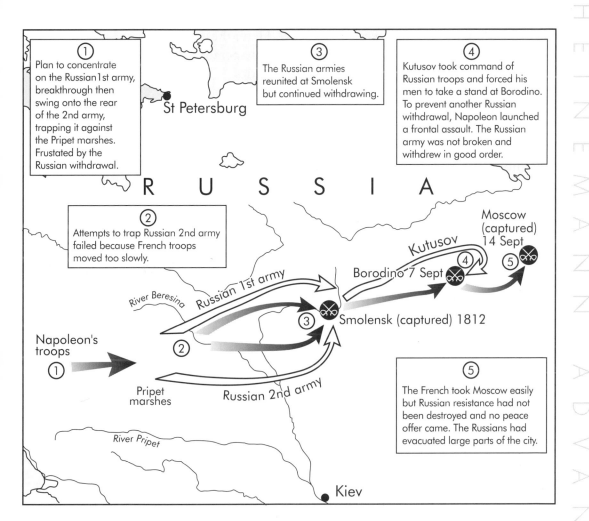

① Plan to concentrate on the Russian 1st army, breakthrough then swing onto the rear of the 2nd army, trapping it against the Pripet marshes. Frustated by the Russian withdrawal.

③ The Russian armies reunited at Smolensk but continued withdrawing.

④ Kutusov took command of Russian troops and forced his men to take a stand at Borodino. To prevent another Russian withdrawal, Napoleon launched a frontal assault. The Russian army was not broken and withdrew in good order.

② Attempts to trap Russian 2nd army failed because French troops moved too slowly.

⑤ The French took Moscow easily but Russian resistance had not been destroyed and no peace offer came. The Russians had evacuated large parts of the city.

St Petersburg

R U S S I A

River Beresina

Russian 1st army

Napoleon's troops ①

Pripet marshes

Russian 2nd army

River Pripet

Smolensk (captured) 1812

Kutusov

Borodino 7 Sept

Moscow (captured) 14 Sept

Kiev

Napoleon's advance to Moscow, 1812.

the Napoleonic armies were drawn ever deeper into Russia. This stretched their supply lines and their advance was slowed by the sheer weight of numbers. To make matters worse, the Russians set fire to crops and villages as they withdrew following a scorched earth policy similar to that which had been so successfully employed against the French in Spain.

Napoleon's usual tactics were not working. The French troops had limited shelter and food. Disease killed around 60,000, some were killed by marauding bands of Cossacks and others died of starvation and exhaustion. The Russians, under Kutuzov, did not turn to fight until they reached Borodino, 60 miles west of Moscow. Here, the Russians were defeated on 7 September, after a desperate battle in which there were around 80,000 casualties. Nevertheless, the result was not decisive, as many Russian troops escaped.

Napoleon's forces were able to take Moscow on 14 September, although it was a pitiful city, deserted and burnt by the retreating soldiers, but still the Russians refused to negotiate. The French army lingered in Moscow for more than a month. The French soldiers were pleased to rest and gather loot to take home, but the delay was fatal.

The **retreat** was not ordered until 19 October, by which time the weather was turning and the cold Russian winter drawing nearer. Napoleon tried to take a more southerly route back, to avoid the barren wastes through which they had come, but the Russian army now took the opportunity to harass them at every turn. They were forced back to their former tracks and had to pass the rotting corpses on the battlefield of Borodino. Attacks by Cossacks and Russian forces, starvation and the weather reduced the Grande Armée to 50,000 by the time they reached Smolensk.

The final straw came when the Russians destroyed the bridges at the river Beresina, before the French arrived, to prevent their escape. Only the discovery of a ford and two hastily improvised bridges permitted 40,000 men of the Grande Armée to get away, although thousands more drowned in the freezing water in the panic of the escape. Only 25,000 survived to reach the safety of the Duchy of Warsaw by the end of the year. Napoleon abandoned the remnants of his army and fled to Paris to deal with rumours of a royalist plot.

Napoleon always blamed the catastrophic failure on the weather and it is certain that the elements did not help his campaign. However, the failures of the French armies cannot be explained away quite so easily. Had Napoleon planned the campaign with greater care, he would have avoided being drawn into the Russian heartland and

KEY THEME

The retreat from Moscow, 1812 With starvation pending, the French armies began their retreat from Moscow in October 1812. The columns of the Grande Armée stretched out over 500 miles. They were the easy victims of the Russian winter, mounted Cossack fighters from southern Russia, and the unseasonal floods of the River Beresina. Napoleon himself fled by sledge to Warsaw and on to Paris. General Caulincourt wrote, 'Never was a retreat worse planned, or carried out with less discipline ... to a lack of forethought we owed a great part of our disaster'.

Defeat in Russia – the retreat from Moscow, 1812.

languishing there until the snows fell. He knew he was commanding a huge army with many raw and ill-disciplined troops, and yet he permitted his supply lines to become overstretched and made insufficient provision for the soldiers' rations. The 'caring general' of earlier campaigns had allowed his soldiers to set off with only four days' rations, inadequate maps, sparse summer clothing and insufficient medical supplies. Of course, not everything could be blamed on Napoleon. Russian tactics and disease also played their part, but the 1812 campaign certainly increased the feeling that the final defeat of Napoleon could not be too far away.

The Fourth Coalition, 1814–15

The final coalition against Napoleon was brought about by Tsar Alexander I's reaction to the events of 1812. He believed that the Russian deliverance had been God-given and he was filled with a sense of a **holy mission**: to free Europe from Napoleon's clutches. He set about organising a coalition and, by the summer of 1813, had been joined by Britain, Prussia and Sweden.

Although Napoleon had returned from Russia determined to build another army, his position had been severely weakened. He managed to raise 300,000 men, but they were mostly raw conscripts from the empire. He had only his satellites, Italy, the Confederation of the Rhine,

KEY POINT

Alexander I's holy mission
Alexander was a deeply religious man. The audacity of Napoleon and the success of the Russian armies in repelling the invader had instilled a new sense of purpose in him. He was influenced by the mystic, Madame Krudener, and came to believe his task was to save not only Russia, but all of Europe from Napoleonic oppression.

Hanover and Bavaria in support, but with his usual confidence he went into action and won some minor victories, which forced the coalition partners to retreat.

However, in June 1813, still dogged by the Spanish campaign, he accepted the Austrian suggestion of an **armistice** and negotiations began for a final peace treaty. The Austrians were keen to arrange this since they distrusted Russo–Prussian ambitions. They had not joined the coalition because the marriage agreement of 1810 had left them an ally of the French, but they were determined to win back some of what Napoleon had taken from them. The armistice certainly provided Napoleon with a breathing space, but it may have been another foolish mistake. He had little intention of accepting a peace on Austria's terms, and the seven weeks it lasted gave Austria time to build up its army.

When Napoleon proved unwilling to make concessions, Austria also declared war on France, in August 1813. Fighting recommenced. The coalition cleverly adopted the strategy of avoiding pitched battles with inferior numbers. This frustrated Napoleon's attempt to defeat each of the allied armies in turn. After a number of inconclusive encounters, the coalition partners then converged on Leipzig. A three-day battle ensued (16–19 October), which became known as the Battle of the Nations because it involved the combined armies of Austria, Russia and Prussia. Napoleon, with an army of 200,000, was heavily outnumbered, surrounded on three sides by allied forces of 350,000. He lost 70,000 men and retreated to the Rhine. He hoped that the coalition partners would quarrel, as they had so often done in the past, and allow him to make a comeback.

However, it was not to be. Britain prevented the disintegration of the coalition by persuading the partners to sign the Treaty of Chaumont on 1 March 1814. By the treaty, the allies bound themselves together in a Quadruple Alliance. They promised to continue to fight together and not to make separate peace arrangements until Napoleon was defeated. What is more, they pledged themselves to

KEY TERM

Armistice This is a cease-fire that takes place while negotiations for a peace treaty are going on.

Napoleon's defeat at Leipzig, 1813, by Russian, Prussian and Austrian forces.

preserve their alliance and maintain whatever settlement they drew up for 20 years thereafter.

The myth of Napoleon's invincibility began to crumble and the satellite states gradually deserted him. In the remaining months of 1813, Baden, Bavaria, Württemberg and the other states of the German Confederation joined the allies. Jérôme was driven from Westphalia, Saxony fell to Prussia, and the Duchy of Warsaw to Russia. A popular revolt in Amsterdam drove the French from Holland. The Illyrian Provinces had to be abandoned, Spain was lost and Napoleon was left with Belgium, Switzerland and Italy.

Within France, there was widespread discontent as Napoleon tried to raise and equip yet another army. The financial situation was dire and the hostility to conscription, after 20 years of war, intense. Morale was low but, although the allies offered peace terms on the basis of France's 'natural frontiers', Napoleon refused to agree. By mid-January 1814, when he did accept negotiations, the allies' offer was withdrawn. They had already made the decision to invade France.

Although Napoleon won some small victories in the Rhineland and France in early 1814, this failed to prevent the allied advance. By the end of March 1814, an allied army, led by Tsar Alexander I, captured Paris. On 6 April, having lost support in Paris and from many of his marshals, Napoleon reluctantly abdicated. He attempted suicide, but failed because he had kept the poison too long. Instead, he had little choice but to accept a generous offer from the allies to retire to the island of Elba, off the coast of Italy.

The First Peace of Paris (May 1814) set about establishing a peace settlement. France was to be returned to its frontiers of 1792 and the Bourbon monarchy restored. Everyone thought that Napoleon had gone for good, but they were wrong.

Invasion of France, 1814. After refusing peace terms with the Rhine as frontier, Napoleon failed to counter the allies' advance with a surprise attack on their rear. His tactics were discovered and the allies took Paris.

The 100 Days

After the first Peace of Paris, the allies began to argue over the future of Europe, as Napoleon had anticipated. Louis XVIII, the brother of Louis XVI had been brought back from exile to take the French throne, but he was very vulnerable and totally dependent on outside support. This gave Napoleon hope.

In March 1815, he left Elba and landed in southern France with a few hundred supporters. He **marched through France**, gathering supporters on the way. Many Frenchmen had been dismayed to find a Bourbon back on the throne and there were rumours circulating that he would soon reclaim the land of the *biens nationaux*. The continuance of high taxation and conscription, together with some of the old stirrings of patriotism and loyalty ensured Napoleon a good following. Although the new king sent Marshal Ney to capture him and 'bring him back to Paris in an iron cage', the general defected to his former master. As Napoleon entered Paris, Louis XVIII departed in fear to Brussels where he could be protected by the coalition.

Napoleon had undertaken a gamble, and he tried to win it by announcing his intention to reform the constitution, giving freedom of the press, universal suffrage, and making ministers responsible to the elected assembly. This **Acte Additionnel** was presented to the French people in a plebiscite. Only about a fifth of electors voted in this, but there were over 1.5 million in favour, as opposed to 6000 against. This showed some support for the change, but also a marked apathy on the part of the majority. Although Napoleon referred to the act later as part of his careful plans to liberalise France, most remained unconvinced.

Napoleon tried to negotiate separately with the allies. He rightly believed this his best chance of re-establishing himself, but his presence only served to reunite the coalition. It was clear that he would have to fight for victory and he advanced against the British and Prussians in Belgium. He hoped a defeat would force the Russians and Austrians to make terms. He nearly succeeded.

The 100 Days, 1815.

Napoleon's return It took Napoleon just three weeks to re-establish himself as master of France, after landing at Antibes on 1 March. His progress was made possible by his promises, his military reputation and the magnetism of his personality, as well as concerns about the newly restored Bourbon government. He informed the first troops sent to capture him that he had been summoned to Paris by the allies, so the soldiers joined him and helped his march.

Acte Additionnel Benjamin Constant (see page 88) was invited to draw up this act as an addition to the existing constitution, bringing greater democracy. Napoleon claimed that he had always intended a liberal empire to grow out of his authoritarian one when the time was ripe. He said, 'I am not an enemy of liberty but I set it aside when it obstructed my way'.

He showed some of his old military talent by adopting a central position to divide the Prussians and British before they could join forces, with the aim of defeating each in turn. He crossed to Belgium at Charleroi and sent Ney to hold off the British advance while he defeated the Prussians at Ligny. He then turned to face the British army under Wellington, leaving Marshal Grouchy to pursue the Prussians. Wellington, expecting Prussian help, had taken up a position at Waterloo and was waiting. Napoleon delayed his attack, waiting for the ground to dry a little after a night's rain, and this gave Wellington time to contact Blücher, the Prussian commander. The battle of Waterloo took place on 14 June and was, in Wellington's words, 'a damned close thing'. The arrival of 81,000 Prussians finally swung events in Wellington's favour and Napoleon was pursued back to Paris.

KEY TERM

Regency This is when a person or group is appointed to run a state until a child ruler comes of age. Napoleon's son was only four years old.

Even after this, he was ready to try again, but the French Council of State would have none of it. Napoleon had to accept a second abdication and his proposal of a **regency** for his young son was ignored. This time, Napoleon was exiled to the island of St Helena, 5000 miles away in the mid-Atlantic. Here, he spent his remaining years under British guard, dictating his version of events, until he died in 1821, probably from cancer of the stomach. On 8 July 1815, Louis XVIII again rode into Paris, the empire came to an end and the Second Peace of Paris reinstated France's borders of 1790.

SUMMARY QUESTIONS

1 Which played the greater part in Napoleon's downfall, the Peninsular War or the Russian campaign? Explain your answer.

2 'Napoleon never stood any chance of success during the "100 Days"'. Explain why you agree or disagree with this view.

CHAPTER 12

Why was the Bourbon monarchy established in 1815 and overthrown in 1830?

The impact of the Vienna Settlement

The victors of the revolutionary and Napoleonic wars spent 1814–15 trying to arrange a settlement that would prevent any future French aggression and ensure peace in Europe. They arrived at their decisions at a great congress in Vienna, attended by **Charles Talleyrand**, as representative of the restored French Bourbon monarchy. The Vienna Settlement involved restricting France by establishing a **cordon sanitaire** of buffer states around the country. Austria was again placed in a position of authority over Germany and Italy, Prussia was given the left bank of the Rhine while a new Kingdom of the Netherlands was made to the north and a neutral Switzerland to the east. The settlement was not unduly **punitive** but it nevertheless humbled France. France had its frontiers reduced to those of 1790, an indemnity of 700 million francs to pay and an army of occupation, which was to be paid for by the French and to remain until the indemnity was paid off. The new king of France had an unpromising start.

THE REIGN OF LOUIS XVIII

The charter

The allies had accepted Louis XVIII as king of France because of their fear and distaste of republicanism, and because he was the only **legitimate** heir. It was felt that he would divide France the least, but he was far from a popular choice. A fat and elderly 59 year old, he had spent the last 20 years in exile, and had a limited understanding of the changes that had taken place in France during that time. In an attempt to make his position acceptable, he was asked to sign a charter, as a condition of his return. This was designed to ensure that the new king would retain and obey some of the fundamental changes of the

KEY PERSON

Charles Talleyrand-Périgord (1754–1838) Talleyrand had been the chief negotiator on Louis XVIII's behalf with the allies in 1814. At the Vienna Congress, he tried to exploit the differences between the other powers to France's advantage.

KEY TERMS

Cordon sanitaire This involved the setting up of buffer states, under the influence of other strong powers, to prevent France attempting to expand again. It was a 'healthy' barrier designed to keep the peace.

Punitive This is something that punishes and takes revenge. The allies, particularly the British, were fearful of weakening France too much, for fear this would tip the balance of power in favour of the authoritarian Russia, Austria and Prussia.

Legitimate This referred to the right of a ruler to hold power by strict hereditary law. This had been the normal pattern in the *ancien régime*, but had been disrupted by the revolution. At the Vienna Congress, the principle of legitimacy was upheld where it was feasible to do so.

revolutionary and Napoleonic period. The charter promised basic civil rights, fair taxation, freedom of the press, property rights, pardons for former revolutionaries, the abolition of conscription and religious toleration (although Catholicism was to be the state religion).

The charter also made Louis XVIII's position as a **constitutional monarch** clear. France was given a parliamentary system of government, with two chambers (councils). Members of the Chamber of Peers would be nominated by the king, while those in the Chamber of Deputies would be elected by property owners in a two-tier system of voting. The king was allowed to choose his own ministers, introduce laws, veto amendments, dissolve Parliament and control all military and civil appointments.

The charter certainly made Louis XVIII's return more acceptable, but the government was far from democratic. From a population of 29 million, only around 88,000 had the right to vote, and around 15,000 had the right to stand as deputies. Furthermore, Louis XVIII had determined that the charter should not undermine his position. He had therefore added a **preamble** in which he made it quite clear that the freedoms granted by the charter were his personal gift to his people, not their basic right. He strongly believed in his own divine right to rule and accepted no responsibility to his new Parliament.

Louis XVIII's successes

In many respects, Louis XVIII handled France well. He tried to rule in the spirit of the charter and pursued fairly moderate policies, helped by capable ministers such as the Duc de Richelieu, and later, the Duc de Decazes. He tried to work with his chambers, and chose ministers they trusted. He did make some mistakes. For example, he replaced the Tricolore flag of France, which symbolised the revolution, with the white flag carrying the gold Bourbon *fleurs-de-lis* and he reformed the household guard and restored several thousand noble officers. However, he tried, with some success, to resist the demands of his more extreme supporters in the early years and was supported by most of those that mattered: the voters who made up the *pays légal.*

KEY TERMS

Constitutional monarch
The powers of a constitutional monarch are limited by a written document that guarantees basic rights, such as freedom of speech, and gives power to an elected assembly, or parliament.

Preamble This was an introductory section explaining the basis of the charter.

Pays légal was the term given to those with a franchise (right to vote) in the new constitutional regime of Louis XVIII. They represented the social elite in France, made up of rich landowners, bankers, merchants, officials and lawyers. They exercised an influence out of proportion to their numbers, which amounted to under half of 1 per cent of the population.

The Chamber of Deputies

Year	No. of Seats	Deputies' qualifications		Electors' qualifications		Size of electorate
		Tax (fr)	Age	Tax (fr)	Age	(000s)
1816	258	1000	40	300	30	88–110
1831	459	500	30	200	25	166–241

The French electoral system, 1816 and 1831.

He was assisted by a general economic recovery after 1815 in which French industry prospered. By accepting tighter controls on government spending, the war indemnity was soon paid off and by 1818 the foreign troops had left France. At the Congress of Aix-la-Chapelle the same year, Louis achieved another success, when France was readmitted to the **Concert of Europe** regaining some of France's international prestige. He even felt strongly enough to send an army of 100,000 men, under the Duc d'Angoulême, to assist the Spanish king, Ferdinand VII, who was appealing for help against liberal rebels in 1823. His troops were victorious and Louis XVIII was able to boast that he had achieved something even Napoleon had failed to do, establish control in Spain.

The revival of the Ultras

Despite his successes, Louis's reign was constantly unsettled by the demands of the **Ultras**, who used their power and influence to gain positions in the new Chamber of Deputies. Louis referred to his first chamber of 1815 as *la chambre introuvable* (the impossible-to-find chamber) because it was more royalist than he was himself, something he had not deemed possible! They hoped to do away with the charter and with parliament and wanted the return of the lands lost by aristocrats and the church during the revolution. They constantly tried to push Louis XVIII further than he seemed prepared to go.

For example, it was the Ultras who encouraged the **White Terror**, which led to a spate of imprisonment and executions, particularly in the south of France, in 1816. There was a public outcry at the execution of Marshal Ney, but Louis XVIII was powerless to do much about it in view of the Ultras' strength in the chamber. They also pressed Louis XVIII for a purge of the civil service and local government, replacing Napoleonic officials with their own nominees and, despite Louis XVIII's promises of 'freedom of the press', they demanded the censorship of political news and comment. Worse still, to the horror of the buyers of *biens nationaux*, they continually asked for the return of *émigré* and church property.

Louis XVIII did his best to counter the Ultras' influence. The electoral system was reformed in September 1818 to permit annual elections at which a fifth of the chamber would be replaced. This measure succeeded in bringing more moderates into parliament in the short term but, in 1820, the assassination of Louis's nephew, the Duc de Berri, presented the Ultras with the perfect excuse to press their demands. The duke was the only male member of the Bourbon royal family capable of providing an heir to ensure the succession. The Ultras regarded the assassination as a clear warning of the power of the moderates and left-wing radicals and demanded tougher policies.

The moderate minister, the Duc de Decazes, was dismissed. The electoral system was again changed, this time in favour of the wealthy. Around 15,000 of the richest men in France would now be responsible for choosing over a third of the deputies. In addition, more press censorship was introduced in 1821, the clergy were given greater influence in education and plans were drawn up to compensate the many *émigrés* who had lost land during the revolution.

This was a turning point for the monarchy. Louis XVIII was racked by **gout** and lacked strength to resist the Ultras. However, their demands upset many who had previously been prepared to tolerate, if not support, the monarchy. To make matters worse, in September 1820, the wife of the Duc de Berri gave birth to a son, some months after her husband's death. Some thought it a divine miracle, others, evidence of **the lengths the Ultras were prepared to go to** in order to ensure the succession. It was far from welcome news to those who feared the way the government was heading.

KEY TERM

Gout This was a disease causing inflammation of the joints, particularly in the legs. Louis XVIII suffered badly and parts of his toes actually dropped off.

KEY THEME

The lengths the Ultras were prepared to go to
The Duc de Berri was the son of Louis XVIII's brother, Charles X, and the second in line to the throne. With his death it might have been expected that the Bourbon line would die out. The arrival of a son, Henry, to his widow, Caroline of Naples, a few months later, was greeted with dismay and scepticism by the moderates. They accused the Ultras of falsely producing a miracle baby to ensure the Bourbon succession.

In the later years of Louis XVIII's reign, the chamber was heavily dominated by the Ultras, and led by the Comte de Villèle. He was to remain as chief minister into the next reign from 1822 to 1827. He carried through important financial reforms, which helped him to balance the budgets, but his support for the Ultras made him unpopular. There was an outcry when he persuaded the ageing Louis XVIII to dismiss his foreign minister, the **Vicomte de Chateaubriand**. Louis XVIII was condemned at every turn. When he sent the French armies into Spain and looked for public acclaim for asserting France's authority and power, cynics complained that he was merely showing his support for a despotic king. So, when Louis XVIII died in 1824, he not only left a well-established pro-Ultra parliament, but also a good deal of underlying discontent within the country.

Radical opposition

Although there was friction between the moderates and the Ultras during the reign of Louis XVIII, they both accepted the idea of monarchy. Of greater significance for the future was the survival of the radical republicans, who regarded the restoration as a betrayal of the revolution. With the changed political circumstances, many of these had been forced into hiding, but they thrived in secret societies, on the model of the Italian **Carbonari**.

In the early 1820s, the French Carbonarist movement had around 40,000 members and it even managed to attract some dissatisfied upper-class followers, such as Lafayette, the old revolutionary. However, the numbers fell as government spies uncovered their activities and a planned rising in 1822 failed, when the army did not give its support. By 1824, radical opposition to the monarchy had become less organised, but it had certainly not disappeared. Left-wing intellectuals and students had begun to take an interest in the writings of socialists such as **Saint-Simon**. They spread their socialist ideas among the working men of Paris, who were willing to support any movement that promised them a better future. Although few realised it at the time, such developments were far more dangerous to the monarchy than the dispute between the moderates and Ultras in the Chamber of Deputies.

KEY PERSON

François René, Vicomte de Chateaubriand (1768–1848) An ex-*émigré* who had been forced to flee to America in 1791 and had fought in the counter-revolutionary armies. He had returned to France to serve under Napoleon but resigned his commission in 1804. He supported the restoration and acted as Louis XVIII's foreign minister. He was regarded as too moderate by the Ultras, who forced him out of office. Nevertheless, he refused to serve Louis-Philippe, and spent his retirement writing.

KEY TERM

Carbonari This began as an Italian society of liberal thinkers who based some of their rituals on the practice of the Freemasons. Their name literally means 'charcoal burners'.

KEY PERSON

Claude Henri, Comte de Saint-Simon (1760–1825) Saint-Simon fought for the republicans in the American War of Independence and returned to France to buy land during the revolutionary period. In his writings he argued that bankers, industrialists, scientists and engineers were the men of the future and that churches and kings were things of the past. By allocating the profits of industry fairly, poverty could be eliminated and a perfect society created.

THE REIGN OF CHARLES X

The policies of Charles X

Although Charles X was 67 when he came to power in 1824, he was an energetic man, with firm convictions. He intended to play an active role in government and declared, 'I had rather chop wood than reign after the fashion of the King of England'. He was also profoundly religious and insisted on a pompous coronation at Reims, surrounded by **medieval pageantry**. This frightened the anticlerical *pays légal*, which viewed him suspiciously.

Charles X's association with the Catholic Church provoked opposition. He encouraged the return of the religious orders, and restored the influence of the **Jesuits**. He made **heresy and sacrilege** punishable by death and continued to extend the control of the Church over education. In 1821, bishops had been made responsible for secondary education and, in 1824, they were given the right to put forward suitable candidates for primary school vacancies. Clerics were also encouraged to fill teaching posts in the universities. By 1827, 66 out of 80 philosophy teachers in colleges were priests, and about a third of all teachers were clerics by 1830.

In 1825, a law was passed to compensate the *émigrés*. In many respects it was a fair measure. There was to be no return of land. Even Charles X knew how politically dangerous such a step would have been. Instead, the act confirmed existing ownership, while providing an annual grant of money as compensation to the former holders. It aimed to provide financial security for ex-*émigrés* and to reward their loyalty. However, it met with strong opposition. To raise the compensation money the scheme involved reducing the interest payable on the national debt. This meant that the value of government bonds, many of which were held by the *pays légal*, fell. Although the sums involved were not as large as opponents made out and were insufficient to satisfy many *émigrés*, it was the principle that caused trouble.

KEY TERMS

Medieval pageantry
Charles liked elaborate ceremonial and encouraged his courtiers to behave in a respectful manner. He revived ancient royal customs, such as visiting hospitals to cure those inflicted with scrofula, an unpleasant swelling of the glands, by his holy touch.

Jesuits The Jesuits were members of the Catholic Society of Jesus. They had been dissolved in 1773, but recreated in 1814, and resumed their duties of teaching and encouraging conversions to the faith during the restoration period.

Heresy and sacrilege
Heresy was the denial of the teachings of the Catholic Church, sacrilege, the destruction and abuse of the Church's sacred objects. The law passed against these proved unenforceable.

To counter the opposition he faced, Charles X extended royal control over the press. Opposition newspapers were bought out, postage rates and stamp duty on paper increased, and legal action was threatened against printers who produced material contrary to regulations. By 1827, all books and journals were censored. Royalist control of the army was also assured by the dismissal of 56 ex-Bonapartist officers.

Charles X upset all shades of political opinion with his policies. Relying on Villèle as his chief minister, he maintained the rule of the Ultras by increasing the term deputies were elected for from five to seven years. He also abolished the annual elections introduced in 1818. Consequently, the moderate, middle group of men who believed in the charter and had held the balance in Louis XVIII's chamber dwindled and turned into the 'liberal' opposition. They were firmly opposed to the Ultras, who refused to consider any political reform.

Like Louis XVIII, Charles X enjoyed one foreign policy success. In 1830, an expedition against the **Barbary Pirates**, who attacked shipping in the Mediterranean, led to the capture of the pirates' base in Algiers. However, the *pays légal* was so hostile to his domestic policies by this time that he received little credit for his daring.

The mounting crisis of 1827–30
By 1827, there were mounting signs of discontent in France:

- In March, the Parisian National Guard was disbanded when some members shouted '*à bas les Ministres*' (down with ministers) during a review by the king.
- A liberal political society, '*Aide toi, le Ciel t'aidera*' (God helps those who help themselves) was founded by **François Guizot** and backed by his friend, the banker Jacques Laffitte. This helped to coordinate the opposition. Chateaubriand also mounted a campaign in the Chamber of Peers.
- In November 1827, Charles X attempted to alter the chambers again, creating new peers and announcing new elections. The move backfired, as Guizot's society

Barbary Pirates A band of superb seamen based in Algiers who made their living from piracy off the coast of northern Africa. They were a particular hazard for French cargo vessels, which had to pass their bases as they entered the Mediterranean on their way to the ports of southern France.

François Guizot (1787–1874) Guizot was a Huguenot Protestant from Nîmes who became Professor of History in Paris in 1812. He led the moderate liberal opposition of the *pays légal* to Charles X's policies. He later became a minister under Louis-Philippe.

succeeded in increasing the number of liberal deputies and even some former Ultras began to change sides.

- In January 1828, Villèle was forced to resign and Martignac was appointed first minister. He was regarded as a man of moderate views, but this only encouraged the liberals to press their demands.

- By August 1829, government was virtually at a standstill and Charles X determined it was time for strong action. He ignored the chambers and completely changed his ministerial advisers in line with his own beliefs. Martignac was dismissed and Prince Jules de Polignac appointed. He was an ex-*émigré* who believed he was guided by visions of the Virgin Mary. La Bourdonnaye, who was remembered as an ardent supporter of the White Terror, became minister of the interior. Courvoisier, a priest, became minister of justice, and Bourmont, who had deserted Napoleon just before Waterloo, was chosen as minister of war. When the election of 1829 returned a large liberal majority, the few remaining moderates joined the opposition.

- On 3 January 1830, *Le National*, a liberal, middle-class paper, was founded. It was again supported financially by Jacques Laffitte and one of its editors was the politician, **Adolphe Thiers**. It produced many articles attacking the government and its ministers.

- In March 1830, the chamber passed a vote of no confidence in the government. Charles X responded by dissolving the chamber and calling elections in June/July 1830. Although the chamber refrained from a direct attack on the king, there was a growing demand for the dismissal of his unpopular ministers.

- The capture of Algiers on 9 July 1830 increased Charles X's confidence. He decided to use a clause in the charter, which would allow him to change the voting system by royal edict and, on 25 July 1830, published four edicts, known as the Four Ordinances of St Cloud. The edicts reduced the electorate to the 25,000 richest members of the *pays légal* and forbade the publication of unauthorised newspapers and pamphlets. Although this move was legal within the terms of the charter, to Charles X's opponents it seemed as though he was undermining the constitution on which his monarchy was based.

KEY PERSON

Adolphe Thiers (1797–1877) Thiers was a lawyer, journalist and historian. As editor of *Le National*, he was able to attack Charles X's advisers and policies and he did much to precipitate the revolution of 1830. He became minister of the interior and later prime minister under Louis-Philippe.

THE JULY REVOLUTION

The events of 1830

Charles X had overestimated his subjects' loyalty, without any thought for the consequences. He had few troops stationed in Paris, since the best were in Algiers, and the commander of the Parisian garrison (and other ministers) were not even informed of his edicts before they were published. There had been no attempt to round up opposition leaders before the ordinances were released. Charles X was seemingly so unconcerned that he went hunting that day.

Naturally enough, the edicts caused an outcry and the radical republicans, led by Lafayette, began mobilising support. Discontented printers, the very men asked to print the ordinances, journalists who were threatened by the curbs on the press, students who believed in radical change and discontented working men all joined in the protests. By 28–29 July, there was severe rioting and barricades started to go up in the streets of Paris. The few remaining troops were forced out of Paris and Charles X had little choice but to go. On 1 August 1830, he abdicated in favour of his 9-year-old grandson, Henry (V), son of the assassinated Duc de Berri. On 17 August, he fled to England.

'Liberty Leading the People' – painting by Eugène Delacroix, 1830.

KEY PERSON

**Louis-Philippe
(1773–1850)** (King of the
French 1830–48) Louis-
Philippe was a direct
descendant of Louis XIII, and
the eldest son of Philippe,
Duc d'Orléans. His father
had supported the revolution
and favoured the execution of
Louis XVI. This had earned
him the nickname 'Égalité',
(equality), although it had
not saved him from the
guillotine. Louis-Philippe was
the next in line to the throne
after the family of Charles X.
He had served as a military
commander in the
revolutionary armies of 1792
and, although he had fled to
Austria in 1793, as the
revolution grew more
extreme, he had never
supported the enemies of
France. He had remained in
exile in Switzerland, the USA
and England until 1815,
returning at the restoration.
From 1815 to 1830, his
home, the Palais Royal in
Paris, was a focus for middle-
class opposition to the
monarchy and he was
strongly associated with the
bourgeoisie.

By the end of July 1830, the republicans and working men
had Paris under their control and the Tricolore flag of the
revolution was hoisted over the cathedral of Notre Dame.
These developments alarmed the moderates. If the liberal
bourgeoisie was to retain control, they had to act quickly.
Adolphe Thiers assumed the leadership of this group and
rapidly distributed posters in favour of **Louis-Philippe,
Duc d'Orléans**, around Paris, backed by a campaign in his
newspaper, *Le National*. Louis-Philippe, son of Philippe
Egalité, whose Palais Royal had been a centre for the early
revolutionaries (see Chapter 1), had a royal claim to the
throne, and it was believed he could win the support of
both the middle and lower classes.

Thiers succeeded in persuading the republicans to give
their backing and, to the cheers of a large crowd, Louis-
Philippe dramatically embraced Lafayette at a window in
the Hôtel de Ville, wrapped in a Tricolore flag. Henry V
was to 'rule' for merely one week. On 9 August, Louis-
Philippe was recognised as 'King of the French by the
grace of God and the will of the nation'.

The causes of the July Revolution

Both Louis XVIII and Charles X can, to an extent, be held
responsible for the collapse of the Bourbon monarchy in
1830. Both were elderly ex-*émigrés*. Louis XVIII was fair
but uninspiring, while Charles X seemed unable to
compromise. Both showed their insensitivity by stressing
their divine right to rule and insisting on using the
Bourbon flag and, while they shared great hopes for
France, seemed dull after the glories of the Napoleonic
period.

In some respects, the restored Bourbon monarchs were
unlucky. Factors such as the 100 Days, which set Louis's
reign off to a bad start, the assassination of the Duc de
Berri, which gave the Ultras the upper hand, and Louis
XVIII's poor health were beyond personal control.
However, they added to their troubles by showing little
regard for public opinion and gradually allowing the
provisions of the charter to be undermined.

Their attitudes and policies offended the very group that the monarchs most needed for support: the *pays légal*. It was Charles X's failure to respond to this powerful and influential group in society that sealed the fate of the dynasty.

Nevertheless, it would be unfair to suggest that the Bourbons were solely to blame for their fate. They had been restored, by France's erstwhile enemies, to a country that had experienced plenty of political turmoil and was not afraid of changing its government. The continuing influence of republicanism, the growth of the Carbonarist secret societies and the influence of the socialists ensured a continuing body of opponents ready to seize any opportunity for change.

Slumps, unemployment and high food prices, particularly after 1826, when an economic depression hit France once again, created a willing Parisian 'mob' prepared to follow those who promised a better future. At the same time, the bourgeois middle classes were growing in Paris and France, and the property-owning beneficiaries of the revolution were determined not to lose all they had gained.

The leadership of Thiers, the existence of a moderate 'middle-class' royal, in the person of Louis-Philippe and the willingness of Lafayette to accept the liberals' choice were all factors in the establishment of the July Monarchy.

SUMMARY QUESTIONS

1 What factors made it difficult for Louis XVIII to establish his royal authority in France in 1814–15?

2 'Louis XVIII could have been a great monarch had he had better supporters.' Explain why you agree or disagree with this view of Louis XVIII's reign.

3 Assess the relative importance of (a) social and economic; (b) personal and (c) political factors to the downfall of the Bourbon monarchy.

AS ASSESSMENT: NAPOLEONIC AND BOURBON FRANCE

STRUCTURED QUESTIONS IN THE STYLE OF AQA

Read Source A and then answer the questions that follow.

Source A
The exclusion of Britain from the economic life of continental Europe was to be a starting point, the foundation upon which the rest of the Continental System had to rest.

> From M. Broers, *Europe under Napoleon 1799–1815*, Arnold (1996).

(a) Explain, briefly, what is meant by 'the Continental System' in relation to Napoleon's economic policies. (3)
(b) Explain why Napoleon's Continental System was unsuccessful. (7)
(c) 'The economic problems of Napoleonic France and the Empire cannot all be blamed on the Continental System.' Explain why you agree or disagree with this statement. (15)

Reading
Before answering these questions you should re-read Chapter 9. You will also need to look at parts of Chapters 10 and 11 for references to the economy of the empire and the workings of the Continental System.

How to answer the question
Sub-question (a). As a simple, 3-mark question, this requires a straightforward definition, linked to the context. A good answer might state:

• The Continental System was a form of economic blockade, whereby Napoleon attempted to prevent British goods entering Europe. It was established by the Berlin and Milan decrees of 1806 and 1807 to help promote the self-sufficiency of the Napoleonic Empire and to defeat Britain, by removing the source of its prosperity, trade. It was undertaken as a retaliatory gesture against the British blockade on French goods, but developed into an obsession demanding that Napoleon defeat or ally with Russia, Prussia and Spain in order to effect the ban.

Sub-question (b). To answer this you will need to present a range of relevant factors in such a way that you show some links and understanding of their relative significance.

The answer might focus on the opposition from other European and imperial territories, or that within France from the shipbuilding and export trades. It might stress the practical difficulties of enforcing the ban, such as French naval weakness and the success of smuggling encouraged by the continent's need for British goods, which the French proved unable to supply. Alternatively, answers could argue that the Continental System was based on mistaken economic beliefs and that it underestimated the strength of the British economy. In drawing a conclusion about the significance of the factors mentioned, it is sometimes a good idea to leave the most convincing point till last. The final paragraph might begin:

- While all these factors played their part in the failure of the Continental System, it was the contribution of the system to Napoleon's defeat which showed, more than anything else, how flawed the policy was. The system demanded military campaigns in Spain and Russia for its enforcement, which were directly linked to the collapse of the empire and caused an economic depression that alienated the bourgeoisie who were therefore not prepared to save it.

Sub-question (c). In planning this answer it would be a good idea to start with a list of economic problems. You could then go down the list and note which were caused or made worse by the Continental System and which could be blamed on other factors such as the inherited economic state of France, the British blockade, military demands and defeat and natural disasters. Remember also that you should consider whether the Continental System had any benefits in order to provide a balanced answer. Economic problems you might include are:

- inflation, loss of foreign markets, labour shortages, trade deficits, balance of payments problems, rising industrial costs, scarcity of raw materials, poor harvests, stagnant agriculture, lack of technological advance, banking and commercial crises, monetary problems, depressions.

STRUCTURED SOURCE-BASED QUESTIONS IN THE STYLE OF EDEXCEL

Study Sources A and B and then answer questions (a) to (c), which follow.

Source A
If you can discover how a young, unknown man inspired a ragged, mutinous, half-starved army, and made it fight; how he gave it energy and momentum to march and fight as it did; how he dominated and controlled generals older and more experienced

than himself – then you will have learnt something. Napoleon did not gain so much by a study of rules and strategy, as by a profound knowledge of human nature in war.

A British general's opinion of Napoleon during the Italian campaign.

Source B

Although the campaign had only lasted two months we were barefooted ... worn out with fatigue, wet through with rain and snow, nipped with cold, and camped in the mud ... The Emperor knew of our wants and our fatigue, which he shared. He was aware too, that the soldiers grumbled and he said, 'They are right; but it is to spare their blood that I make them undergo these hardships.' When we heard that, he could have made us do what no one else could.

Recollections of Captain Charles François who served under Napoleon during the Austerlitz campaign.

(a) What do these sources reveal of the reasons why Napoleon was such a successful general? (5)

(b) Explain how Napoleon's military successes enabled him to gain control of France between 1799 and 1804. (7)

(c) Why did the military success of the empire give way to failure and defeat? (18)

Reading

Before answering these questions you should re-read Chapters 8, 10 and 11. You would also find it useful to read Section 5 of the A2 part of the book.

How to answer the question

Sub-question (a). This question is based on the given sources, so you will need to read them carefully before starting to write. Try to extract some linking themes and support your statements clearly, without relying on excessive quotation. Themes might include:

• determination, energy, attitude to his men, understanding of human nature.

Sub-question (b). Answers will need to make a clear link between military factors and political change. A two-column plan, headed military and political, would help organise the relevant material. The body of your answer will probably be chronological, showing awareness of the stages by which Napoleon increased his power – as consul, First Consul (for life) and finally Emperor – but the best responses will make some overall conclusion, perhaps about his growth in prestige, self-confidence, or about the weakening of opposition and other factors contributing to his political ascendancy.

Sub-question (c). This answer demands an examination of a range of causes of defeat, focusing on the difference between Napoleon's later years (after 1808) and those of his years of military glory. Try to write thematically, rather than chronologically, and make links between the causes. Before you begin, decide which factor or factors you regard as the most important, so that you can argue to this end and lead to a strong conclusion. Themes you might include in your answer are:

- Napoleon's ambition and confidence, the over-extension of the empire and the part of the Continental System, the lack of resources and weakening of Napoleon's military strength, the improvement in the allies' military strategies, the strength of the Fourth Coalition.

QUESTION IN THE STYLE OF EDEXCEL

Identify and explain any **two** factors that helped to bring Louis-Philippe to power in 1830. (30)

Reading
Before answering this question you should re-read Chapter 12. You would also find it useful to read Section 6 of the A2 part of the book.

How to answer the question
Perhaps the most difficult part of this question is deciding which two factors to write about. It would probably be sensible to choose two broad factors, which you can then subdivide, rather than focusing on a very marginal or limited factor, such as the part of Lafayette. Nevertheless, if you do have a lot of specialist knowledge about one particular issue, this question does provide you with an opportunity to use it. The most likely response will pick two broad, or more specific factors from:

- economic and social factors – the growth of working class discontent as revealed in the republicanism of 1830, the power of the bourgeoisie and the influence of the *pays légal*
- personal factors – the failure of the Bourbons, the appeal of Louis-Philippe, the influence of individuals e.g. Thiers
- political factors – the problems of the Bourbon restoration, the reaction against the Ultras, the political ineptitude of Charles X, the importance of the July Ordinances.

Answers should focus clearly on the accession of Louis-Philippe and it should be remembered that the failure of the Bourbons did not automatically mean the triumph of Louis-Philippe.

A2 SECTION: REVOLUTIONARY, NAPOLEONIC AND BOURBON FRANCE

INTRODUCTION

This section offers a more detailed and analytical examination of some of the issues that have given rise to historical debate about this period of French history. History is never static. It is only to be expected that, because historians have different personal views and interests, and work with evidence that is often ambiguous or incomplete, their interpretation of events will differ. This section examines how different historians have interpreted some of the major issues concerning revolutionary, Napoleonic and Bourbon France. This gives students the opportunity to consider how and why interpretations differ and to begin to make their own judgements about the relative importance of the differing factors that help explain historical events and issues. The section ends with some advice on how to tackle the types of questions set by the main examining bodies at A2 level.

Areas of debate are discussed as follows:

Section 1: Why did revolution break out in France in 1789? examines the development of the historiography of the French Revolution and assesses the influence of different schools of thought.

Section 2: How significant was the part played by crowd action and the Sans Culottes in the development of the revolution? develops from Section 1 and examines the influence of one very significant social group as a revolutionary dynamic. It helps explain the links between the French revolutionary regimes, their leaders and urban politics.

Section 3: To what extent did the war affect the course of the revolution? examines the impact of war on domestic politics and assesses whether the revolution was 'blown off course' as well as investigating what provoked the Terror.

Section 4: Did Napoleon develop or destroy the revolution? examines the continuing controversy over Napoleon's contribution to the revolution. Arguments about his aims, methods and achievements and the degree to which Napoleonic rule represented change or continuity from the French Revolution are considered.

Section 5: How can Napoleon's military successes be explained? focuses on the debate as to whether Napoleon deserves to be described as a 'great' military leader. It analyses some of the factors that contributed to his success in battle.

Section 6: Why did the restoration of the Bourbons (1814) end in revolution (1830)? offers an in-depth analysis of the failure of the Bourbon restoration and the causes of the July Revolution, examining the extent to which political, economic, social, ideological and religious developments can be linked to change.

Why did revolution break out in France in 1789?

The apparently simple question, 'Why did revolution break out in France in 1789?' has given rise to endless research and debate. Why in 1789? Why in France? Historians have been fascinated by the coincidence of events, movements and ideas that created, in the words of the historian R.R. Palmer, 'the great turning point of modern civilisation'. They have answered the question in different ways, depending on their own particular standpoints and those of the era in which they lived.

KEY POINTS

- The French Revolution had no single cause but was the product of a unique combination of events.
- The ways in which historians have interpreted the causes of the French Revolution have largely been determined by their own political and personal standpoints.
- Any attempt to explain the outbreak of revolution must take both long-term and short-term factors into consideration.

HISTORICAL INTERPRETATION

For around a hundred years after the French Revolution, it was normal practice for historians to view the events in political and ideological terms. Writers belonging to this 'school' can be divided into four groups:

- The opponents of the revolution, such as **Edmund Burke**, who condemned the revolution as early as 1790 as the 'conspiracy of a few', and **H. Taine** (1876), regarded the revolution as evil and sought individuals and groups to blame.
- The French 'liberal-monarchists' of 1815–30, including **Adolphe Thiers, Germaine de Staël** and **François Mignet**, approved of the early stages of revolution but condemned the Republic and the Terror.
- Later 'liberal' or, in Britain, 'Whiggish' historians, the most famous representative of whom was **Alexis de Tocqueville**, favoured the 'freedom' brought by the revolution in principle, but were suspicious of the notion of 'equality'.
- The 'liberal-democratic' historians, beginning with **Jules Michelet** (1856), favoured all revolutionary developments, including the birth of the Republic. **F. Aulard** (1901), who set a new standard of scholarship

by his systematic and critical use of sources, also belonged to this group.

Despite their differences, these historians all regarded the revolution as coming 'from above'. In their writings, the revolution was the product of a battle between old and new 'enlightened' ideas or between differing factions – the king, court, aristocracy and the Third Estate, which was generally regarded as a single group led by the middle classes.

In the early twentieth century, there was a shift in focus away from the political–ideological to a more social–economic interpretation of events. This change owed a good deal to the rise of socialism and the influence of **Marxist ideas**. It also reflected a growing concern for the 'common man' and an interest in working-class movements which was common to much historical study. Beginning with **Jean Jaurès** in France in 1901, the emphasis moved to a study of the peasants and Sans Culottes as groups in their own right, and the revolution came to be regarded as a struggle between differing classes. Jaurès' work was developed by **A. Mathiez** (1932), **Georges Lefebvre** (1924–34) and **Albert Soboul** (1958).

This new concern with history 'from below' stirred up huge debate and led to major clashes between historians. It is not feasible to list here all the writers who have contributed to the arguments, but the views of the major voices are provided below. The continuing controversy includes those who question this social interpretation and those who have placed a greater emphasis on the 'cultural' history of the revolution.

It is possible to divide twentieth-century historians into two broad schools of thought. One group followed the Marxist interpretation, based on a belief that all history is the history of class struggles and that economic factors are the key to an understanding of the process of historical change; the other followed the **Revisionist** view, which opposed this and emphasised political and cultural factors.

The Marxist interpretation

The Marxist school explained the French Revolution by looking at the rise of the bourgeoisie (middle classes) and in turn the working classes, and the challenge this posed to the old nobility and the structure and practices of the *ancien régime.*

Albert Mathiez added to Jaurès' studies of the *menu peuple* (humble people) with his own work on the Parisian Sans Culottes and a favourable reassessment of Robespierre.

Georges Lefebvre provided important social studies, including work on the peasants, the Great Fear of 1789 and the behaviour of the revolutionary crowds. In his book *Quatre-Vingt-Neuf* (1939), he argued the classic

Marxist ideas
These were based on the teachings of Karl Marx (1818–83), a German philosopher who lived in exile in England. He argued that class conflict was an inevitable and necessary consequence of capitalism and that it would eventually lead to revolution.

Revisionist A historian who revises, or challenges, what has been written before. In a sense, all historians are Revisionists revising the work of others, but the term is often used when different broad schools of historical thought emerge, the more recent challenging the established view. There are differences of interpretation within each school.

Marxist case. The bourgeoisie had been growing in numbers and wealth throughout the eighteenth century and the Enlightenment was the result of their new ways of thinking. When the king's political authority was undermined by debt, and reform was blocked by nobles anxious to retain their privileges and influence, the bourgeoisie were able to overthrow the old aristocratic society. There were four clear stages to the revolution:

- the revolt of the aristocracy (1787–8)
- the revolution of the bourgeoisie (September 1788–June 1789)
- the popular revolution (July 1789), inspired by the economic problems of urban workers
- the peasant revolution (later 1789), following the escalating economic crisis and ending with the abolition of feudalism in August 1789.

For around 20 years this view remained largely unchallenged. **Ernest Labrousse** analysed price movements up to 1789 and these gave strength to Lefebvre's arguments. He showed how the economy developed in 18th-century France and made links between the outbreak of revolution and severe economic crisis, as well as between popular intervention and economic misery.

Albert Soboul, Professor of the French Revolution at the University of Paris, like Mathiez and Lefebvre before him, also provided material in support of the Marxist interpretation. This included a detailed study of the urban Sans Culottes in 1958. He wrote, 'The revolution of 1789–94 marked the arrival of modern bourgeois capitalist society in the history of France'. To him, 1789 was a necessary stage in Marxist evolution.

Although the older, more political interpretations of the causes of revolution were not entirely forgotten, this social interpretation dominated teaching in the French universities and, although **Daniel Guérin**, himself a Marxist, questioned whether the Terror was really in the interests of the people, it was left to an Englishman to mount the first effective challenge.

The Revisionist interpretation

Alfred Cobban first questioned the Marxist interpretation in a lecture, entitled 'The Myth of the French Revolution' in 1955, but his views were expressed more clearly in his *Social Interpretation of the French Revolution* in 1964. He challenged the argument that the revolution was led by a rising bourgeoisie and suggested that it was the peasants rather then the bourgeoisie who overthrew the old system. He claimed that France was not a predominantly capitalist society, and the small group that might be termed 'bourgeoisie' was not hostile to traditional society, merely anxious to join it.

Cobban's views were soon backed by others. They took some while to be accepted in France but **François Furet**'s *Interpreting the French Revolution*

(1978) and his combined two-volume history of the revolution with **Denis Richet** (1965–6) eventually questioned the orthodox approach. The Americans, **Robert Foster**, who published a study of *Toulouse* (1960), in which he showed how the nobility and bourgeoisie shared the same economic outlook, and **George Taylor**, who also demonstrated similarities between the nobility and bourgeoisie (1964), gave further support. Taylor wrote, 'it was essentially a political revolution with social consequences, not a social revolution with political consequences'.

In 1973, **Colin Lucas** gave another twist to the Revisionists' arguments. He claimed that the revolution occurred because the political crisis of 1786–8 convinced the privileged bourgeois members of the Third Estate that the social structure was becoming more closed. He argued that it was fear of being shut out from their ambition of obtaining noble status, not revolutionary class-consciousness, which motivated them to revolt. He spoke of 'an intra-class conflict over basic political relations'. Other historians, such as **Roland Mousnier**, have emphasised the diversity of the bourgeoisie and suggested that the Marxist idea of division into classes by wealth was inappropriate in eighteenth-century France.

By the 1980s, however, most Revisionists accepted that the revolution did have social as well as political and cultural origins, but did not agree that the capitalist bourgeoisie was the driving force. **William Doyle**, writing on the *Origins of the French Revolution* in 1980, believed that what occurred was the product of circumstances rather than any preconceived plan. He wrote, 'the principles of 1789 cannot be identified with the aspirations of any one of the pre-revolutionary social groups. The development of the revolution was neither inevitable nor predictable'. Revisionists have also challenged the view that the revolution was an agent of modernisation, necessary to move France forward. The popular historian, **Simon Schama** is among those who have decried the whole idea of revolutionary change being 'liberalising'. In his book, *Citizens* (1989), the revolution is associated with fanaticism and excess.

In challenging the Marxist view, some Revisionists have emphasised the political and cultural causes of revolution. One group has suggested the revolution was the product of trends, not only in France, but throughout the whole of western Europe. **R. R. Palmer** and **J. Godechot** (1970s) have both taken this 'Atlantic' view, linking developments in France to those in America and elsewhere, while **Emmet Kennedy** has written of the French Revolution as a 'profound cultural event', the product of much wider developments in the growth of science and rationalism and the loss of religion.

Post-Revisionism
Since 1989, there has emerged a third historiographical 'school', sometimes known as that of the post-Revisionists. These are historians

who have tried to look for yet different ways of interpreting the revolution. Although Marxist views have been almost totally discredited, particularly since the fall of the communist regimes in Europe, some of the most important recent developments in the historiography of the revolution have involved a reversion to the idea of the aristocracy as a distinct political group. The views of the post-Revisionists do not as yet form a coherent whole. However, there has been a good deal of interest in the role of public opinion in the generation before the revolution. Borrowing from the ideas of the German left-wing philosopher, Jörgen Habermas, it has been suggested that it was a loss of respect and reverence for the monarchy that sapped its political strength and led to revolutionary change. Those wishing to examine recent views on the causes of revolution would be advised to read the work of **Tim Blanning**, who has summarised viewpoints in *The French Revolution, Class War or Culture Clash?* (1998) or Colin Lucas (ed.), whose *Rewriting the French Revolution* (1991) has drawn attention to some key areas of study.

The important lesson to be drawn from this historiographical survey is that the French Revolution cannot be considered the product of any one factor. It was a mixture of intellectual, social, economic and political factors that gave rise to this unique event.

INTELLECTUAL FACTORS

The Enlightenment

The Enlightenment, an intellectual movement that spread through 18th-century Europe, challenging age-old assumptions about society and authority, no doubt played a part in the timing and location of the revolution. The enlightened thinkers applied logic and reason to politics and believed it was possible to create a perfect society on a rational basis. The ideas of the *philosophes*, as they were known, led to a questioning of existing arrangements in society, politics and religion and led to concepts like the '**social contract**', '**citizen**', '**nation**' and the '**general will**'.

Unlike the 'enlightened despots' in Austria, or even in Russia, the French monarchy had not risen to the challenge that the new thinking posed. Yet the *philosophes* of the Enlightenment were primarily French. It was in the salons of Paris that much of the questioning, arguing and resort to 'reason' encouraged by the Enlightenment took place. The works of the *philosophes* were quoted by the French *parlements* in the 1760s and 1780s. Their attacks on 'ministerial despotism' were peppered with references to the writings of Montesquieu, Rousseau and others – with the direct intention of winning public support in their struggles.

The Enlightened Philosopher: Jean-Jacques Rousseau.

The intellectual debate was disseminated throughout France. The 18th century saw the development of literary societies in many provincial towns, extending the influence of the Enlightenment to the educated bourgeoisie. Even the artisans and workers, particularly in Paris, were encouraged to question authority by the many pamphlets and cartoons, satirising in particular the monarchy and the Church, which were distributed at this time. It became fashionable to be sceptical and irreligious. Although Louis XVI did not realise it, the Enlightenment undermined the divine right on which his system of government was based.

It is important to remember, however, that although standards of literacy were rising, the *philosophes* did not enjoy mass readership and even political pamphlets had a limited circulation. In any case, as the spirit of criticism increased, so did censorship and control. The *philosophes* never offered a clear-cut programme of reform; nor did they (apart from Rousseau) question the institution of the monarchy. Although important, the ideas of the Enlightenment did not so much cause the revolution as provide a framework within which it could take place. Once underway, it was to the ideas of the enlightened thinkers that the revolutionaries turned for guidance.

The influence of the American War of Independence

There was some precedent for the overthrow of a legitimate ruler in the interests of the ruled in the American War of Independence. The American Revolution of 1778–83 set an example of liberty achieved by an army of citizens inspired by the doctrine of no taxation without representation and equal rights. What is more, Frenchmen such as Lafayette had fought on the side of the rebels, absorbing some of their enthusiasm. Some historians, such as the American, **Forrest Macdonald**, have tried to show a connection between the return of French soldiers from the American wars and the outbreak of rural violence in 1789. Although Macdonald's research has been questioned, there was a good deal of revolutionary fervour in the Île de France (to the south of Paris), which sent more troops to America than anywhere else. The educated classes were certainly interested in American events. They drew parallels between the 'tyranny' of George III of Great Britain and his 'despotic' ministers and their own country. Federal and state constitutions were studied in the **literary societies** of France. It is sometimes said that the American Declaration of Independence (1776) helped shape the revolutionary Declaration of the Rights of Man and the Citizen (1789). Certainly Thomas Jefferson, the author of the former, was in Paris at the time and may even have been consulted but, despite similarities of style, the content shares little in common.

The coincidence of timing suggests that the American war did have an effect on the outbreak of revolution in France, although it would seem that the economic impact was greater than the political and intellectual.

KEY TERM

Literary societies
Literary and debating societies had been set up in most of the major cities of France in the course of the eighteenth century. Typical of their interests was the prize essay competition, sponsored by the society at Toulouse in 1784. Entrants were asked to write on the importance of the American Revolution. The competition was won by a Breton army captain who wrote that it was a 'beacon of virtue and happiness and a model to emulate in France'.

The influence of the War of American Independence: the inscription on the pedestal reads 'America and the Seas acknowledge you, O Louis, their Liberator'. Engraving after Jean Duplessis-Bertaux, 1786.

The war forced the French government to take out loans (on five- to seven-year terms beginning in 1778–81) at interest rates it could ill afford. The costs of the war itself, coupled with the disruption to trade that followed, all helped weaken the monarchy and provoke the financial crisis of 1786–8, which preceded the political upheaval.

ECONOMIC AND SOCIAL FACTORS

Whatever historical arguments are accepted, there must be some place given to economic and social factors in any survey of the causes of the French Revolution. We have already seen in Chapter 1 how French society was, despite its apparent stability, full of contradictions. The monarch was not as absolute as he appeared, the nobility was divided and resentful, the bourgeoisie was denied social status, while the peasants and urban workers were grossly overtaxed and yet the first to suffer when food was in short supply.

The privileged classes

According to the traditional Marxist interpretation, the clergy and nobility worked in harmony with the monarch and were set apart from the rest of society by their privileged position. A closer examination of French society in the second half of the eighteenth century shows, however, that this was hardly the case.

Ever since the **Frondes** of the seventeenth century, the traditional nobility – the Noblesse d'Épée – had been excluded from political office and, despite their status, still harboured direct grudges toward the monarchy. The Noblesse de Robe, who had acquired noble status and ran the royal bureaucracy, including the *parlements*, were no more content. There had been a series of clashes between the *parlements* and Louis XV, Louis XVI's grandfather, whose extravagance and laziness provoked their exasperation. Nevertheless, it was their own vested interests that had stood in the way of the reforms proposed by the king's minister, Maupeou. Such developments weakened the monarchy by encouraging criticism and loss of respect, and also, ironically, damaged the position of the privileged classes that depended on the monarch.

KEY TERM

Frondes Groups of nobles who had rebelled against the king, causing civil war in the 17th century.

It is always dangerous to generalise about any group or class and the privileged orders are no exception. The nobility were not simply divided by 'robe' and 'sword'. There were, as the historians George Taylor and **Guy Nogaret** have shown, some who invested heavily in industry, particularly coal and textiles and who therefore shared a similar lifestyle to the industrial bourgeoisie. They had little in common with the rich nobles who lived at court or dominated the salons of Paris and, again, neither shared the problems of some of the impoverished nobility of the provinces who were struggling to maintain a reasonable income from their estates. The clergy were even more divided, with the lower clergy identifying with the peasants and artisans and often openly hostile to their 'noble' superiors.

The privileged orders were not a closed caste and, while it is certainly true that the exemption of the privileged from most taxation exacerbated France's financial problems, to claim that all were united in defence of those privileges is not. The idea that the French Revolution was the product of class antagonisms is therefore highly suspect. Nevertheless, since it was the Assembly of Notables, which included many higher-ranking clergy, that refused to endorse ministerial reform in 1789, the privileged must bear at least some of the responsibility for the outbreak of revolution in 1789.

The bourgeoisie

For most of the eighteenth century the wealth of the French bourgeoisie had been growing, thanks to the expansion of manufacture and trade. However, according to the research of historians such as Mathiez, Lefebvre and Godechot, the social and political opportunities presented to this class had not grown accordingly. They believe that the normal avenue to status – the purchase of a hereditary office of state or an army commission – had been blocked during the second half of the eighteenth century. The Army Law of 1781 excluded the recently ennobled from the higher ranks and throughout France the number of offices for sale in the *parlements* had declined, and those that remained had become less lucrative. Fewer than 20 per cent of 680 new magistrates in *parlements* 1774–8, for example, were non-noble. The more numerous, the wealthier and the more educated the bourgeoisie became, the scarcer became the number of posts to which they could aspire. Marxist historians have described this as an 'aristocratic reaction', but it is more likely that there were simply too many wealthy job seekers for the administration to absorb.

Frustration was made worse by inflation, which hit at fixed incomes on which office holders and lawyers depended. According to the traditional Marxist school of historiography, this 'resentful' bourgeoisie was responsible for the outbreak of revolution. However, not all historians accept this view. Schama wrote that 'the historian seeks in vain for a revolutionary class – the bourgeoisie – thwarted in upward social mobility and bent on the destruction of the privileged orders'. He believed it was still easy to gain access to the Second Estate and pointed out that, in 1789, a good number of powerful leaders came from within the ranks of the nobility and clergy. 'They were not the product of an "aristocratic reaction" but its exact opposite, "an aristocratic modernisation".'

As we have seen, an expanding number of aristocrats were involving themselves in capitalist ventures by the second half of the 18th century, so it is not really possible to speak of a clear-cut division between the classes. Furet and Richet have suggested that antagonism within the ranks of the bourgeoisie – between the increasingly wealthy merchants and manufacturers as against those in the less prospering legal professions and administration – was more significant.

Whether or not the bourgeoisie, or parts of it, were 'resentful' and ready for change in 1789 will no doubt continue to be debated, but it is important to remember that their position did not suddenly alter in 1788/9. Their circumstances had not provoked revolution before this and even then, although the bourgeoisie wanted a share in 'privilege', they made no attempt to demand social equality until after the *parlements* and nobility had begun the process that was to lead to revolution.

The peasantry and urban workers
The peasantry was also increasingly dissatisfied in the later years of the eighteenth century. The French population had been rising steadily throughout the century and much of the strain of demographic change had fallen on the peasants. The growth in the rural population had forced land prices up and wages down. So, while French peasants were not as impoverished as those in some other European countries (and about one in four owned some land), their conditions were deteriorating.

Thanks to a series of bad harvests from as early as 1730, food prices had increased by around 48 per cent to 65 per cent (1730–89) while wages increased by only 11 per cent to 26 per cent. The two principal supplements to farm work, the wine trade and weaving, were also troubled by fluctuations in demand, particularly in the 1770s and 1780s, while taxes continued to rise.

There was another recession in French agriculture after 1778, the year France entered the American war, as a result of which prices fell. Small tenant farmers, peasant proprietors and wine growers were particularly badly hit. On top of this came the catastrophic harvests of 1787–8, which doubled the price of wheat in the north of France, taking it to record levels in the midsummer of 1789. The peasantry suffered as both consumers and producers and through the resultant lay-offs in the domestic industry, which many relied on to bolster their incomes. Some were forced to join the ranks of the landless and drifted to the big cities, particularly Paris, in search of work.

Economic pressures had also encouraged landlords and the more prosperous peasant farmers to enclose common land, scrutinise title deeds, revive or impose new obligations and squeeze yet more from the hard-pressed small proprietors, **sharecroppers and landless labourers**. Once again, the Marxist historians have seen this as part of the 'feudal reaction' but, according to Cobban, what the landlords were doing was 'less a reversion to the past than the application to old relationships of new business techniques'.

In the towns, the lower-paid urban workers were also victims of similar economic pressures. Unemployment grew, partly because of the ill-advised Eden free trade treaty (see page 16) with Great Britain in 1786, which hit the French textile trade particularly hard. More people were chasing fewer jobs. In Paris the 'floating' population of casual labourers and immigrants, criminals and vagabonds grew to around 50,000. Falling standards of living, longer hours, and ever-rising bread prices dogged the urban worker's life. The proportion of income spent on bread rose 50 per cent in the summer of 1788 to 80 per cent of the total and, in 1789, there were economically motivated riots, both in Paris and elsewhere.

So it could be argued that the economic situation and the rise in food prices brought urban craftsmen, workers and peasants and, to some extent manufacturers, together in a common bond of hostility towards government, landlords, merchants and speculators. However, these common links were not clearly visible in 1788 and only gradually became so in the course of 1789. The peasants played no significant part in the unrest that started the revolution and not until after the calling of the Estates-General and the proclamation of the National Assembly did the workers of Paris add their weight to the course of revolution by storming the Bastille.

KEY TERMS

Sharecroppers and landless labourers
Although around three-quarters of the peasants had some land, about half of these were sharecroppers. This meant that they had to give half their produce to their landlords instead of rent. This usually left them with insufficient to live on, so they supplemented their income with domestic work such as cloth weaving. The remaining quarter of the peasants had no land and were dependent on their lord for work. Bad weather or illness could soon turn these into beggars and vagrants.

PERSONAL FACTORS

The responsibility of the French monarchy

Historians have argued over the role of Louis XVI. Cobban regarded him as 'one of the most uninterested and uninteresting spectators of his own reign', while **George Rudé** said he was 'eager to bring about substantial reform in the administration' and 'had a high sense of personal responsibility'.

Cobban's comment derives from Louis's apparent detachment from the real world in which he lived. Encased in the splendour of Versailles and surrounded by fawning courtiers, Louis had little comprehension of life in the rest of France. He was reluctant to leave the vicinity of Paris, and appeared uninterested in matters that did not directly concern him. He had a strong sense of his own divine right and tried to maintain the absolute monarchy of Louis XIV, even in the atmosphere of Enlightenment and reform before the outbreak of revolution. Cobban would argue that his indifference made him slow to accept that his system of government was unworkable and therefore hastened the revolution.

Rudé, on the other hand believes that Louis XVI began his reign with good intentions. He was prepared to reduce expenditure and bring about reform and he appointed Turgot, who had the respect and support of the 'enlightened' and the bourgeoisie, as his chief minister. That Louis's dreams were shattered, Rudé claims, was because of the intransigence of the *parlements*, upper clergy and nobles who fought to protect their own interests and forced Turgot out of office within two years.

Historians have also criticised Louis XVI's methods. He could be high-handed as, for example, when he exiled the Paris Parlement in 1788, or called up the troops in 1789. When he was forced to back down on these and similar occasions, he just looked ridiculous. His indecisiveness did not ride easily alongside his attempt to retain absolute status. He failed to support his ministers' schemes for reform in 1788, until it was too late, and the government was paralysed by Louis's failure to rule on voting procedure in June 1789. He appeared unable to see the likely consequences of his own actions and his gathering of troops and abrupt dismissal of Necker in July 1789 led directly to the storming of the Bastille. Furthermore, his constant double-dealings and intrigue made the revolutionaries doubt his sincerity although, interestingly, it took until 1792 before he was forced to relinquish his position.

Louis was not helped by his wife Marie Antoinette, an Austrian whose marriage to Louis XVI in 1770 symbolised an alliance with an old enemy. She was frivolous and extremely unpopular, even after she bore an heir in 1781. Her reputation for extravagant living became one of the targets of the scurrilous journalists, and although some of the stories (such as the purchase of a diamond necklace in 1785) were subsequently disproved, they were still commonly believed. She was regarded as immoral and unprincipled and stories circulated of her lovers, debauchery and gambling debts. All this did little for the reputation of the monarchy and, while Marie Antoinette largely kept to her own private circle at court, it is probably fair to say that her influence on Louis XVI was almost invariably to encourage him to resist change.

Marie Antoinette painted by Louise Vigee-Lebrun, 1783.

SHORT-TERM FACTORS

The economic crisis of 1789

The immediate cause of the revolution was, of course, the economic crisis that the monarchy faced in 1788. The crown's dependence on credit to finance war had proved disastrous. France's three major wars between 1740 and 1783 had cost around 4000 million livres. Added to the costs of running the administration and court and maintaining royal patronage, the crown was 112 million livres in debt. By the 1780s over half of royal revenue went on interest payments.

The royal government faced a dilemma. How could it raise the revenue it required when the French tax system was so inefficient? Privilege prevented the direct taxation of the wealthy and any challenge to that privilege would meet the opposition of the court, church and *parlements*. Furthermore, it would so weaken the crown's position that it would make it even more difficult to raise credit. Calonne, appointed in 1783, did his best to stave off trouble, but only by yet more borrowing. Although sacked in 1787, it was his reform proposals that led to the summoning of the Assembly of Notables, that year, to consider the crisis, and in turn provoked the 'aristocratic revolt' as the nobles refused to endorse the reforms and demanded an Estates-General.

For the first time there was the feeling, as Arthur Young, an English traveller in France in 1787 wrote, that 'some great revolution in government' was imminent. But although the 'nobles' revolt' brought rioting and disorder in the provinces, the royal troops remained loyal and there was little serious trouble or widespread support in Paris. The disruption would probably have passed, like similar localised disturbances before, but for the continuing financial problem.

On 16 August 1788, the royal government suspended interest payments to its creditors, revealing that it was bankrupt. The monarchy was left with no choice but to give in to the demand for an Estates-General. **Gwynne Lewis** wrote, 'The French Revolution was born in a state of bankruptcy'. Although the summoning of the Estates-General did not, in itself, amount to a revolution, it set in motion a process whereby the various groups that made up French society were forced into a position of defining their aims. What emerged was something far different from that which king, nobility and even bourgeoisie, peasants and urban workers ever expected.

CONCLUSION

Our survey has shown that, by the 1780s, there was economic hardship, social discontent and a good deal of resentment within French society. There was also an intellectual climate that fostered criticism and a monarch moulded in the absolutist tradition. However, as Rudé has written, 'It is doubtful whether any intelligent person living in 1787 could have found good reason to predict that a revolution was close at hand'.

Bankruptcy in 1788 precipitated the revolution but, even then, the French government might have weathered the storm but for the failure of the harvest and the agricultural crisis that followed. To the political and financial crisis was added a social and economic crisis because of long-term developments in the economy and the disastrous harvest of 1788. The calling of the Estates-General focused attention on grievances and forced the various parties to define their positions and expectations – most practically in the *cahiers*. Alignments changed after the Estates-General met, and the clash moved from *parlements*, aristocracy and bourgeoisie versus the king's ministers towards the bourgeoisie and sympathetic clergy and nobles versus privilege. The action was joined by the peasants and urban workers in July/August 1789, and only then did it really become appropriate to talk of revolution.

Why did the revolution occur in France and not elsewhere? Historians, including Jacques Godechot and **Claude Manceron**, have pointed out that political and social disquiet was not unique to France and that there were similar developments in Northern Italy, the Netherlands and, of course, America. There were riots and uprisings in several large cities including London, Brussels and Amsterdam during the 1780s. However, nowhere else experienced the complete collapse of royal power and the administrative and social upheaval that we call 'revolution'. The answer can only be that the factors that made up the French Revolution did not appear in a similar combination in any other part of Europe. It was the unique coincidence of long-term and short-term factors that provides the answer to the question why the revolution occurred in France in 1789.

How significant was the part played by crowd action and the Sans Culottes in the development of the revolution?

The development of the French Revolution was punctuated by the involvement of the crowds of Paris and the Sans Culottes. These red-capped revolutionaries helped drive events forward at key points to at least 1794. Specific examples of involvement can be easily charted: the storming of the Bastille and the October March, 1789; the Champs de Mars attack, 1791; the two marches on the Tuileries, June and August 1792; the September Massacres 1792; the fall of the Girondins, 1793; and the *journée* of 4/5 September 1793. In each case, the *menu peuple* (humble people) acted decisively and contributed to political change. However, there has been some historical argument over the exact role they played, once again dominated by the Marxist and Revisionist schools of thought.

KEY POINTS

- The 'crowd' is necessarily a vague term. Any serious historical study must analyse who formed the crowd and the Sans Culottes.
- The term 'Sans Culottes' came into use in the spring of 1792 and is used to describe the more organised groups of Parisian workers that formed at that time. The 'crowd' refers to earlier groups (although not all historians are consistent in their use of terms).
- An examination of the crowd and Sans Culottes leads to a focus on Paris. It must not be forgotten that the provinces also played a part in the revolution.
- The most controversial area of the Sans Culottes' involvement concerns the Terror.

HISTORICAL INTERPRETATION

The Marxist interpretation

According to the Marxist school of thought, the involvement of the Parisian crowd and the Sans Culottes represented the third stage of the revolution that had, until then, been bourgeois led. The Sans Culottes supplied the revolutionary dynamic that overthrew the king and gave power to 'the people'. They developed a political programme to combat the oppression of modern capitalism and tried to put this into effect in the Terror. In support of this thesis, **Albert Soboul** published the first fully documented study of the everyday activities and social and political ideas of the Sans Culottes, in 1958.

Thanks to some painstaking research, Soboul was able to identify the Sans Culottes. He showed that they were made up of a variety of elements and included some quite wealthy men, like Santerre, a brewer. Some were smaller employers, but most were tradesmen and craftsmen. He quoted a contemporary definition of a Sans Culotte as someone 'who always goes on foot, who does not have any millions stashed away, no castles, no valets to wait upon him, and who lives quite simply with his wife and children, if he has any, on the fourth or fifth floor'. He dismissed the nineteenth-century 'liberal' view that they were the 'down and outs', although he accepted that they were affected by the problem of food supply.

Soboul used this evidence to propound the view that the Sans Culottes formed a distinctive group, held together by hunger and a particular 'moral' outlook. They shared a revulsion that a few should have vast economic power and believed that wealth should be related to the everyday needs of the ordinary family. They valued honesty, despised 'aristocrats' (which they used as a term of abuse) and favoured violent political solutions to problems. They hated secrecy and believed politics should be open and vulnerable to popular pressure. As Soboul put it, 'The Sans Culotte did not think of himself as an isolated individual, he thought and acted en masse'.

Challenges to the Marxist interpretation

Alfred Cobban (1964) and other Revisionists attacked the whole Marxist interpretation as too rigid. Using Soboul's own research, they pointed to the diversity of the Sans Culottes. They came from varied economic backgrounds and shared much of the economic outlook of the bourgeoisie. **M. Sonenscher** (1989) put it clearly when he wrote 'artisans who became Sans Culottes did not always do so because they were artisans'. According to **François Furet** and **Denis Richet**'s survey in 1965–6, after the fall of the monarchy the revolution was 'blown off course'. The 'middling bourgeoisie' assumed control and the Sans Culottes only acted in a supporting role. **Richard Cobb**, in 1969, challenged the view that the Sans Culottes were early socialists. They did not, he stressed, believe in enforced equality. At the most they wanted protection from the worst abuses of the free market, such as price controls on bread.

Although the Marxist interpretation of the revolution and the primacy of the role of the crowds and Sans Culottes has been challenged and largely discredited in more recent years, at least the interest which Soboul sparked in the *menu peuple* encouraged historical enquiry into the role of the clubs, popular societies, newspapers, pamphlets and the part played by the Paris *sections* during the revolution.

Nevertheless, modern 'post-Revisionist' historians now regard the part of the crowds and Sans Culottes as only one of the many influences that helped shape the revolution. **D. M. G. Sutherland** (1982) has stressed the violence in the countryside as being of at least equal importance. Evidence for this includes disturbances in Flanders and around Macon, even before the storming of the Bastille and the 1789 riots, which grew into the 'Great Fear' and led to the August decrees, which destroyed feudalism. Similarly, **Gwynne Lewis** (1993) wrote, 'It was the involvement of the peasants (not just artisans and shopkeepers) which provided the main dynamic of the revolution during its early years'. Another view is that of the French historian **J-P. Hirsch** (1990), who felt that the 'bourgeoisie' played the more decisive role and were 'more attentive, better educated, better equipped than others to face up to the unexpected'.

THE ROLE OF THE CROWDS AND THE SANS CULOTTES

The power of the crowds and the Sans Culottes was centred on Paris. There were Sans Culottes in the provinces, most notably in the revolutionary armies, but the power and influence of this group lay in their use of the Parisian *journées* to effect change and their dominance in the National Guard, the Parisian *sections* and the revolutionary *commune* formed in 1792.

Why did the Sans Culottes develop in Paris?

Paris enjoyed a unique position in France. The court at Versailles was only 20 kilometres away. News of the latest political developments reached Paris long before they could be disseminated to the provinces and in Paris there were plentiful **journalists and pamphleteers** eager to spread gossip. Literacy rates in the capital were fair and probably extended to around half the men and a quarter of the women, but even those who could not read could be reached by the radical orators who thrived in the populous city.

Paris was also extremely vulnerable to any variations in food supply. Its inhabitants depended on a guaranteed, regular supply of bread at affordable prices, and any threat to this could rapidly provoke riots and disorder in its crowded streets. In an attempt to control supply and counter a healthy 'black market' in goods, much hated ten-feet-high barriers had been built around Paris in 1785 where *octrois* (entry taxes) were levied on goods entering the capital.

Conditions in Paris favoured the emergence of a vociferous and active band of citizens. It was large, with 600,000–650,000 inhabitants (six times greater than its nearest rival), and the majority of these lived and worked in close proximity to one another. While the rich had largely moved out of the city to the western suburbs and the redeveloped districts to the south, in the centre, the majority of the population was poor, particularly in the eastern suburbs, the cheap areas to the north of the river and on the two central islands. Studies have shown that 39 per cent of those who married had no property worth recording. Areas like the Faubourg Saint-Antoine, a furniture-making centre, which ended near the Bastille, housed a large population of skilled artisans with a strong sense of common identity (see the map of Paris on page 28).

How and why did the crowd become involved in the outbreak of revolution in 1789?

Rioting was a fairly common phenomenon in eighteenth-century Paris. Protests mainly concerned food prices but some demonstrations were of a political nature.

For example, when the Paris Parlement held out against the king in September 1787, there were demonstrations of support in opposition to the king's minister, Brienne. Similarly, there were several weeks of celebrations when Necker was restored, but it was all relatively orderly. It was not until the spring of 1789, when political stagnation coincided with economic distress, that the crowds showed their collective power and became a force that could not be ignored.

KEY POINT

Migrants There were normally around 100,000 migrant workers in Paris, but in 1789 there may have been as many as 30,000 more than usual as a result of the economic crisis.

KEY PLACE

Palais Royal The home of the Duc d'Orléans (see page 166).

The harvest of 1788 was catastrophic and bread prices rose to a level they had not seen for almost 20 years. Paris swelled as even more **migrants** than usual drifted to the city seeking work and putting even more pressure on the precious food supplies. The Parisians looked for someone to blame as widespread hunger led to violence. Attacks on granaries and rioting against bakers, farmers, corn dealers and speculators assumed a political dimension, as complaints were encouraged by those collating material for the *cahiers*, to be addressed by the Estates-General in May. Rumours spread of a 'plot' to subdue the people and, in April 1789, there were riots at the house of the wallpaper manufacturer, Réveillon. Although disputes over working conditions and pay were not unknown, cries for the 'Third Estate' suggested revolutionary ideas were beginning to spread. The gardens of the **Palais Royal** swelled with disaffected crowds anxious for the latest news. It was no coincidence that the price of bread rose to its highest point on 14 July.

It was Necker's dismissal on 11 July that set in motion the events that led to the storming of the Bastille. For all his faults, Necker was popular and the Parisian crowds had a blind faith in him as the man to right their

Busts of Necker and the Duc d'Orléans held aloft by the crowd as heroic trophies, 12 July 1789. Contemporary painting by Le Sueur.

wrongs. They regarded his dismissal as deliberate provocation. The arrival of German cavalry troops in the centre of Paris to maintain order did nothing to reduce their alarm. Encouraged into action by the pamphleteers, journalists and orators, they forced the closure of the Paris theatres, occupied the Tuileries Palace (12 July), burnt 40 of the 54 customs posts around the city and attacked prisons and those suspected of hoarding grain or arms (12–13 July). In search of weapons, they marched to the Invalides and the Bastille in a frenzy of excitement and desperation on 14 July.

The *journée* of 14 July saw the outpouring of the anger and frustration that had been building up over the previous three days and more. Around 8000 overwhelmed the Invalides, taking muskets and cannon, and marched on to the Bastille. It is significant that the Bastille stood at the end of the Faubourg Saint-Antoine, where it towered above the homes of the working-class population as an ever-present symbol of the power of royal despotism.

Historians have tried to analyse the composition of the crowd that stormed the Bastille and the professions of 700–800 have been traced. Five-sixths were skilled artisans such as joiners, locksmiths, cobblers, shopkeepers and clockmakers. The remaining sixth were more prosperous tradesmen, soldiers, officers and members of the professions. All lived within two kilometres of the Bastille, although at least half were newly arrived from the provinces. The very poor, criminals and vagrants do not appear to have been involved. However, the rioters were supported by a number of those responsible for the maintenance of order, including the lower ranks of the **Paris garrison** and the Paris police.

The storming of the Bastille created a myth, which is to some extent still celebrated today in the French national festival on 14 July, that the action

KEY POINT

Paris garrison
Paris had a permanent garrison of Gardes-français (French guards), a well-organised crack corps of soldiers. However, their loyalty was uncertain, and there were those among them who had joined the disaffected at the Palais Royal. In the events leading up to the storming of the Bastille, many had simply stood by. It was doubtful how many would have obeyed an order to shoot.

of the people of Paris forced a revolution in the name of liberty. The reality was rather different. The revolution was already underway, with the deadlock over voting procedure in the Estates-General and the first moves towards the creation of a National Assembly already in progress. However, as **William Doyle** pointed out, 'Without the intervention of the hungry people of Paris the bid for power which began on June 10 might well have been defeated. The Parisians knew they had saved the revolution and they were proud of it'.

What marked this economic riot apart from the many thousands that had previously occurred in the city, was that it came at a time of political turmoil and absorbed the political slogans and demands of the politicians of the newly formed National Assembly. It showed the weakness of authority and the power of mob violence. The attack was not part of any careful plan, nor even particularly well organised, and yet it led to the recall of Necker, the king's acceptance of constitutional change and, within a month, to the destruction of the feudal system and the *ancien régime*.

How did the involvement of the Parisian crowd and the Sans Culottes affect the development of the French Revolution to 1793?

After the events of 14 July, the 'crowd' became more organised. Although some historians, such as **Simon Schama**, feel much of the violence still represented 'the arbitrary brutalities of the mob', some Revisionists as well as those of the Marxist school believe a 'Sans Culottes mentality' developed in the following years and revolutionary violence was deliberately orchestrated. Historians of the Soboul tradition allege that it was the influence of the Sans Culottes which prevented the revolution ending with the moderate changes of 1789, and drove it on to become more radical. It was the Sans Culottes who prepared for a 'Second Revolution' to create a republic. Even **Tim Blanning**, a Revisionist, commented, 'if the bourgeois had had their way, the revolution would have been closed down by 1791 at the latest. It was only insistent pressure from below which drove them on to destroy feudalism in its entirety'.

KEY INSTITUTION

National Guard
Army of citizens to keep order in the city.

The power bases for Sans Culottes activity were twofold. First, there was the establishment of the Paris Commune and the formation of a **National Guard** in Paris in 1789. These provided the Sans Culottes with powerful central organisations for the direction of operations. Although initially instruments of the bourgeois property holders, established to prevent the sort of chaos seen in July, in an atmosphere of uncertainty, change and anticipation, they were soon infected by the radical fervour. Secondly, the home of the Sans Culottes themselves was in the Cordeliers District of Paris, where the club of that name was to be founded in 1791. Here, working men were invited to listen to popular leaders such as

Danton, Desmoulins and Marat debating the proceedings of the assembly. Several newspapers were also published in this district and there is evidence that plans were made here. For example when, in April 1791, the king was prevented from attending Easter Mass at Saint Cloud, it was a Cordeliers battalion of the National Guard that was sent to unharness his horses.

The image of the 'good revolutionary' was born in these institutions. The Sans Culottes took upon themselves the role of defenders of the revolution, prepared to fight for its principles. **G. A. Williams** believed, 'a central feature of Sans Culottes psychology was its permanent anticipation of betrayal and treachery'. Examples of popular activity bear this out. The March of the Women (supported by 20,000 of the National Guard), which forced the king to confirm the August Decrees and the Declaration of the Rights of Man in October 1789 was provoked by fear of Louis XVI's imminent 'betrayal'. Similarly, the first cries for a republic came when a crowd of 50,000 assembled at the Champs de Mars (17 July), following the disenchantment spread by the king's flight to Varennes, 1791. It only needed the 'threat' posed by the outbreak of war (April 1792), and rumours of royal double-dealings, for the Sans Culottes to organise the two *journées*, to the Tuileries, which sealed the king's fate in 1792.

As the revolution progressed, the Sans Culottes gained in confidence and power. By 1792, the term was synonymous with republicanism, patriotism, and radicalism. **Passive citizens** were absorbed into the National Guard and the assemblies of some of the Paris *sections* in response to Sans Culottes pressure in 1792 and in 1793. Their direct influence could be seen in another Declaration of Rights, which accepted the right to work, to be educated and 'to defend equality by insurrection'.

However, the Sans Culottes' activities were not all inspired by idealism. The threat of hunger was never very far beneath the surface and there was a clear connection between their activities and the economic state of Paris. It is significant, for example, that the October Days were led by women at a time of further rises in bread prices. Probably there was a strong pro-revolutionary, pro-republican belief among the leaders, but it seems unlikely that this can be ascribed to all those who supported their activities.

The effect of the Sans Culottes' intervention can also be questioned. Did their actions, as **D. G. Wright** wrote, 'secure the consolidation of the gains of the revolution' or did they weaken it by challenging the new 'revolutionary' authority of the assembly? At the Champs de Mars in 1791, revolutionaries even fired on revolutionaries, so it is hard to accept Soboul's argument that all the Sans Culottes activity was inspired by, 'the coming of democracy in the politics of the revolution', and popular pressure was essential for the revolution's success.

What was the part of the Sans Culottes in the Terror?

There are two opposing views of the Terror. At one extreme, there is the attitude that it was the work of a bloodthirsty mob of frustrated men who enjoyed a taste of power and revelled in an orgy of violence and, at the other, that it was the work of sincere revolutionaries trying to clear France of privilege, corruption and the enemies of revolution. The truth, as always, probably lies somewhere in between. Albert Soboul regarded the Terror as the final stage in the class struggle. Tim Blanning, on the other hand, thought it a 'knee-jerk' reaction to the emergency posed by the war.

Many historians, including both Marxists and Revisionists, such as Williams, Sutherland, **D. Townson** and Wright, believe that the overthrow and execution of the king (1792–3) and the removal of the Girondins (June 1793), was a key turning point in the Sans Culottes' influence (the Girondins had labelled the Sans Culottes *buveurs de sang* (drinkers of blood) for their involvement in the September massacres). **George Rudé** wrote, 'Thus a new and distinctive phase of the revolution had opened to which the common people by their constant intervention, had made an essential contribution'. Of course, not all agree: Furet and Richet believed that the Sans Culottes were no more than a minor prop to the Jacobin government during the critical period of the summer of 1793 to spring 1794. This argument is supported by the attitude of Robespierre. Although popular in Paris, he had little sympathy with 'the masses' and although he happily 'used' the Sans Culottes to oust the Girondins, he was less interested in granting their demands for better food supplies and price controls in Paris.

However, the Sans Culottes certainly forced some change, and this must reflect the degree to which they had become an **organised body**. They maintained support through nightly meetings in church halls and other suitable venues and they used the power of numbers to exert pressure. A *journée* on 4–5 September 1793 forced the Convention to grant the Law of the General Maximum, which fixed the price of basic commodities. This was accompanied by another Sans Culottes demand, the creation of *les armées révolutionnaires* (revolutionary armies) to force grain requisition in the provinces and defeat 'counter-revolution'.

Whether the Sans Culottes were the sole force behind the anarchic Terror of the autumn and winter of 1793, or whether it was the influence of the war or the work of Robespierre or his colleagues in the Committee of Public Safety is another area of debate, details of which will be dealt with more fully in Section 3. There are certainly those that subscribe to the view that the Sans Culottes bear a good deal of the responsibility.

KEY THEME

The organisation of the Sans Culottes

Although the Sans Culottes became more organised in the course of 1793, the number of activists must not be overestimated. Recent research by the historian Richard Cobb puts their number at no more than 10 per cent of the adult male population of Paris – with similar numbers in the provinces. Although their meetings might grow large in moments of crisis, numbers fell once that crisis was over. So, in 1793, when the movement was at its height, the Sans Culottes in Paris comprised no more that 2–3000 committed revolutionaries, although they were capable of mobilising armed crowds of tens of thousands.

Richard Cobb, for example, emphasised the bloodthirstiness of the Sans Culottes, writing, 'the armées came closest to realising the dream of every sectionary militant – a guillotine on wheels, casting its long shadow over grain hoarders, counter-revolutionary priests and foreign spies'. Certainly, the Sans-Culottes-dominated Paris *sections* set up their own *comités de surveillance* (watch committees), which spied on suspected traitors.

The Terror represented the peak of organised Sans Culottes influence. Some joined the **Enragés**, while others were attracted by the ideas of Jacques Hébert, a member of the Paris Commune who had led the Hébertistes in a demand for radical change. It was Hébert who began a violent campaign against the Church, demanding the closure of churches, the abolition of the Sabbath and saints' days and the use of the non-Christian calendar.

Why did the Sans Culottes' influence wane after 1794?

The Terror gradually moved beyond the Sans Culottes' control. As the Committee of Public Safety became more ruthless and sought strong centralised government, ardent supporters of the Terror, including the Hébertistes (March 1794) soon found themselves its victims. The popular leader, Danton, was also guillotined. The revolutionary armies and the popular societies in the *sections* were disbanded and, worse still for the Sans Culottes, despite continuing food shortages, the Law of Maximum was extended to control wages as well as food.

After 1794, the Sans Culottes became more fearful and the Thermidorian Reaction that toppled Robespierre broke their power. Weakened after the lawlessness of the Terror, they failed to rise to save him. The price was the closure of the Jacobin Club and the Paris Commune. The Law of Maximum was repealed and protests against the rising price of bread (April 1795 and 20–21 May 1795) led to large-scale arrests, the disarmament of Sans Culottes and the execution of 42 National Guard leaders. The Sans Culottes could not survive without leaders and power bases and, in any case, their political interests were, by 1795, largely discredited by the excesses of Jacobin government.

What was the role of the provinces?

Political activity was not, of course, solely confined to Paris. One of the features of the revolution (at least until reversed by Robespierre and the Jacobins in 1793–4) was decentralisation. During the 1788–9 period, radicalism was centred in the provinces, with peasant involvement in 'The Great Fear' (see pages 31–2). The most 'revolutionary' *cahiers* presented to the Estates-General in 1789 came from provincial areas and the dominant speakers at that body were not Parisians but provincial representatives, such as Robespierre from Arras and Lafayette from the Auvergne. Furthermore, the centre for radical ideas, although established

The Enragés
These were a group of orators and politicians who believed in absolute equality. They believed the revolution had failed to make sufficient provision for economic equality and that hoarders and speculators should be punished by death. If the government refused to do this, they believed that the people should launch new massacres of the 'blood suckers'. They also became involved in the dechristianisation campaigns.

Revolutionary committee. These administrative bodies, manned by activists, sprang up all over France from 1792 onwards.

in Paris, was known as the Breton Club (later the Jacobin) in respect to its origins in Brittany.

KEY POINT

La Feuille Villageoise had 15,000 subscribers by 1791 and was probably read by four or five times that number.

The provinces certainly maintained a healthy interest in revolutionary change. Local Jacobin clubs were established in most provincial cities and a steady stream of newspapers, including *La Feuille Villageoise*, which was specifically aimed at the rural areas, had a wide readership. The involvement of the provinces and acceptance of revolutionary ideas can be seen in the militancy of the *fédérés*, the provincial soldiers whose arrival in Paris in 1792 had at least as much influence on the overthrow of the king in 1792 as that of the urban Sans Culottes.

The counter-revolution and the federal revolt that provoked the Terror were also centred in the provinces. Horror at the religious changes, and opposition to the military *levées* in particular, inspired the resistance that was unusually strong particularly in Brittany and the Vendée from February 1793. This was, of course, to have a major effect on the course of the revolution, bringing the Terror, the domination of the Committee of Public Safety and ultimately the collapse of that era of revolutionary radicalism. Some have suggested that the overthrow of Robespierre in 1794 was, in part, a provincial reaction to the Parisian dominance he had tried to assert.

What other factors influenced the development of the revolution?

As well as the provincial involvement, there were, of course still other influences on the course of revolution, most notably the war (which is examined in Section 3), economic pressures, and the role of particular individuals. The **Duc d'Orléans**, who may well have been the financial force behind the Sans Culottes in the early days, the king himself and key revolutionary leaders such as Robespierre, all played an important part. In examining the influence of the Sans Culottes, it is therefore important to keep their contribution in perspective.

CONCLUSION

Few historians now hold to the pure Marxist theory that the crowds and Sans Culottes had a specific class-consciousness that demanded a particular political programme. Indeed, **Dr Geoffrey Ellis** has questioned the traditional view that the Sans Culottes were commoners at all, although there is a danger here that the leaders, who were often the more prosperous tradesmen, craftsmen and professionals, are being confused with their followers. Equally, the French historian **Hippolyte Taine**'s theory that they represented a 'criminal element' has been shown to have little substance. What is accepted is that the Sans Culottes were often at the forefront of the revolution and 'their excitability, gullibility, conceit, deprivation, suspicion of plots and betrayal, of moderates, rich men and priests' (D. G. Wright), provided at least some of the fuel for revolutionary politics between 1789 and 1794. The crowds and the Sans Culottes may not have been the only influence on the course of the revolution, but they did remain a constant factor. While modern historiography may play down the role of the crowd, in relation to other influences, as George Rudé has written, 'An essential and quite distinctive element of the French Revolution (was) the active participation of the common people from 1789 onwards and all the consequences that flowed from it'.

KEY PERSON

The Duc d'Orléans (1747–93) The part of the Duc d'Orléans remains unclear, but he was one of the forces that helped steer the mobs. He presumably had ambitions to be king or regent for Louis XVI's young son. He encouraged the press in the Diamond Necklace affair, directed against Marie Antoinette (and may have started the rumour). See also page 18.

To what extent did the war affect the course of the revolution?

From 20 April 1792 to the final fall of Napoleon Bonaparte in 1815, France was more or less continually at war. Naturally enough, this affected French domestic affairs and coming, as it did, shortly after the beginnings of a revolution in government and society, its effects were more marked than they might have been in a country that enjoyed greater stability. This section looks at the effects of war up to 1799 and examines some of the questions historians have argued over.

KEY POINTS

- Did the war drive the French Revolution 'off course'?
- Was the failure of parliamentary democracy in France the result of war or was it doomed to fail anyway?
- To what extent was the Jacobin Terror a direct consequence of war?
- Did the war benefit or harm France?

HISTORICAL INTERPRETATION

The central problem concerns the changes in the structure and control of government that accompanied the war. Historians are more or less agreed that, up to 1792, the revolution appeared to be developing along 'democratic' lines. The old centralised structure of the *ancien régime* had been swept away and a new decentralised administration established, in which elections at every level ensured the direct participation of the people in the running of the country. Although there was a rather fine distinction between active and passive citizens, the basic principles of democratic government had been established under a constitutional monarchy and the revolution seemed to be well on the way to establishing freedom from oppression and the 'rights of man'.

After 1792, all this changed. The monarchy was overthrown and a republic established. Moderate elements were forced out of government and the Jacobins constructed a strong centralised administration, dominated by the Committee of Public Safety. There was enforced conscription, requisitioning, summary justice and a network of spies and informers that effectively stifled freedom of speech. The Terror passed through various stages and eventually gave way to the calmer period of the Directory but, by then, much had changed. The government of 1795–9 was never fully endorsed by the electors and its resort to military intervention to alter the constitution showed how far government had moved from the ideals of the early revolutionaries.

As historians have sought to explain this change, some have placed much emphasis on the effect of war. According to **Tim Blanning**, for example, 'war inflicted permanent social, economic, and political damage … ending with the destruction of the revolution'. **François Furet**, on the other hand, put the case that the revolution would have grown more radical anyway, and that the war was not the decisive influence on the coming of the Jacobin Terror. Furet believed the political views of the leaders of revolution were so influenced by Rousseau that any attempt to create a parliamentary democracy in France was doomed. The problem, he felt, was the idea of the 'general will', which Rousseau had put forward as the guiding principle in government. Since the task of a nation's leaders was to discover the general will and follow its course unswervingly, the revolutionary leaders of 1793–4, believing they knew best, had no option but to follow the path of Terror as a way of 'forcing men to be free'.

In **Pierre Nora**'s view (quoted in Furet's *Dictionary of the Revolution* in 1988), the essence of the Republic was already in place by June 1789 when the Estates-General accepted their role as a National Assembly. The revolution was bound to become increasingly radical, war or no war. Put more bluntly in **Simon Schama**'s *Citizens* (1989), 'violence was not just an unfortunate side effect … it was the revolution's source of collective energy. It was what made the revolution revolutionary'.

What arguments can be made for the influence of the war?

Many connections can be established between the development of the war and the politics of the revolution. For example, it could be claimed that the first casualty of the war was the monarchy. With the danger of invasion imminent in 1792, it became harder than ever for the Girondins to argue in favour of a moderate constitution that retained a king whose sympathies were in doubt. Louis XVI's veto on the decrees ordering the deportation of refractory priests (27 May), and a *levée* of 20,000 *fédéré* volunteers from the provinces to help defend Paris (8 June), did not help matters. The resulting storm of protest led to the attack on the Tuileries (20 June). However, had it not been for the continuing bad news from the front and the publication of the Duke of Brunswick's manifesto in Paris in July, the subsequent moderate behaviour of the king might still have enabled him to survive.

The *journées* of 9–10 August can also be directly linked to the events of the war, the influence of the *fédérés* and the defection of Lafayette. These heralded the overthrow of the monarchy (August 1792), the birth of the Republic (22 September 1792) and the execution of the king

KEY THEME

The influence of the *fédérés* Many of the *fédérés* came from areas of France where the revolution was under challenge, such as Brittany, the Midi and the east. They were therefore responsive to the efforts of the popular orators, such as Marat, who asked why 'the rich alone should have the fruits of the Revolution … while you have won the sad right only to continue to pay heavy taxes'. Many were lodged in the Cordeliers Club or in the home of revolutionary patriots and, not surprisingly, soon joined the ranks of the most militant in Paris.

(January 1793). War, it can be argued, made Louis XVI's death inevitable. Had his life been spared, he would almost certainly have been used by foreign powers as a figurehead.

The September massacres (1792) can be seen as another radical product of war. Popular orators, particularly Danton, had played on the Parisians' fears of invasion to whip up enthusiasm for the war effort. When news of the fall of the fortress town of Longwy reached the capital, the Paris Commune, filled with radical Jacobins who had believed the French army of 'free men' was invincible, could only credit this loss to treason. So it organised the September massacres, bringing the deaths of around 1400 prisoners. The popular violence displayed also owed something to another effect of war – inflation. The *assignat*, which was already debased to the extent that a 100-livres *assignat* was only worth 82 livres in gold in September 1791, fell to 57 livres in June 1792 and was to sink to 36 livres by June 1793. As always, economic hardship encouraged violence and extremism.

According to **Gwynne Lewis**, the radicalisation of politics was not inevitable. The Girondins had tried to bridge the gap between the demands of the people and a successful war. Lewis argued that this moderate line might have worked, but for the scale of the crisis afflicting France. The problem was not just the external enemy. Another unpopular effect of war had been the return of conscription (previously abolished by the Constituent Assembly), and the rising in the Vendée directly followed the *levée* of 300,000 men (24 February 1793) and the execution of the king. Threatened with invasion and an internal rebellion the Girondins proved unequal to the task. The defection of Dumouriez in April 1793 brought their loyalty into question and they fell because they appeared incompetent and cowardly.

KEY CONCEPT

Total war This is a term more frequently used of 20th century warfare, when all the resources of a country, both material and human, are harnessed for the purposes of war (for details see pages 59–61).

So Lewis believes the advent of the Jacobins and the radicalisation of the Terror was the result of the war and its accompanying counter-revolution in France. The Terror was established to bring victory, solve economic problems and deal with traitors, and it did so with reasonable success, producing an early form of '**total war**'. **Duncan Townson** claims that, thanks to the Terror, 'the threats to the existence of the revolution in the spring of 1793 … had been removed or brought under control' by the end of the year. Without the centralising policies of the Terror, France would not have been able to raise and feed the armies and fight to win. So, in that the Terror saved France, so the Terror saved the revolution.

The war affected subsequent developments too. When defeat turned to victory in 1794 at Fleurus, the rationale for the Terror disappeared, Robespierre was overthrown and the new Directory was established. However, internal stability proved an impossible goal while the war continued. The damage had been done and attempts to find a workable constitution proved elusive. According to Gwynne Lewis, 'After 1795 the French Revolution continued, but wearing a military uniform and without the active support of the masses'. War had made unified command and force necessary and this resulted in the Directory's reliance on the army to annul **unwelcome election results**. In reaction to the left-wing radicalisation of the Terror, the government veered to the right in response to the pressures of maintaining an effective command in war.

The influence of the war on the strength and popularity of the Directory is straightforward to chart. Babeuf was easily defeated in 1796 during the spate of victories 1796–7, but from the autumn of 1798, when Russia, Austria and England formed the Second Coalition against France, the military situation deteriorated and renewed conscription (September 1798) made the government unpopular again. Bad news from the war fronts in Italy and the Netherlands led to the plans for the final coup, which brought Napoleon to power in 1799. Bonaparte's subsequent career, which was based on his position as Supreme Commander of the armed forces as well as head of state reversed the revolution's original aim to curb arbitrary central power.

What arguments can be used against the influence of the war?

Furet's argument that the revolution was bound to grow more radical, regardless of the war, certainly has some validity. The Jacobin leaders, and in particular Robespierre, were immersed in the teachings of the enlightened thinkers. Marat had long since called for a one-man dictatorship on the Roman model, although he had no direct influence on the new form of government established from December 1793, since he was stabbed by Charlotte Corday in July of that year. Robespierre's own sincerity has sometimes been questioned, but he certainly tried to convey the view that he knew what was best for the nation as a whole. This was his guiding premise and he used it to justify the Terror, or the 'Republic of Virtue' as he preferred to call it.

Furthermore, the influence of the *philosophes* had always been towards the development of more rational government. From the outset, the revolution had been intent on destroying the chaotic, complex and unequal structures of the *ancien régime*. The revolution had entailed a quest for simplicity and uniformity as seen, for example, in the reforms of the Constituent Assembly. So it could be argued that what happened after 1792 was merely a continuation of this tendency. The rulers of France persisted in their efforts to rationalise government, even when this was at the expense of personal liberty. Perhaps there was an inherent contradiction in what the revolution stood for. Fraternity and equality did not necessarily equate with liberty.

KEY THEME

Unwelcome election results

In 1797, when large numbers of monarchists were elected to the councils of the Directory, troops were used to quash the results and exile two pro-royalist directors. In 1798, when the Jacobins won almost a third of the seats, the government again overturned the election. These were known as the coups of Fructidor and Floréal. Such acts undermined the credibility of the Directory (see page 69).

Seeing the developments of 1793 as part of the wider cultural picture of the revolution, Furet and his followers believe it is impossible to consider the effects of the war in isolation. They have even cast doubt on specific links of timing. For example, Furet pointed out that the Vendée rising had been crushed in December 1793 and that, by the summer of 1794, the French army was advancing beyond its borders into the Low Countries, Spain and Italy. Therefore, he argued, it was Robespierre's political and cultural agenda that created the Terror, not a state of emergency and panic.

This argument is not, of course, conclusive. Writing of the Terror, **George Rudé** commented, 'to conclude that this was intended all along and that "revolutionary" government corresponded to the long-cherished ambitions of the Jacobin leaders is to misrepresent both their principles and the evolution of their policies'. He argued that the type of government established by the Terror did not conform to that of the enlightened thinkers anyway. 'These prescribed not dictatorship or Jacobin style "revolutionary" government but a strong **legislature**, a weak **executive** and the **separation of powers**. The system of government that took legislative shape in the law of 4 December 1793 was the product of neither Rousseau or Montesquieu.'

DID THE WAR BENEFIT OR HARM FRANCE?

What were the benefits brought by the war?

A case can be made that the war brought considerable benefits to France. Coming in 1792, at a time when the religious issue was dividing French society and opinions over the fate of the king were threatening to weaken the assembly, the war helped instil a sense of public duty and pull the nation together again. Admittedly, not everyone rallied in support, but the critics of governmental policies, including the king, could be branded traitors and dealt with. Panic induced a sense of patriotism, which turned into euphoria when all went well.

The war also provided an opportunity for young men to escape provincial life, to travel and perhaps acquire some political education. Conscripted soldiers were encouraged to read radical newspapers and attend the meetings of the local Jacobin Club where they were garrisoned. There were new opportunities open to those who showed military talent, of which Napoleon was the prime example. The departure of ex-noble officers provided opportunities to men within the ranks of the army – corporals and sergeants who, because of their birth, would never have been promoted in the royal regiments. The idea of career open to talent was established in war and helped change the nature of the French army. Soldiers had new political rights and could denounce their own officers, but officers talked the same language as the men and there was greater mutual respect.

According to Marxist historians, such as **Soboul**, war acted as the catalyst that enabled the Committee of Public Safety to move towards a controlled economy that, in turn, helped lay the foundations of a fairer and more equal society. The committee mobilised the resources of the whole of French society in the service of national defence. This was progressive and opposed to traditional privilege. The economic controls of the period of the Terror brought speculation and inflation under control. The *assignat*, which had reached 22 per cent of its value in August 1793, rose to 33 per cent in November and 48 per cent in December. The supply of food to the cities was more regularly assured than at any time since the autumn of 1791. The peasants' debt to their landlords was written off (Summer 1793) and some (though not very successful) efforts made to encourage peasants to combine and purchase ex-*émigré* land, which was put up for auction in smaller lots.

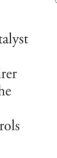

A soldier of the Republic, carrying his bread ration on his bayonet.

It could also be argued that, in strengthening Jacobin control, the war gave them an opportunity to develop their social programme. The Committee of Public Safety considered laws relating to education, industry, the civil code and public assistance. Not all made the statute books, but some of their drafts influenced subsequent legislation. The Directory also accomplished a good deal. Although it could be argued that some of this was in spite of, rather than because of the war, nevertheless it was partly because of the success of the war effort that it was able to reduce the public debt (September 1797), overhaul the tax system, standardise weights and measures, reform education, the army and hospitals and lay the basis of the modern civil service.

Finally, it should also be remembered that the war brought extensive military achievement. The army was reorganised by Carnot and the conquest and success achieved by the French armies, particularly under the Directory, increased French prestige and power and laid the foundations for the Napoleonic Empire.

In what ways was the war a destructive force?

The opposing argument suggests that the war took much of the idealism out of the revolution and promoted the case for Terror and political intolerance. War consumed so much time and so many resources that other revolutionary ambitions could not be pursued and achieved. It prevented the government from dealing adequately with the problems of its earlier reforms and in some cases weakened what had already been achieved. This was particularly true of the workings of local government, the judicial reforms, the problems created by the Civil Constitution of the Clergy, issues of taxation, the *assignats* and the sale of church land.

Economic liberals suggest the strong control that the war demanded destroyed some of the early revolutionary gains. **Florin Aftalion** (1990), for example, believes that the early measures against the guilds and corporations had been extremely beneficial in freeing trade from its 18th-century restrictions, but that the war was a turning point. 'The protectionist tradition which the revolution might well have broken with, was, in fact, definitively established in this period, and was to last, with incalculably destructive consequences, up until the present time.'

The war was a disaster economically and in other ways too. Defeats at the hands of the British led to loss of vital French colonies and the virtual immobilisation and destruction of the French navy. This meant a near strangulation of French trade as the British naval blockade inflicted grave economic damage. Furthermore, the prosecution of war was expensive and, although the Jacobins were initially successful in controlling inflation, it soon spiralled out of control until tackled by the Directory.

The war also had consequences for the 'image' of France and the revolution abroad. Initial reactions to the revolution from liberals elsewhere had been favourable. There had been signs of support from Holland, Britain, Switzerland and many German states. However, the experience of war reversed this. The cause of liberty and self-determination seemed to have been sacrificed to French ambition and conquest. The war probably did more to delay than to spread 'liberty, equality and fraternity'.

CONCLUSION

Whether or not the war drove the French Revolution 'off course', it certainly affected its development. The king may have been doomed, but it was the war that explains the timing of his demise. Similarly, there may have been radical tendencies within the revolution, but the establishment of the Jacobin government and the Terror were directly linked to the crises of war. The war brought some benefits but, on balance, its negative effects seem to have been greater. War was, according to **William Doyle** 'a great polarising issue'. By forcing people to take sides and identifying the defeat or survival of the revolution with that of the nation itself, it undermined much of what the revolution had stood for.

SECTION 4

Did Napoleon develop or destroy the revolution?

Napoleon's life and career were full of paradoxes. What he said, what he did and what others said about him were often quite contradictory. Historians therefore face a hard task in trying to interpret his rule, and their work is not made easier by the existence of the conversations that he had while in exile on the island of St Helena, which were recorded and later published. In these, Napoleon painted a picture of himself as the 'heir' of the French Revolution. He created the legend that he had fulfilled the intentions of the revolution and, as ruler of France, had constructed a new type of society. Furthermore, he had spread this 'liberal' society throughout the rest of Europe.

Not all, at the time or since, have agreed with this interpretation. Even Napoleon himself had talked of 'healing the wounds' left by the revolution, and of helping the other sovereigns of Europe 'stem the revolutionary torrent', in his later years as emperor.

KEY POINTS

- The image that Napoleon later created does not fit easily with the facts of his rule.
- It is probably impossible to categorise Napoleon. He preserved some revolutionary principles, but destroyed others.
- Interpretations of Napoleonic rule have been influenced by historians' attitudes to the revolution itself.

HISTORICAL INTERPRETATION

When nineteenth-century historians examined the Napoleonic era, they tended to view it as a separate political development, divorced from the revolution itself. However, as the interest in longer-term social and economic developments grew during the twentieth century, it became less appropriate to make such a rigid division, and historians concentrated more specifically on Napoleon's relationship with the revolution. When Napoleon came to power, the changes made by the revolution had still not been firmly absorbed, and historians have tried to assess the extent to which Napoleonic rule consolidated or undermined these.

The division of views does not necessarily follow the Marxist/Revisionist divide. On this issue, the Marxist historian **Soboul**, who wrote that Napoleon 'essentially belonged to the line of the revolutionary heritage', is supported by the modern 'liberal' historian, **William Doyle**, who described Napoleon as the man who 'tamed and harnessed the energies unleashed by the revolution'.

François Furet also accepted that Napoleon was 'the heir of the revolution' but, unlike Soboul and Doyle, he held this accountable for his despotic, not liberal tendencies. Furet believed the revolution had been blown 'off course' after the destruction of the monarchy and had become an authoritarian dictatorship, which Napoleon went on to perpetuate. He believed that Napoleon continued the despotism of the Convention. Furet wrote, 'his domestic policies daily revealed the corruption of his domineering character by the exercise of absolute power, by his mania to control everything and make every decision ... and by his development of a police state of which Louis XIV could never even have dreamed'. According to this view, Napoleon consolidated the radical principles of the revolution and continued the revolution's path towards administrative unity and political centralisation at the expense of people's freedom.

Another interpretation has suggested that Napoleon was more like an eighteenth-century enlightened despot, ruling for the benefit of his people, providing efficient and rational government, religious toleration, equality before the law, education, a career open to talents and basic freedoms. However, the absence of freedom of speech and of the press, as well as the question of motivation, casts doubts on this view. His attitude to women, workers, slavery, arbitrary arrest and inhumane punishments was far from enlightened.

Napoleon's regime has also been likened to that of Louis XVI. He did, after all create a court and an imperial nobility and he ensured that the whole edifice was supported by the Catholic Church. The Council of State has been likened to the old Royal Council, which supervised a centralised bureaucracy, legal system and police state with prefects rather similar to the old *intendants*. William Doyle has resoundingly refuted this, writing that 'apart from its gaudy trappings, the monarchy of Napoleon had little in common with that of Louis XVI'. Indeed, in comparison with Napoleonic France, the whole edifice of Louis XVI's government looked remarkably weak. No institution could oppose Napoleon like the *parlements* or the provincial estates, which troubled Louis XVI. The church that propped up the Napoleonic regime had none of its former independence and influence. Napoleon's nobility was smaller, more compliant and dependent on the ruler's protection. Napoleon's drive for order and efficiency was indeed a far cry from the chaotic governmental apparatus of the *ancien régime*.

The heir of the revolution

Napoleon certainly owed a great debt to the revolution. His own rise to power was only made possible through the revolution, and he became the most famous example of one of its precepts, 'careers open to talents'. There is also evidence that he was a supporter of the revolution in the early years. As a young officer, he had read Rousseau, declared himself in favour of the revolution and supported Jacobin policies to the extent that he was imprisoned for a month after Thermidor on suspicion of being a Robespierrist. He fought on behalf of the revolutionary governments, against counter-revolution at home in Toulon, and to 'spread the revolution overseas', in Italy and Egypt.

His return to France in 1799 and the establishment of the Consulate can be seen as an attempt to reconcile revolutionaries and royalists. He always claimed that the establishment of strong government was essential for the consolidation of the revolution and that his constitution of 1799 helped carry revolutionary principles into effect by establishing the 'sacred rights of property, equality and liberty'. Furthermore, this, like all his subsequent constitutional changes, was approved by plebiscite, which he deemed a show of support from those he ruled.

As First Consul and Emperor, Napoleon went to some lengths to emphasise the continuity of his rule with that of the revolutionary period. Many of the same **personnel** continued in governmental office and the words *République française* continued to be used on official documents to 1804 and on the reverse of coins to 1809. The Republican calendar was not abandoned until the end of 1806.

Furthermore, Napoleon carried out many great reforms that did, to a greater or lesser degree, continue and complement the work of the revolutionary governments. That Napoleon chose to give a good deal of his personal time to chairing meetings and supervising the drawing up of legislation, is an indication of how important such reform was to him.

Probably the most famous and enduring of these reforms was the Civil Code, of which **George Rudé** has written, 'Napoleon was to take greater pride in this achievement than in all his forty battles'. By continuing the codification of the law, begun by the Convention and Directory, Napoleon quite literally consolidated earlier work and helped to formulate a code of law that embraced revolutionary principles. He has been much criticised for adopting the Roman law emphasis on authority, particularly of men over women, but the basic principles of 1789, the destruction of feudalism, liberty of conscience and employment, and equality as in the division of estates between all children were also included in it.

Personnel Half the 29 members of the Council of State had served under the Directory and 240 of the first 300 members of the Legislature and 69 of the first 100 members of the Tribunate had served in the Directory councils. In addition, 76 of the first provincial prefects had been members of various revolutionary assemblies and this gave stability and continuity to Napoleon's government from the revolutionary period.

Napoleon's religious attitudes and the Concordat The revolution had undermined the Catholic Church in France, building on an already underlying hostility to its riches and power, but also going further and attempting, in 1793, to wipe out religious practice entirely. Napoleon recognised the folly of encouraging too much anticlericalism. He did not like the outside influence of the Pope, but he did want to use the Church to increase social order and authority in France. He referred to organised religion as 'the mystery of the social order'. He was therefore prepared to make the Concordat, although he did all he could to limit the Pope's powers and, from imprisonment on St Helena, later claimed that he had planned to abolish the papacy.

Napoleon's concern for equal opportunity could also be seen in his educational reforms, which set up the *lycées*, complete with state scholarships for the able, and the creation of the 'Legion of Honour', which was open to all who served the state. The honoured had no tax exemptions or legal privileges and awards were based on loyal service not birth. The later Imperial Notables were a similar institution, while within the army, the 'career open to talents' permitted able generals like Murat and Ney to rise from the ranks.

It could be argued that Napoleon followed some of the earlier revolutionary principles in his reform of the economy. He strengthened France's finances with a reform of the currency, placed limits on the exports of grain and, in 1812, a maximum on the prices of bread and flour. Such actions followed the example of the Convention for, like the Jacobin government, he understood the importance of an adequate and affordable supply of food.

Napoleon might have been accused of flying in the face of the revolution, with its anticlerical and atheistic associations, in his **Concordat** with the Roman Catholic Church in 1801. However, it is worth noting that he appended the organic articles to the promulgation of the Concordat, guaranteeing equal rights for Protestants and Jews, and that the agreement was made on France's terms. Church lands seized in the revolution were never to be restored, Napoleon retained the right to nominate the bishops, and clergy remained salaried by the state and under oath to the constitution (although not the same oath as in 1790). In all essentials, even this settlement maintained revolutionary principles.

In 'exporting' the revolution to Europe, Napoleon also continued where the revolutionary governments had left off. The principle of waging war in the interests of liberty, after some fine wrangling in the early years, had already been accepted by the Convention and Directory. Annexations and 'sister republics' had been established in the name of liberty and new laws and political institutions, modelled on those in France, established in them. Napoleon built on this principle to create an empire that spread over the greater part of Europe. He adopted an almost romantic approach to his work and George Rudé has written of his conquests, 'in so far as they followed any master plan they were inspired by memories of the universal monarchy of Rome or Charlemagne'. Napoleon claimed to have dreamt of liberating peoples everywhere and providing them with national unity, although it is hard to reconcile this boast in its entirety with the reality of his dynastic ambitions and governmental and territorial arrangements.

Nevertheless, Napoleon did carry through some drastic political and social reforms within the empire. Wherever the French armies conquered, written constitutions were established. Religious toleration was spread, bringing civil rights for Jews, secular education, civil marriage, the secularisation of church lands and the dissolution of monasteries. There was internal free trade and priority was given to the building of roads and canals and standardising of weights and measures. The Civil Code created uniformity and brought equality before the law and the abolition of serfdom where it still existed. Privileges, corporate bodies, tithes and feudal dues disappeared, while the rights to the ownership of property and inheritance were confirmed. According to Rudé, 'Napoleon tore up the institutions of the *ancien régime* by the roots'. He may have had dynastic ambitions but he was still the 'heir and soldier of the Revolution'.

Destroyer of the revolution

It is not difficult to find support for the alternative view that Napoleon destroyed the revolution. Most of the evidence stems from Napoleon's style of government. For example, although Napoleon claimed to use elected bodies, the system of election was so indirect as to make the universal suffrage meaningless. Furthermore, while every constitutional change was put to the people in an apparently democratic plebiscite, in practice, these were rigged and unrepresentative.

From the very beginning of his rule, Napoleon sought ways to bypass elected bodies. The provision of *senatus consultum* (having consulted the Senate) in the constitution established in 1800 allowed Napoleon to ignore the elected law-making councils by issuing decrees. He did this regularly as a consul and it also provided the means by which the Napoleon-nominated Senate was able to create the empire. Thereafter, Napoleon was able to do as he wished. It would appear that the boast that he fulfilled the revolutionary principle of 'national sovereignty', giving the people a say in how they were governed, was little more than a slogan to legitimise his dictatorship and establish his own hereditary rule.

His action in crowning himself emperor might be said to be symbolic of the development of his views. By assuming 'sovereignty', Napoleon claimed to have taken the burden from the people and vested it in himself and his heirs. Napoleon justified this action with talk of governing in the people's interests and providing a strong government that was best for all. However, his methods seem very different from those of the early revolutionaries to whom popular sovereignty was **sacrosanct**. Napoleon's 'people' were now referred to as 'subjects' not 'citizens'.

Napoleon's style of government contained many of the trappings associated with dictatorship. There was strong central control. Napoleon reversed the principle of local election and, although he retained the *communes* and *départements* created in 1790, he placed prefects, which

KEY TERM

Sacrosanct Holy and very precious. It could not be changed.

may have been modelled on the *intendants* or perhaps the representatives-on-mission, in charge of these. Tax collection was also vested with these prefects. He used secret police, censorship, propaganda, spies and informers to retain control and root out any opposition.

In the administration of justice too, the more liberal practices of the revolution were abandoned. The judicature was once again placed in the hands of judges appointed by the ruler, rather than elected by the people, and a form of sale of offices re-emerged among notaries and other legal officials. State juries were suspended in several *départements* in the interests of security and processes similar to the old *lettres de cachet* were resurrected to deny trials to extreme political offenders.

Even the great Napoleonic reforms can be criticised as little more than the product of a man who was motivated by ambition and a desire for order and authority and who paid little heed to abstract principles. His law codes, particularly the criminal and penal codes, with their insistence on Roman law, clearly appealed to the authoritarian side of his nature and his disrespect for women was hardly enlightened. The insistence on the rights of property, rather like his belief that education was to be restricted to boys, and particularly the sons of civil servants and officers, also reflected his overriding concern for traditional order. In legal matters, Napoleon could hardly be described as a supporter of civil rights, and it has been considered significant that he abandoned the Declaration of the Rights of Man and the Citizen, with which the revolution began, in his successive constitutions.

The revolutionary principle of equality of opportunity was also greater in theory than in practice under Napoleon. He spoke of rewarding talent and courage but, while the new **notables**, made up of officers and wealthy administrators, could buy hereditary rights, opportunities for improving status lower down the social scale were very limited. Entry to high government posts was dependent on income, and from 1800 a rich man could even avoid conscription by paying a substitute to serve. Given the dearth of educational opportunities, however, there was little prospect of advancement for agricultural workers or artisans, who remained subject to the full force of Napoleonic demands.

Taxation too, was unequal. Indirect taxes on goods, which had already been re-established by the Directory, were increased to provide revenue for war. This shifted the burden from the property owners to the poorer peasants and workers. While taxes on land rose slowly, indirect taxes, including taxes on tobacco, playing cards and alcohol, rose by 50 per cent between 1804 and 1814. In 1806, a tax on salt reminiscent of the old *gabelle* was introduced and, in 1810, the old state monopoly on tobacco was re-established. Such moves were contrary to the policies of the early

KEY POINT

Notables

Historians have debated whether Napoleon reconciled the old aristocracy with the newer bourgeoisie of the revolution to form a new governing elite. Research shows that 3500 men were ennobled 1804–14 and, of these, just over 20 per cent came from old nobility, nearly 60 per cent from bourgeoisie and nearly 20 per cent from other groups, who virtually all gained titles because of their military service. Studies of the army suggest very few of ordinary rank rose to the top. Murat and Ney are among a handful of exceptions. Work on electoral colleges and lists also supports the view that the main beneficiaries of Napoleon's rule were the bourgeoisie, with few men of humble origin and a limited number of ex-nobles.

revolutionary assemblies, which had sought to lift the burden from the poor.

Napoleon's 'reform' of the economy as a whole was in favour of greater state control, defying the revolutionary and enlightenment trend towards freedom from restraint. Napoleon went further than the controlled economy of the Committee of Public Safety. The economy was regulated to supply food, weapons and soldiers for his wars and to protect French industry and agriculture from foreign competition. While Napoleon ensured the provision of bread, which he knew to be necessary in the interests of order, he was uninterested in the material conditions of the workers. They were forbidden to form unions and had to carry a *livret*, which restricted their freedom of movement. He even considered resurrecting the trade guilds of the *ancien régime*.

The reinstatement of the Catholic Church was another reminder of the *ancien régime*, after the dechristianisation of the revolution. Napoleon's expressed view that 'in religion I do not see the mystery of the Incarnation but the mystery of the social order' tells us much about his attitude. The Concordat was neither a religious nor a libertarian move. It was yet another step in Napoleon's quest for power and control and suited Napoleon because it ensured loyalty, with priests paid out of state funds, and conformity. However, Napoleon's re-establishment of clericalism made possible the revival of church influence after 1815 and, as William Doyle wrote, 'a casual observer might be forgiven for concluding that all the destructive zeal of the Revolution had achieved nothing'.

Napoleon's conquests in Europe flew in the face of the 'no conquests' formula, established in the constitution of 1791, although admittedly that had already broken down with the outbreak of war and the conquests of the Directory. The string of titles given to the various members of his family bore witness to his dynastic ambitions, and his continuing desire for conquest, even though he already had an empire of half a million square miles and a population of 44 million in 1812, suggested **megalomania**.

While the empire benefited from some of the 'enlightened' principles of the Napoleonic government, with these came an arrogant lack of concern for popular sovereignty. Napoleon denied rights of democracy and election to subject peoples, and established a strong and centralised administration in the hands of his trusted notables. All freedom of political expression was crushed. He wrote to Jérôme, 'It is ridiculous to quote against me the opinions of the people of Westphalia. If you listen to popular opinion you will achieve nothing'. As in France, it was only the rich, particularly those who had acquired wealth through trade or the purchase of land, who had much to thank Napoleon for.

CONCLUSION

Although Napoleon appeared the 'popular' saviour of France in war, many of the basic principles of the revolution, such as popular sovereignty, equality and liberty were not fulfilled in the way that had been envisaged in 1789. Admittedly, there had been changes to these before Napoleon and he did preserve some elements. It is probably fair to say that, where a revolutionary principle, such as freedom of speech, threatened him, he abandoned or modified it, but where it helped him, as in religious toleration and the abolition of 'feudalism', he maintained it. His overriding concern seems to have been to preserve order. Whether this was for the altruistic motive of maintaining or extending the revolution or the selfish one of preserving himself in power must remain a matter of debate. As George Rudé has written, 'His intentions were certainly never as pure as he claimed, yet the legend has not proved entirely false ... the image of the "soldier of the revolution" has as great a claim to reality ... as that of the despot and conqueror'.

SECTION 5

How can Napoleon's military successes be explained?

The exiled Napoleon once boasted 'I have fought 60 battles and I have learned nothing which I did not know in the beginning'. Many of Napoleon's contemporaries would probably have agreed. The success of the French armies under his command, at least up to 1808, certainly suggested that Napoleon possessed an unrivalled military genius that allowed his armies to go on winning one victory after another. He acquired a reputation as an outstanding, perhaps invincible, general and, although events from 1809 to 1815 shattered the myth of his invincibility, the belief that he had been one of the greatest generals in history persisted, with the development of the 'Napoleonic legend'. Even Wellington, his adversary, referred to him as 'a great *homme de guerre*, possibly the greatest who ever appeared at the head of a French army'.

KEY POINTS

- Napoleon was a highly successful military general up to 1808.
- Napoleon's success was not entirely dependent on his own skill.
- Napoleon's failures after 1808 were at least in part a result of his own mistakes.

HISTORICAL INTERPRETATION

Napoleon's reputation mainly rests on his early campaigns. If his career had finished in 1807, no one could have questioned his military success, although the reasons for this would still have been debatable. However, his failures after that date and his eventual defeat have encouraged historians to question whether he really was the 'military genius' his memoirs would have us believe. Research into the origins of the Napoleonic army, the military tactics adopted and specific studies of campaigns and battles have enabled military historians such as **R. W. Phipps**, who produced a five-volume study of the revolutionary forces, to analyse Napoleon's contribution to the achievements and failures of the French forces.

Napoleon's military advantages

The **size and quality of the French army** was in sharp contrast to that of his opponents, at least up to 1808. By the time of the Consulate, France had already abandoned the small but highly trained armies of rarely more

KEY THEME

Army size The vast armies which Napoleon amassed were only made possible through conscription – the enforced enrolment of soldiers. The expansion of military manpower had begun with the French *levées* of 1792 and had been extended by Carnot's *levée en masse* in 1793. Lots were drawn so that *départements* could meet quotas. Conscription was unpopular, but over 90 per cent of the expected *levées* were raised without difficulty to 1808. Not all conscripted men were actually enrolled in the army, however. Many were able to claim exemption because they were married (until 1813), only sons, or physically unfit. The shortfall was made up by auxiliary troops from the satellite countries.

Napoleon at the Battle of Wagram, July 1809. Contemporary painting by Horace Vernet.

than 24,000 that had dominated warfare earlier in the eighteenth century. The result of the French *levées* of 'volunteers' in 1792, and the general conscription brought by the *levée en masse* from 1793, was to increase the size of the French armies quite dramatically. Consequently, Napoleon had both large numbers of men at his disposal and the means with which to increase that number. France had the largest population in Europe and conquest and empire offered the prospect of an endless supply of men.

The military historian R. W. Phipps has provided us with some figures. It is obviously difficult to be exact, but Napoleon seems to have fought with around 65,000 at Austerlitz, 85,000 or more at Jena, 165,000 at Wagram, 135,000 at Borodino and 190,000 at Leipzig. We must also remember that these figures refer to specific battles. In 1808, on the eve of the Austrian campaign, Napoleon had 300,000 troops in Spain, 100,000 in France, 200,000 in the Rhineland and 60,000 in Italy. One military historian, **A. Meynier** calculated that between 1800 and 1815, 2 million Frenchmen were enrolled in the army.

The size of Napoleon's forces must go some way towards explaining his success. There is, of course, no reason why Napoleon's enemies could not have matched these numbers, since they were frequently in alliance one with another. However, a general lack of enthusiasm to raise too many raw recruits, perhaps for fear of ill discipline, plus a lack of cooperation between the allies, which Napoleon was ever keen to exploit, prevented them doing so before 1813–5. In 1812, the French forces could still outnumber the Russians and, while Wellington never had more than 80,000 troops at any one time in Spain, Soult had over 200,000. Not until the Battle of Leipzig, in 1813, did the allies muster overpowering forces. By the '100 Days', the allies were able to mobilise three-quarters of a million men, and direct 225,000 to Waterloo.

The weapons used by the French armies seem to have had no particular superiority over those of their opponents, although Napoleon did make good use of the mobile field artillery, developed in the pre-revolutionary era by General de Gribeauval, the Inspector-General of the Artillery in France after the Seven Years War. The French gun carriages were lighter, stronger and easier to maintain by the use of iron supports, and interchangeable wheels, pins and bolts, but the weapons of the infantry, standard flintlock muskets, which were inaccurate above 100 metres and the slightly better longer muskets, gave no particular advantage.

French battle tactics certainly proved superior to those of France's enemies for the greater part of the war period. Here again, Napoleon built on developments already under consideration in France before the outbreak of the revolutionary wars. The military debate had concerned battle formations. Did the traditional *ordre mince* (thin line) of troops or *ordre profond* (thick line) provide the best results? The resort to the huge French *levées* had more or less decided the outcome. It was impossible to use vast numbers of virtually untrained soldiers to good effect in the *ordre mince*, so the *ordre profond* or an *ordre mixte*, combining the two, became the likely formation. Napoleon built on his inheritance, favouring the *ordre mixte*, and supporting his footsoldiers with cavalry actions, as **du Teil** had advised, for maximum effect.

Napoleon's tactics were therefore taken from the best of the *ancien régime*, although he developed and refined them into a winning battle formula. He kept his enemies guessing, deliberately made misleading moves to place them in a weaker position or lure them into the open, attacked where it was least expected – often from the rear – and used constant bombardment by infantry, artillery and cavalry, with devastating results. One other feature of his battles which, according to the historian **Franklin Ford**, revealed 'his debt to the revolution', was his relentless pursuit of the retreating enemy, resulting in horrific ensuing carnage.

The allied troops in Europe, still fighting by eighteenth-century methods, slowly and carefully deploying in line for battle, were no match for the French armies. At Ulm, the Austrians seemed to be 'rooted to the ground' and did not know which way to turn when confronted with the swift and unpredictable French forces. It was not until the Battle of Leipzig in 1813 that the Prussians and Russians adopted tactics similar to those employed by the French, wearing out the Napoleonic army with their repeated attacks. However, it should be remembered that victory was also dependent on using the right tactics for the terrain. It was the British adherence to the disciplined *ordre mince* that worked in Spain and triumphed at Waterloo. Wellington certainly showed skills in his use of troops that rivalled Napoleon's own.

KEY THEME

Du Teil's advice
Du Teil was a military expert whose battle tactics Napoleon used to good effect. He particularly recommended that the artillery should play a prominent part in battles. He advocated concentrating artillery fire in a barrage to make gaps in the enemy front line in the opening stages of battles. This provided space for the infantry or cavalry to attack. As the battle evolved, du Teil recommended that the artillery be used to mow down reforming or retreating troops and so cause constant disarray in the enemy lines.

Napoleon also used the systems of army organisation that he inherited from pre-revolutionary days to good effect. Following the advice of Guibert's *Essai Général de Tactique* of 1772, which had been incorporated into the French army's drill book of 1791, he adopted foraging, or **living off the land**, as the normal method of feeding troops on the move.

Napoleon was fortunate to inherit some fine military engineers, educated at the Central School of Public Works established by the revolution and renamed the École Polytechnique in 1795. This was Europe's leading centre for technological instruction and provided the Napoleonic armies with men skilled in the arts of fortification and demolition, bridge construction and similar skills. Trained engineers were in short supply among France's enemies who only gradually came to learn from the example of the French themselves.

The command and organisation of the French army worked in Napoleon's favour. Breaking with revolutionary tradition, he gained a unique advantage when he assumed the position of Commander-in-Chief of the army on becoming First Consul. Thereafter, there was no conflict

KEY TERM

Living off the land This was cheap and convenient and permitted a manoeuvrability that contrasted with that of the enemy forces who moved slowly, in long columns, with enormous supply trains. However, its limitations were clear, both in Spain and Russia, where the systematic destruction of crops was to slow the French army's advances. In Spain, the British used light high-wheeled carts to accompany and supply the forces, which helped bring victory against the rampaging French legions there.

Contemporary illustration of Napoleon dictating to his secretaries. Napoleon always maintained absolute emphasis on the punctual fulfilment of administrative duties.

of civil and military interests and all decisions were made by Napoleon himself within the war committee of the Council of State. He was able to exercise a centralised control over military planning and operations, harnessing state resources for the war effort and setting a standard that the allies, where there was a separation of control between army and state, could never match. His resources of men, money and materials were unrivalled. The Ministry of War was also expanded and divided into two, one for the army itself and another for administration, which increased efficiency.

The internal organisation of the army was partly based on an experiment that had first been tried in the French armies of the 1770s. This involved the use of divisions or corps of 15,000 to 30,000 men, incorporating elements of cavalry, artillery and infantry. Each corps was capable of fighting on its own or could be used in combination with other corps, which permitted flexibility. Formed into a *bataillon carré* (a diamond formation), four corps could change direction while retaining the same shape, if an enemy were detected by a cavalry screen riding in front. A commanding general was placed in control of a corps, which helped to simplify communication with Napoleon, who had the overall direction. The traditional organisation by regiments was not entirely abandoned, however, as Napoleon liked a strong central control. Regiments were commanded by officers who had been promoted to fill the vacancies left by the former aristocratic officers' corps. The new officers, who had gained promotion through their own talent, were loyal and extremely successful, and the French army was considerably weakened by the loss of many such men in the Russian campaign.

Again, Napoleon's enemies were slow to recognise the advantages of the French arrangements. Divided command structures and a reliance on generals drawn from the semi-independent aristocratic gentry made planning difficult and the organisation of campaigns problematic. The allies also had the additional problem of needing to coordinate the armies of different nations. Victory was made even easier for Napoleon when, for example, the Austrians and Russians failed to cooperate at Austerlitz, or he was able to take on the Austrians before the Russians arrived at **Ulm**. Napoleon certainly never lost an opportunity to divide his enemies. Again, experience eventually led to improvement, and the allies managed to cooperate effectively in their final campaigns from 1813. The quality of the Prussian officer corps also improved, following Scharnhorst's military reforms which were put into effect after the disaster of Jena.

Napoleon's troops were also high in morale. This was again inherited from the revolutionary era when troops were called upon to fight for a cause they were conditioned to believe in. Training then, and under Napoleon, was rudimentary, but the policy of *amalgame* (mixing veterans

KEY POINT

Ulm Napoleon was able to win the battle as the Russians arrived late because of confusion over the calendar. The Austrians used a different calendar from the Russians, who were 12 days behind.

with new conscripts) helped both teach and inspire the recruits. The psychological effect of seemingly endless victories must also have helped motivation, and Napoleon seems to have appreciated the need to inspire his men with promises of *la Gloire* (military glory), booty and promotion. According to Ford, Napoleon's 'ringing exhortations … marked him as one of history's true masters of the technique known in modern jargon as *opinion control*'. In contrast, the armies of his enemies were more often held together by fierce discipline, cruelty and contempt, than by loyalty and respect. They incorporated mercenaries and press-ganged soldiers from the lowest ranks of society, as well as conscripted serfs in the Russian army. It was not until after 1806 that the Prussian reformers saw the value of replacing brutal floggings with fair discipline. Napoleon was to comment at Waterloo, 'these animals have learned something'.

Napoleon's generalship

Clearly, most of the advantages the French armies possessed stemmed from the reforms and practices of pre-Napoleonic times. Napoleon inherited an army that was already superior to that of his enemies, and that superiority was maintained at least up to 1808 and, in some cases, to 1813. Napoleon's own contribution to this was twofold. On the one hand, he was an excellent military strategist who was ready to apply a high level of calculation to the winning of battles. On the other, he had what can only be described as a 'magnetic personality', or a way with his men that ensured they rarely failed him.

Napoleon's debt to former generals and theorists does not make his achievements any the less. It took a commander of Napoleon's ability to use his inheritance to best advantage. It was Napoleon who ensured that his huge armies moved at unprecedented speeds across unimaginable distances. It was through Napoleon's detailed planning that the French armies were able to take up superior positions in battle, fragment the opposition, cut off enemy supply lines and prevent the drawing up of reserves. It was Napoleon who developed what became a winning formula. He manoeuvred the enemy into a weak position, outnumbered it with troops, wore it down with mass artillery, bayonets and cavalry charges and then pursued it relentlessly.

Napoleon's other contribution was unique. He deliberately cultivated his men. They naturally held a special respect for him as their First Consul and then Emperor, but it was his way of travelling with the troops and appearing, at least, to share their sufferings and privations that helped gain him their confidence. He would visit his men before a battle, issue daily bulletins and show a personal involvement in the campaign. Napoleon also ensured the army enjoyed a special status. He rewarded bravery and used the Legion of Honour, decorations and titles to encourage acts of valour. He tried to ensure they were well fed and paid and it says something for his achievement that, even when hundreds were starving in Russia, he still retained their loyalty. A sergeant in the Imperial Guard involved in the Russian campaign wrote, 'the Emperor in our midst, on foot … he so great, who had made us all so proud of him, inspired us by his glance in this hour of misfortune'. Napoleon's personal abilities certainly contrasted favourably with those of the allies. Although there were some able men such as Kutuzov, Blücher, Archduke Charles and Wellington, most allied generals were old and cautious and held themselves aloof from their men.

However, Napoleon's generalship has been subjected to some criticism. One factor we have already noted was his lack of interest in technological innovation. Despite the efforts of his military engineers and scientists, Napoleon rejected such new ideas as a mechanical semaphore telegraph which he regarded as expensive, cumbersome and easily intercepted, underwater warships (submarines), first tested in France 1800–1, explosive rockets (as used by the British at Copenhagen in 1801) and ground balloons for reconnaissance. He was even disinterested in such relatively simple innovations as a sharp knife attached to a musket to open cartridges without having to bite them. Wherever Napoleon's talents lay, they were not in the field of invention. Napoleon made little innovation in organisation, introduced no new training methods and the developments in the army were more of size.

Even his organisation and tactics can be questioned. He took risks that could have led to disaster, his reconnaissance was often poor, he frequently failed to provide himself or his troops with adequate maps, he underestimated supply problems and he tried to save money by reducing medical supplies. In *Blundering to Glory*, the historian **O. Connelly** has criticised Napoleon's reputation as a great general, pointing out that some of his victories were close run and that he was often just lucky. His ignorance of weather and climate meant he lost men needlessly, for example in Egypt, in the mud of the Oder, 1806 and in Russia, 1812. He was even worse on naval matters and yet refused advice. His projected invasion of Britain was little short of a fiasco.

Napoleon failed to appreciate that his methods and tactics, while highly successful in most of his early campaigns, were not the only ways of winning victories. They were only suited to certain terrains and types of battle and when his enemies began to understand them, proved all too predictable. His insistence that his soldiers live off the land, for example, was clearly an inappropriate demand in Spain and Russia. Similarly, when he was unable to force a quick battle, in line with his normal practice, in Russia, he failed. His 'surprise' tactics of attacking from the rear were eventually countered and his relentless pursuit mimicked by his enemies at Leipzig. Clearly he could absorb and put his understanding of known

KEY THEMES

The contribution of Napoleon's generals The battle of Marengo in 1799, which was so crucial to Bonaparte's future career, was very nearly lost, when the Austrians launched a surprise attack of 30,000 against 18,000 French. It was only when General Desaix, who had earlier been sent away by Napoleon, reappeared with 6000 fresh troops that the tables were turned and the battle won, at the cost of Desaix's own life.

Napoleon's health From 1807 many of those close to Napoleon spoke of the change in their master's health. He became more irritable, intolerant and unpredictable. He grew more openly contemptuous of others and made the comment, 'power comes through fear'. His formerly brilliant memory seemed to fade and he appeared lethargic and slow.

tactics to good effect but, as in the realm of military technology, he was not an innovator or unqualified genius, even in strategic matters.

It could even be argued that many of Napoleon's great victories were dependent on the **contribution of his generals** and that it was only Napoleon's own writings and the legend that grew after his death that denigrated them to a lesser role than they really deserved. While the skill of his subordinates, men like Murat, Ney and Davout, should not necessarily detract from Napoleon's own ability to plan campaigns, it was nevertheless an important ingredient in their success.

While Napoleon's position as Commander-in-Chief and Head of State was an advantage in many ways, the way Napoleon used this position could be said to have been harmful rather than beneficial to the French armies in the longer term. Napoleon was so protective of his own power that subordinates were given little experience of command. He preferred to mastermind everything himself, causing one of his marshals to remark, 'the Emperor needs neither advice nor plans of campaign … our duty is just to obey'. Such control proved disastrous when Napoleon was forced to leave others in command. The losses of the Peninsular War were partly the result of the failure of the generals to cooperate or take effective decisions. Caulaincourt, a trusted general who accompanied Napoleon on campaigns, wrote 'Even the Chief of Staff … who knew the Emperor's plans, decided nothing … The Emperor occupied himself with the most minute details. He wanted everything to bear the imprint of his genius'.

So Napoleon's generalship was entirely personal. There was no permanent general staff to serve the army and, as Napoleon's own mental and physical health deteriorated, there was no other 'brain' to take over the planning and conduct of campaigns. After 1807, piles and bladder and stomach problems troubled **the increasingly corpulent Napoleon**, and may have been responsible for his seemingly hysterical outbursts, which have been likened to epileptic fits. Certainly he seemed to lose something of his earlier skill and control, although it may simply have been that his formerly unbroken run of success had led him to believe that he was invincible. However, he still continued to plan and fight and had the energy to return in the '100 Days' in 1815.

Historians, such as Ford, have often referred to his decisions to control Spain (1808) and invade Russia (made some time before 1812) as 'fateful'. Both were launched with little forethought, and conducted in a less sophisticated manner than his earlier wars. In Russia, for example, he grew increasingly frustrated and apparently confused when the campaign failed to follow its expected course. His own ill health and lethargy might well explain why he allowed his armies to languish in Moscow for a fatal month, so delaying until the winter set in. However, it would be inaccurate to say that all Napoleon's strengths had deserted him. He did fight vigorous campaigns in 1813–14 (never considering surrender, for good or bad) and his strategy at Waterloo was almost successful.

How can Napoleon's military successes be explained?   189

SNUFFING OUT BONEY!

Other factors contributing to the decline in French fortunes from 1808

It would therefore be unfair to attribute the decline in French fortunes after 1808 solely to a decline in Napoleon's own generalship. There were many other factors at stake. The size and quality of the French armies, for example, declined in later years as Napoleon was increasingly forced to recruit from the empire and satellite states rather than the mother country, and losses in battle meant many more raw recruits and fewer veterans. By the time of the Russian campaign, only half the army was French and the flank commands were in the hands of Austrians and Prussians. This reduced reliability and reduced the amount of flexibility, as displayed by the earlier French armies.

The gradual improvement in the generalship and organisation of Napoleon's enemies must also be taken into account. The Austrians, under Archduke Charles's leadership, considerably improved their recruitment and organisation by 1813 and began to copy French tactics. Prussia also made dramatic improvements following the shock of defeat at Jena in 1806 and the loss of half its territory and a hefty 600 million francs indemnity in the Treaty of Tilsit (1807). The shame helped foster unity and led to social and military reform. While **Humboldt and Stein**

KEY PEOPLE

Humboldt, Stein and Scharnhorst
Wilhelm von Humboldt, Karl Baron vom und zum Stein and General Scharnhorst were among those figures who helped reorganise the Prussian state after its humiliating defeat at Jena. Stein was Minister of Home Affairs 1807–8 and in his short period of office ended serfdom in Prussia, allowing the free sale of land, and reformed local

government. Humboldt founded the University of Berlin in 1810, and supported reforms to provide a more open and practical education for citizens. Scharnhorst, alongside other military reformers, introduced a Great General Staff to co-ordinate operations and founded the War Academy. This provided advanced training for officers and was open to non-noblemen. A universal reserve service was also established to provide back-up troops.

Robert Stewart, Viscount Castlereagh (1769–1822)
Castlereagh was British foreign secretary 1812–22 and appreciated the need for the chief powers of Europe (Britain, Austria, Russia and Prussia) to work together against Napoleon. It was he who engineered the Treaty of Chaumont in March 1814, by which the allies bound themselves together against Napoleon in the Quadruple Alliance (see page 122).

modernised education and government, the army was reorganised by **Scharnhorst**. By the Battle of Leipzig, the Prussian army had abandoned its old eighteenth-century tactics, relaxed the traditional harsh discipline, created a well-organised system of compulsory military service, which provided 150,000 trained men, and established promotion by merit in the officer corps. In addition, volunteer forces of students and urban workers responded to the call for a war of liberation.

Given the length of the wars, economic factors were also bound to play a part. The historian **J. U. Nef** (1950) has referred to this era as the opening of the modern world's experience of total war – fought by mass armies with tools supplied by mass industries. In the initial stages, France had the advantages of size and strength but, after 1808, the Continental System brought depression to France and loss of manpower and an undeveloped industrial base gradually sapped the French effort. On the other hand, Britain with its superior industrial economy and control of the seas remained undefeated. Britain was able to provide its allies with the material resources needed to pursue the fight and, given its commanding position, was able to ensure that its allies eventually learnt the value of working together. By the later stages of war France's enemies had the economic ascendancy and, thanks in part to **Castlereagh's** interventions, had learnt the value of collective action. This placed them in a far stronger position than France.

CONCLUSION

Napoleon's run of military successes up to 1808 certainly owed something to the quality of Napoleon's generalship, even if that needs to be balanced against his military inheritance and the weaknesses of his opponents. He was no innovator, except in terms of scale and elements of organisation, but he did show outstanding skill as a commander and strategist. His later losses stemmed from his personal failings, both as a military general and as a leader who refused to face reality and lay down arms and consolidate his gains when it became clear that his enemies' position was growing stronger and his own advantages declining. His military skills never totally deserted him, but it might be suggested that he grew too arrogant and ambitious. According to Franklin Ford, 'year by year Napoleon seemed to lose the capacity for dealing with other governments or even tolerating their independent existence'. Even when virtually all governments turned against him in 1813, he was not prepared to negotiate or compromise. The same qualities of self-confidence and control, which had enabled him to enjoy such unparalleled military success in the early years, thus contributed to his downfall.

SECTION 6

Why did the restoration of the Bourbons (1814) end in revolution (1830)?

In many ways, the term 'restoration' is a misnomer. The Bourbon monarchy was 'restored' in that the new kings of France from 1815, Louis XVIII and Charles X, were brothers of the martyred Bourbon, Louis XVI. However the position enjoyed by Louis XVI was never 'restored'. So much had changed in the intervening years that it would have been impossible, even if it had been desirable, to return to the days of the *ancien régime*. In the 23 years since the abolition of the monarchy, France had been transformed socially and politically by the revolutionary and Napoleonic administrations. The 'restoration' of the Bourbons was a compromise and the product of military defeat. Louis XVIII was put into power by France's erstwhile enemies because it was felt that he stood the greatest chance of 'healing the wounds of the revolution'. In 1814, it was expected that if the Bourbons were restored 'on conditions', they would prove acceptable to the French and provide the peace and political stability that all craved. By 1830, that expectation was shown to be false. This section looks at some of the key questions that this failure poses.

KEY POINTS

- The restored Bourbons began their reign with a number of advantages.
- The collapse of the Bourbon monarchy in 1830 cannot be deemed inevitable, although underlying factors, such as social division and economic insecurity, weakened it.
- The collapse of the dynasty was the product of personal as well as other factors.

HISTORICAL INTERPRETATION

Historians have examined the reigns of Louis XVIII and Charles X in the light of what happened in 1830, when the Bourbon monarchy was replaced by the so-called 'bourgeois' monarchy of Louis-Philippe. Marxist historians, such as Soboul, saw the events of that year as the inevitable result of the rise of the bourgeoisie and the next stage in the process of Marxist revolution. **Soboul** accordingly wrote, 'The revolution of 1789 did not really end until 1830 when, having brought a king to power who accepted their principles, the bourgeoisie took definitive possession of France'. Marxists also stress the part of the urban workers who manned

KEY TERM

The July Days
This refers to the revolution of July 1830, when rioting led to the overthrow of Charles X and his replacement by Louis-Philippe. Following Charles X's issue of the July ordinances, which tried to curb the powers of the press, Parisian workers, republicans and students set up barricades in the narrow Parisian streets in an attempt to force change (see pages 134–6).

the barricades in the 'July Days'. **George Rudé** has gone so far as to write, 'the workers that thronged the streets of the capital to overthrow the Bourbon Charles X were no longer the Sans Culottes of 1789, but were becoming moulded into a new industrial workforce which, barely a dozen years later, would call themselves *prolétaires*'.

This view suggests the failure of the Bourbon restoration was primarily the result of economic and social change. The development of manufacturing industry was creating a working class with specific political demands, and a bourgeoisie determined to replace the old aristocracy as leaders of society and to keep that working class in its place. Even those who do not subscribe to Marxist ideology recognise that the troubles of 1830 had links with economic distress among the lower classes, particularly after the depression of 1826, and most acknowledge the frustration of the liberal bourgeoisie. However, non-Marxists question the inevitability of developments and place greater importance on other factors.

Liberal historians are more likely to view the 1830 revolution as the result of the Bourbon kings' own inadequacies and a strong case can be made for placing the blame firmly on the shoulders of Charles X. Whether or not the revolution is considered inevitable in turn depends on how much emphasis is given to Charles X's attitude, policies and blunders. No one disputes the fact that the Bourbons' inheritance was unenviable, but it is possible to argue that there were a number of factors that favoured the regime and the best proof of this is the comparative success of Louis XVIII.

FACTORS THAT FAVOURED THE BOURBON RESTORATION

The effective compromise

Whatever their political views, by 1815, most French people were tired of war. A generation had grown up knowing nothing else and it must have been tempting to accept the fettered Bourbon monarchy as the price of peace. In any case, the French did not really have a lot of choice. They were at the mercy of the other powers of Europe. There was no consensus for an alternative form of government and those, such as Talleyrand (see page 126), who were in a position to negotiate, regarded the Bourbon monarchy as the most acceptable choice and one that would divide Frenchmen the least.

It should be remembered that monarchism had never been completely undermined in France. Indeed the principle of hereditary monarchy had been so strong that it had split the revolutionaries when they abolished it and had helped forge a powerful counter-revolution. Under the Directory, increasing support for monarchism had led to the various army coups that ultimately brought Napoleon to power. He chose to become an emperor, rather than the King of France with its unfavourable associations, but he created new monarchies throughout the rest of his empire, believing them to be the best guarantors of social and political stability. According to the historian, **David Thomson**, 'Monarchy was at the time, to most people, the most natural form of government in the world'.

The Bourbon restoration upheld the principle of legitimate inheritance and the constitutional charter acted as a sweetener (see pages 126–7). The Bourbon monarchy was pledged to maintain the civil code, equality of taxation, equality in the law, careers open to talent and purchasers of the lands of the *biens nationaux*. The social and political elites were reassured and, even after the period of the 100 Days, the Bourbons were able to take the throne, secure in the knowledge that most of those Frenchmen that mattered wanted the restoration to work.

The structure of government

The Bourbons inherited an established administrative structure, civil service and legal system that were to provide the Bourbon regime with some solid foundations. The simplification and rationalisation of local government by the Constituent Assembly had largely survived the Napoleonic era unscathed, while the great Napoleonic codes had helped considerably in the establishment of effective law and justice, and in the workings of trade and commerce. There was a nationwide system of law courts and juries, and government was centralised and efficient.

The Bourbons were therefore happy to take over the apparatus of the imperial state, including its systems of surveillance and control which no doubt helped to curb criticism during the early days of the regime.

The principle of elective assemblies was another of their inheritances, and this was enshrined in the charter. The revolution had never succeeded in establishing a successful constitutional monarchy, but that might have been blamed on the faults of Louis XVI. There was plenty of experience to draw on and the new constitution of 1814 tried to bring together the best of the various experiments to date. A two-chamber system, with a franchise restricted to property owners and a royal veto, seemed to steer well away from the worst excesses of democracy, while avoiding any concessions to absolutism. Over the next 15 years, the French **electoral system** was amended six times but there was no major overhaul until 1830, and the changes were made in the interests of strengthening government and increasing stability.

The Bourbons also inherited and worked with some experienced and capable ministers. Talleyrand and Fouché had both served ably under

KEY THEME

Changes to the electoral system
From 1818, one-fifth of the members of the Chamber of Deputies was to be elected annually, which left a permanent 'core'. From 1820, 172 extra deputies were added to the chamber – to be elected for seven (rather than five) years for greater stability. The biggest change came after the revolution of 1830 when the tax qualification for the vote fell from 300 francs to 200 francs, and that for deputies fell from 1000 francs to 500 francs.

Napoleon. The Duc de Richelieu, the Duc de Decazes and the moderate Martignac were all capable ministers and even the Comte de Villèle, better known for his faults, proved a successful financial minister to Charles X.

The support of the nobility

The French nobility of 1815 was rather different from the old *noblesse* of Louis XIV, but it was, nevertheless, a natural supporter of monarchy. Of the old nobility, some, like the kings themselves, had been *émigrés* and lost their land, while others had remained in France and had retained their property, although without their titles, privileges or hereditary offices. Alongside these were the surviving new *notables* created by Napoleon who had both titles and estates. Many of the older aristocrats also received lands and titles as 'rewards' from the Bourbons after the restoration and these two groups were generally happy to accept a constitutional monarchy which gave them power and influence, not least in the chambers. However, there was a group of former nobles, encouraged by the Comte d'Artois, the future Charles X, who hoped for more. They wielded considerable power in government and their 'support' was a mixed blessing.

The support of the Catholic Church

There was real enthusiasm for the restoration of the Bourbon monarchy from the Catholic Church. Services of gratitude were held and clerics taught that it was God's will that France had been purged of Jacobinism and atheism. The settlement of 1815 had brought a revival of the Catholic Church throughout western Europe. The Pope had been re-enthroned in St Peter's and the **Index, Inquisition and Jesuits** reinstated. Rulers like the Bourbons could claim to base their authority on Christian principles, and this suited many Frenchmen. The issue of religion had divided France more than any other during the revolutionary period, and the Napoleonic Concordat had acknowledged the desire of Frenchmen to rehabilitate the Church. Of course, its power was not as it had been. Its lands had gone, and its doctrines and teaching were regarded with increased scepticism, particularly among the educated classes. However, the Church provided some backing for royal authority and, with its renewed control in education, could act as a force for cohesion in France.

The support of the bourgeoisie

The people with the most influence in France in this period were the *pays légal* (the property owners who had the vote). Some were of noble rank, but many more formed the upper bourgeoisie of educated professionals and businessmen. It was their skills that maintained the administration, and their commercial and industrial interests were essential to the wealth of the country. The destruction of feudal dues and controls in the revolutionary and Napoleonic periods had helped stimulate the growth of bourgeois society and, for at least the early years of the Bourbon restoration, Louis XVIII was able to count on their support. Businessmen in particular looked forward to renewed prosperity and welcomed the promise of stability. By the charter, the Bourbons guaranteed there would be no return of seized church or *émigré* lands and even Charles X dared not tamper with this. The Bourbon restoration was highly dependent on support from this group.

The support of the peasantry

The restoration was greeted by the masses as a welcome end to conscription and, some thought, taxation. As a whole, the revolution had given the peasants a new status and economic security, which they were anxious to retain. Among the wealthier peasants, there were those, though a minority, that had benefited from sale of church and *émigré* lands, especially after the law of June 1793 allowing the sale of land in small lots. Although below the voting threshold, they supported a monarchy that accepted their gains, and the restoration of the Church also suited the largely traditionalist peasantry. So the Bourbons could generally count on a quiescent and supportive majority in rural France.

Economic recovery

While the peasants' hopes of an end to taxation may have been unrealistic, the restoration did, nevertheless, bring an economic recovery that provided a good basis for Bourbon rule. During the long period of war, much French manufacture had stagnated. Colonies were lost and the commerce of the Atlantic ports had fallen to a trickle. However, the revolution had helped create conditions in which industry could begin to grow, unfettered by restrictions, and technological innovation after 1800 provided an incentive for industrial development, with the return of peace. France itself had escaped much of the devastation of war and agriculture was thriving. During the early years of the restoration, the government stabilised the food supply, reorganised finances, and wise government spending ensured the war indemnity was paid off, thus freeing the country of occupation troops. Although economic depression returned to France (and the rest of western Europe) in the later 1820s, the overall picture of the restoration years was one of fair taxation and economic growth.

Success abroad

Both Louis XVIII and Charles X had reasonably successful foreign policies. The Bourbons inherited a strong militaristic tradition. Yet they wisely avoided costly war, while maintaining a healthy interest in overseas affairs, which showed that France still deserved to be regarded as a 'great power'. Louis ensured that France was readmitted to the Concert of Europe at the Congress of Aix-la-Chapelle in 1818 and used the French

Ferdinand VII restored, despite his despotic nature, with the help of French troops. Contemporary portrait c. 1814.

army to help restore Ferdinand VII of Spain in 1822. Charles X sent a successful expedition against the Barbary Pirates in 1830, which led to the capture of Algiers and helped establish a new French colonial empire in North Africa.

FACTORS THAT UNDERMINED THE BOURBON RESTORATION

The influence of the Ultras

While noble support was, in general terms, an advantage to the Bourbons, the pressure of the Ultra-Royalist group, which wanted revenge, compensation and a return of former status, was not. France's White Terror, which followed the initial defeat of Napoleon in 1814 and was revived with increased ferocity after the 100 Days, was not an expression of royal policy, but its encouragement by the Ultras led others to believe it was.

It was a reflection of the property-based electoral system that the Ultras were able to wield so much influence. Backed by their semi-secret organisation, the *Chevaliers de la Foi*, they packed the chambers and pressed their views. Louis XVIII's first *Chambre Introuvable* of 1815 was made up of around 52 per cent of *ancien régime* nobles, and Charles X's of 1824, 60 per cent, with 50 per cent former *émigrés*.

Louis XVIII's initial attempt to provide broad-based government proved futile after the assassination of the Duc de Berri in 1820 and the political polarisation hardened between the Ultras and the liberals, the nobles and the non-nobles and, in the country as a whole, between the Ultra west and south and other areas. Charles X, a former Ultra leader himself, only extended and reinforced their influence, providing compensation for ex-*émigrés*, preferential treatment for nobles in the army and administration, and favouring Ultra ministers such as Polignac and La Bourdonnaye over constitutional monarchists like Châteaubriand.

The influence of the Church

The support of the Church was also a two-edged sword. The rehabilitation of the Church was one thing, but to have clericalism and practices reminiscent of the *ancien régime* forced upon an anticlerical bourgeoisie was quite another. Charles X's elaborate coronation ceremony, complete with holy oil, probably caused more sneers than distress, but the Law of Sacrilege against defamers of the established Catholic hierarchy was deemed provocative. The renewed dominance of clerics in education and official encouragement for showy 'religious missions' to the provinces calling for collective penance for the sins of the revolution all added to the tensions of political life.

The personalities and attitudes of the monarchs

It is fashionable to contrast the cautious and moderate Louis XVIII with his foolish Ultra brother Charles X. At least Louis XVIII tried to stand by the charter and rule with a mixture of firmness and moderation that allowed him to die a king. Charles X, on the other hand, seemed to epitomise the charge against the Bourbons that they had 'learnt nothing and forgotten nothing' from the revolution. Clinging to his own stubborn interpretation of the constitution, he ignored advice and acted with an arrogance quite unsuited to the circumstances of the Bourbon restoration.

However, both kings shared some common traits. They were both elderly. Their formative years had been spent in the court of the *ancien régime* and they had largely viewed the changes of the revolutionary and Napoleonic periods from a distance. Their friends were ex-*émigrés* like themselves. They had little comprehension of the industrial and manufacturing world of the bourgeoisie and still less of the life of the urban artisans.

They were colourless figures, and all the more so after the flamboyance of Napoleon. How could Louis XVIII's success against Spanish guerrillas or Charles X's against Algerian tribesmen compare with Napoleon's great victories of Marengo or Austerlitz? What is more, they were Bourbons, representatives of a disgraced house and restored 'in the baggage train of the Allies'. Louis's undignified flight in 1814 had hardly been an auspicious start and his size and problems of health did not help him to cut an impressive figure. Their insistence on dating the reign from 1795, the abandonment of the Tricolore, the shooting of Marshal Ney and the attempt to revive the **Divine Right of Kings** indicated a lack of tact and common sense that was to undermine their chances of survival.

The forces of opposition

Leaving aside the Ultras, the opposition to the Bourbon monarchy can be divided into three broad categories – the Bonapartists, the Liberals and the Republicans.

The Bonapartists were not unduly troublesome. Most of Napoleon's former supporters had been disgraced, repressed or converted into constitutional monarchists at the restoration. The main effect of Napoleon's return during the 100 Days had been to reinforce the *notables*' concern for social order, and defeat at Waterloo left little alternative but to accept a fait accompli. Admittedly it was a demented veteran of Napoleon's armies who carried out the fateful assassination of the Duc de Berri, but he acted on his own initiative. Although there were some disgruntled ex-officers and officials who still hankered after the much exaggerated 'glorious days of Empire', these tended to fall in with

KEY TERM

Divine Right of Kings This was the belief that the king had been appointed by God and was God's representative on earth. He owed allegiance to no one but God. This was symbolised in his coronation and coronation oath.

The consequences of Napoleon's death

After six lonely years on the island of St Helena, Napoleon died in 1821. He left a son, the former King of Rome, who had, since his father's exile, been brought up in Vienna as the Duke of Reichstadt. He was accepted by loyal Bonapartists as Napoleon II from 1821, until his death in 1832, although he never personally used the title. In the 1820s, the Napoleonic legend was still gaining momentum, despite an official ban on any material favourable to him to 1830. The public perception of Napoleon's rule was gradually changing. He was no longer viewed as a dictator but as a champion of liberalism and nationalism, and the brilliance of his victories was contrasted with the dull Bourbon court. The Bonapartists were not a strong political group in 1830, but they were soon to become so.

the broad 'liberal' opposition, particularly after the **death of the former emperor** in May 1821 left them without an obvious leader.

The Liberals were initially supportive of the regime. They had less to fear from a constitutional monarchy than any other form of government and had hoped to be able to work with the monarchy through the charter. However, the power of the Ultras threatened the fundamental principles of representative government and, by the 1820s, Liberal opposition groups of landowners, professional men, members of the former imperial service and retired army officers, were beginning to form in cities and industrial towns. Interest does not seem to have extended beyond this narrow circle of men with money and leisure, and police reports claimed most Liberals were lawyers or merchants. However, their leaders, members of the *pays légal*, were more usually from the land-owning elite. Some were nobles, such as the Duc de Broglie and Comte Molé, but the majority were of non-noble background.

They enjoyed a fair degree of electoral success. The Liberal Association *Aide-toi, le Ciel t'aidera* formed by the Liberal lawyer-journalist, Guizot, to ensure the registration of voters, did extremely well in the polls of 1827 and again in the two final Bourbon elections of 1830. However, the Liberals had no intention of overthrowing the monarchy. The worst they suggested was a nationwide refusal to pay taxes.

The Republicans had been muzzled under Napoleon and, given the continuing censorship and surveillance of the royalist restoration, few dared speak out openly.

However, republicanism was far from finished. Since the heady days of the first revolutionary Republic, when the Sans Culottes had virtually been able to dictate policy, the term had acquired a special significance and a powerful attraction for the urban artisans. Republicanism was kept alive through Carbonarist secret societies and student socialist groups, particularly in Paris. As the Liberal opposition became more vocal, these Parisian Republicans saw an opportunity for action. After 1826, the economy had taken a down turn. There had been a 30 per cent wage fall in the building trades in Paris and a 40 per cent fall for textile workers. Poor harvests had again raised the price of bread in the capital and those workers who had migrated to Paris in search of work were particularly hard hit. The Liberals may have provoked Charles X into issuing the Four Ordinances of St Cloud in 1830 (see page 133), but it was the Republicans who came out against him, manned the barricades and frightened Charles X into abdication.

The short-term causes of revolution, 1830

It was, ultimately, the actions of Charles X that provoked the 1830 revolution. His increasingly reactionary government, which brought press censorship and the dissolution of the bourgeoisie's most prized institution, the National Guard (1827), moved further and further from the spirit of the charter. By 1829, Charles X was choosing ministers with no regard for the chamber or electoral process and, by 1830, issuing edicts that bypassed it altogether. This was the final straw. Within two days the street barricades were up in Paris and in nine, in a Liberal–Republican compromise, Louis-Philippe was proclaimed King. **Franklin Ford** wrote, 'An entire conception of monarchy had come crashing down'.

CONCLUSION

The 1830 revolution was not a reaction to the restoration of monarchy as such, for indeed another monarch was soon on the throne. It was a reaction to the Bourbons' understanding of what monarchy was. Their rule between 1815 and 1830 had taught that the major political and social changes of the revolutionary and Napoleonic periods could not be ignored. Politics was no longer the preserve of the monarch and his ministers and it was impossible to rule without reference to the interests of wider social groups, most particularly the bourgeoisie. To promote the nobility and the Church, as the Bourbons did, was to defy the principles, not only of the revolution, but of the entire eighteenth-century Enlightenment. The failure of the Bourbon restoration was a failure to appreciate that Europe in 1815 had changed, and was still changing, from the continent of the mid-eighteenth century. According to Franklin Ford, it was 'a new world of broad confrontations between conservatives and liberals and of bewildering economic change'.

A2 ASSESSMENT: REVOLUTIONARY, NAPOLEONIC AND BOURBON FRANCE

SOURCE-BASED QUESTIONS IN THE STYLE OF OCR

Study the sources below and answer the questions that follow.

Source A

A summary of the views of Madame de Staël. Madame de Staël's salon in Paris attracted prominent critics of Napoleon. She was exiled by Napoleon in 1803. She was an admirer of the ideals of liberty and enlightened, moderate reform.

Napoleon comes to the fore as a soldier. The principles of political warfare do not interest him. He destroys republican idealism, first in the army, then, with the help of the army, in the State. He is the complete egoist, for whom human sympathy does not exist, for whom men are despised tools, pieces on a chess board. He is a foreigner among the French. Having no faith and no fatherland, he pursues no other purpose than his own greatness. He is the sly Machiavellian, who promises peace, but who, when once power is in his hands, can do nothing but make war. He is a man for whom religion and literature mean nothing, except in so far as they minister to his greatness or his power, and under whom both must wither. In short he is the tyrant.

From Peter Geyl's Napoleon: For and Against, Cape (1949).

Source B

The reported view of a nineteenth-century French historian. Thiers was a journalist and politician who wrote a 20 volume history of Napoleon between 1845 and 1868. The early volume, from which this summary was drawn, was written at the time of the growth of the Napoleonic Legend in the 1840s.

For Thiers the peak of Napoleon's career came at the outset: 'The man who ruled France from 1799 to 1815, knew, no doubt, days of intoxicating glory in the course of his career, but surely neither he himself nor the France over which he cast his spell ever again lived through such days as these, days whose greatness was accompanied by so much wisdom, and by that wisdom which prompts the hope of durability.' These words follow his account of the bringing of law and order, of victory (Marengo), of peace (Lunéville and Amiens), of reconciliation (the Concordat and the amnesty), and his description of the public's amazement at the part played by the young soldier in the Council of State towards the completion of the new Civil Code. He sees in him, in accordance with Napoleon's own view of himself, the consolidator of the Revolution at home and its promoter abroad.

This is Peter Geyl's summary in Napoleon: For and Against, Cape (1949), although it includes a quotation directly from volume 1 of Thiers' work.

Source C
A modern historian discusses the relationship between Napoleon and the French Revolution.

The revolutionary ideals of freedom and equality, the notion of popular sovereignty, the goal of rational administration and the rule of law, the liberation of Europe from feudal oppression, and above all the poisoned legacy of war time: all this inheritance formed the basis of his power, and at the same time limited his options. The lasting contributions of Napoleon Bonaparte were those made when his personal destiny conformed with the needs of France and of its revolutionary history.

As First Consul, Bonaparte's persona was that of creative statesman, the lawgiver who brought France peace, reconciliation, and the consolidation of the Revolution's social reforms. After 1804, he was transformed into the Emperor Napoleon, more authoritarian, concerned to protect his dynasty and eager to dominate Europe itself. A final transformation occurred in 1815, when the circumstances of the Hundred Days forced a new metamorphosis into Napoleon the liberal.

Throughout this evolution two main themes stand out. Napoleon was the founder of the modern state. His regime was also the fulfilment of the bourgeois Revolution of 1789–99.

M. Lyons, *Napoleon Bonaparte and the Legacy of the French Revolution*, Macmillan (1994).

Source D
Napoleon describes his relationship to the revolution and his achievements.

Let me charge you to respect liberty; and above all equality. With regard to liberty, it might be possible to restrain it in a case of extremity, but heaven forbid that we should ever infringe upon equality! It is the passion of the age; and I wish to continue to be the man of the age! The great battle of the century had been won and the Revolution accomplished; now all that remained was to reconcile it with all that it had not destroyed. That task belonged to me. I became the arch of the alliance between old and new, the natural mediator between the old and the new orders. I closed the gulf of anarchy and cleared away the chaos. I purified the Revolution.

Extract from Napoleon's conversations in exile on St Helena, 1816–21, quoted in Andrina Stiles, *Napoleon, France and Europe*, Hodder and Stoughton (1993).

(a) Account for the differences between Source A and Source B as historical assessments of Napoleon. (15)

(b) Explain which of the Sources A to D provides the most convincing interpretation of the relationship between Napoleon and the French Revolution. (30)

Reading

Before answering these questions you should reread Section 4. You will also find it useful to look at the AS part of the book on Napoleonic France, in particular at Chapter 9.

How to answer these questions

Part (a) requires an appraisal of two different historical interpretations. You would need to make the obvious distinction that, while Madame de Staël clearly disapproves of Napoleon and condemns his motives and methods, Thiers found much to praise in his reign. However, a full answer requires more than this:

- Specific source references need to be linked to your own knowledge of the context of Napoleon's rule.
- There must be some attempt to explain the differences between the sources.

You might, for example, observe that Source B only refers to the early part of Napoleon's reign, while Source A speaks of the whole period. Source B was written at the time of the growing 'Napoleonic legend', while Source A was written by a prominent liberal critic at the time.

Part (b) requires some source evaluation. You should already have some ideas about Napoleon's relationship with the French Revolution, and you will need to assess each source and judge its usefulness in the light of your own knowledge and understanding. Try to evaluate the sources as pieces of evidence rather than simply for what they say. For example, you might develop some of the following comments:

- Source A is a contemporary account, but the view given is coloured by strong liberal beliefs.
- Source B was written in the immediate aftermath of the period in question but at a time when the Napoleonic legend was growing and influencing historians.
- Source C is the view of a modern historian far removed from the period described and reliant on available evidence
- Source D provides Napoleon's own account, but can he be trusted?

Don't forget that you will also need to make links between the sources and prioritise to show which is the most convincing. Don't merely assert that one is more convincing. Ensure that you have fully explained your choice and also shown why the other sources offer less convincing interpretations.

SOURCE-BASED QUESTION IN THE STYLE OF AQA

Study the sources below and answer the question that follows.

Source A

Paris became very restless at the news that troops were concentrating about the city. Actually, the troops had no definite orders. No one knew what to do, and Louis XVI was not the sort of man to shoot down his own subjects. From July 12 [1789] there were clashes between parties of soldiers and miscellaneous gatherings of civilians. Groups under improvised* leadership began to search for arms ... to defend themselves against nameless evils the army might be ordered to enforce. Word spread that arms were stored at the Bastille ... the crowd that swarmed about the Bastille on the 14 July was not concerned with the prisoners but in general was protesting against dark and unknown forces arrayed against the people and in particular was asking for weapons.

From *The World of the French Revolution*, by R. R. Palmer, Allen and Unwin (1971).

(*unplanned)

Source B

The March to Versailles on 5 October [1789], by ending in the king's return to the capital, completed the Paris revolution of July. ... The idea that the king should return to his capital and reside among his subjects ... was not a new one: it had been voiced in the *cahier* of the Parisian Third Estate. ... Now it was revived, and with greater insistence, to respond to a new political situation. The immediate issue was the 'veto' – the question as to whether the king should have the power under the constitution being debated at Versailles, to amend, suspend or permanently reject legislative proposals of the National Assembly.

From *The Crowd in the French Revolution*, by G. Rudé, Clarendon Press (1965).

Source C

A central feature of sans-culotte psychology was its permanent anticipation of betrayal and treachery. The fevers of war and civil war were ... causes, but the source is surely to be found in that conflict which splintered the former Third Estate after the first aristocratic counter attack had been beaten. At the Champs de Mars on 17 July 1791 the Assembly shot down demonstrators against a defector king who had betrayed his own constitution. It crushed democratic clubs and prints in a repression which drove men like Danton and Marat into hiding and exile ... With the massacre, the atmosphere of the *journées* returns; henceforth, the course of the Revolution is to be punctuated by them.

From *Artisans and Sans-Culottes*, by G. A. Williams, Libris (1988).

> With reference to these three sources, and to your own knowledge, consider the validity of the view that, during the period 1789 to 1794, crowd action was the driving force in revolutionary politics. (20)

Reading
Before answering this question you should reread Section 2. You may also find it useful to refresh your knowledge of the course of the French Revolution by rereading the AS part of the book, particularly Chapters 4 to 6.

How to answer this question
This question is asking you to consider a historical interpretation concerning the part of the crowd in the French Revolution. The debate between the Marxist and Revisionist schools over this issue is fully discussed in Section 2, but you must not allow your answer to become a recital of historians' views. A personal response is required, which debates the issues and incorporates the given sources into the framework of the answer.

Plan. To reach the highest level, you will need to sustain an argument throughout your answer, so it is important that you decide what your line of argument will be before you begin. You might like to consider the following ideas:

- Was crowd action essential to the development of the revolution?
- Was crowd action mainly spontaneous/disorganised (Source A) or carefully planned and executed (Sources B and C)?
- Was crowd action a response to economic factors (Source B) or political too (Source C)?
- What other factors were driving forces in revolutionary politics? Which was the most important factor?

Style. In your answer you will need to make a clear judgement in response to the question and to support it with your own knowledge as well as the source material.

Here is an example of a paragraph from an answer that makes a direct response to the question:

Crowd action certainly became a driving force in the development of the revolution after 1792. Rudé, in Source B, has shown how the crowd intervened when they feared the 'betrayal' of the earliest revolutionary changes by the king in 1789. However, the royal family's attempted flight to Varennes showed even more explicit betrayal of their trust. It was this fear of betrayal, as Williams has described in Source C, that finally destroyed the monarchy. 1792 was a key turning point in crowd influence, a fact stressed not only by Marxist historians such as Soboul, but by Revisionists such as Furet, who felt that the crowd intervention helped blow the revolution 'off course'. Similarly, Williams, the author of Source C, believed the crowd was central to the overthrow of the moderate revolution that had been developing since 1789. Driven by a mixture of political and economic forces the Sans Culottes drove the revolution forwards towards greater radicalism.

ESSAY QUESTION IN THE STYLE OF OCR

> Consider the arguments for and against the claim that Napoleon should be remembered as a great man. (45)

Reading
Before answering this question you should reread Sections 4 and 5.

How to answer this question
The question asks you to consider different interpretations of Napoleon. You are expected to use the sources (as given in the OCR question above), but you will also need to reveal plentiful other knowledge both to support and to refute claims of 'greatness'. Don't forget to draw on material from both his domestic rule and his military leadership. You will need to balance material from both sides in your answer and draw an appropriate conclusion.

Plan. Try to make a list of controversial themes that you can consider, paragraph by paragraph, discussing points for and against Napoleon's 'greatness' in each. Below are some suggestions:

- personal position and style of government
- reforms – legal, administrative, religious
- social change – principle of equality
- conquest/military achievement.

Style. You must try to decide which way you want to argue before you begin, so that each paragraph leads on to the next, taking the reader forwards to a convincing conclusion. Get in the habit of referring back to the key words of the question at the beginning of each new paragraph. This will ensure the answer remains relevant. Part of an answer follows, giving an indication of the direct style you might use:

No peasant or urban worker would ever have described Napoleon as a 'great man'. He did nothing for the masses but tax them and conscript their sons into his armies. The idea that he was the 'Emperor of the Common Man' is no more than a myth that developed from Napoleon's own memoirs. Peasants only supported Napoleon because they feared the alternative – a return to feudalism. Urban workers lived under a cloud of suspicion, forced to carry a livret and closely watched. Equality of opportunity meant little to these groups, for whom any decent education was denied.

ESSAY QUESTION IN THE STYLE OF EDEXCEL

> What, if anything, did Louis XVIII achieve for France in the years 1815–1824? (30)

Reading
Before answering this question reread Section 6 of the A2 part and Chapter 12 of the AS part of the book.

How to answer this question

The question asks for an evaluation of the reign of Louis XVIII. You are not required to write a narrative account of the reign, and it is best to avoid the chronological approach. Instead, think in terms of policies and issues and try to analyse throughout your answer, making supported judgements about Louis XVIII's achievements.

Plan. Themes you might consider include:

- restoration of peace/stability after the Napoleonic wars
- pursuit of moderate domestic policies
- financial successes
- foreign policy successes.

Argument. It should be clear throughout your answer what your line of argument is. You may choose to argue that Louis XVIII achieved nothing, emphasising the weaknesses of the reign and, for example, Louis's inability to control the Ultras. On the other hand, you might give a far more positive assessment, suggesting that much had been achieved, both domestically and in terms of international recognition by 1824. You may, of course, decide that in some areas Louis XVIII achieved a good deal, but in other areas he did not. Whatever view you take you must present points on both sides, and show why you support or choose to refute them.

ESSAY QUESTION IN THE STYLE OF EDEXCEL

> 'His rule was inadequate and his downfall inevitable.' How far do you agree with this assessment of the rule of Charles X? (30)

Reading
Before answering this question reread Section 6 of the A2 part and Chapter 12 of the AS part of this book.

How to answer this question
The question contains two parts. You must assess whether Charles X's rule was inadequate, and also whether his downfall was inevitable. There is no compulsion to agree with the quotation. Indeed a better answer can often be constructed by challenging a given statement. If you are able to include some historiography in your answer, this might help you to achieve high marks, but do explain ideas in your own words. The answer should not consist of a list of views.

Plan. Try to plan thematically. You might want to examine:

- religious policies
- social policies
- attitude to politics
- foreign policy.

Alternatively, you could focus on 1829–30 and look at the short-term causes of Charles X's downfall, and then balance them against the longer-term forces ranged against him.

Argument. Try to think of some points that could be made in Charles's favour. Although you may wish to argue that his reign was inadequate, you still need to assess whether every decision and policy fell into that category. The greater the discussion of the 'adequacy' of the reign as opposed to the inevitability of his fall, the more effective the argument is likely to be.

The following provides an example of a paragraph that could be included in a response to this question. It shows a direct style and clear judgement:

Charles X's refusal to act as a constitutional monarch upset the balance that had provided France with stability since 1815 and made his downfall inevitable. From his accession in 1824, he leaned heavily on the Ultras and the Catholic Church and, when faced with opposition, he merely sought to distract attention by sending an expedition to Algiers. When the chamber demanded the dismissal of his unpopular right-wing minister, Polignac, Charles ignored the demands, dissolved the chamber, altered the franchise and suspended the liberty of the press. This was done in deliberate violation of the charter as the liberals understood it and inevitably led to his overthrow.

BIBLIOGRAPHY

There is a terrific wealth of literature on France in Revolution and students are encouraged to use the following lists selectively according to their course and interests. The books have been divided according to their suitability for AS and A2 students. The books in the AS list have been particularly selected for their language and style and should prove accessible to most students in the first year of their History course. However, AS students wishing to pursue particular interests further would be advised to look at the more advanced reading in the A2 section. Similarly, many A2 students will find many of the books listed for AS useful for their studies.

AS Section – The French Revolution
W. Doyle, *The French Revolution: A very short introduction*, Oxford University Press (2001)
W. Doyle, *The Oxford History of the French Revolution* (more detailed than the above and also dealing with the impact of the revolution on Europe as a whole), Oxford University Press (1989)
N. Hampson, *The Terror in the French Revolution*, Historical Association pamphlet, General Series 103
J. Hunt, *The French Revolution*, Routledge (1998)
C. Jones, *The Longman Companion to the French Revolution*, Longman (1988); a useful compendium of information for reference.
E.G. Rayner & R.F. Stapley, *The French Revolution* (History at Source), Hodder and Stoughton (1990)
J.H. Shennan, *France before the Revolution* (Lancaster pamphlets), second edition, Routledge (1995)
D.M.G. Sutherland, *France 1789–1815: Revolution and Counter-Revolution*, Fontana (1985)
D. Townson, *France in Revolution* (Access to History), Hodder and Stoughton (1990)
D.G. Wright, *Revolution and Terror in France* (Seminar Studies), Longman (1974)

AS Section – Napoleonic and Bourbon France
I. Collins, *Napoleon: First Consul and Emperor of the French*, Historical Association (1986)
G. Ellis, *The Napoleonic Empire*, Macmillan (1991)
G. Ellis, *Napoleon*, Longman (1997)
C. Emsley, *The Longman Companion to Napoleonic Europe*, Longman (1993)
K. Randell, *Monarchy, Republic and Empire* (Access to History), Hodder and Stoughton (1986)
A. Stiles, *Napoleon, France and Europe* (Access to History), Hodder and Stoughton (1993)
D.G. Wright, *Napoleon and Europe* (Seminar Studies), Longman (1984)

A2 Section – Revolutionary, Napoleonic and Bourbon France
A. Cobban, *A History of Modern France, Vols1 (1715–99)* and *2 (1799–1945)*, Penguin (1957 and 1961); parts are now outdated, but this provides a basic overview.

The French Revolution
N. Aston, *Religion and Revolution in France 1780–1804*, Macmillan (2000)
T.C.W. Blanning, *The French Revolution, Class war or Culture Clash?*, Macmillan (1997)

T.C.W. Blanning, *The French Revolutionary Wars 1787–1802*, Arnold (1996)

T.C.W. Blanning, *The Origins of the French Revolutionary Wars*, Longman (1986)

A. Cobban, *The Social Interpretation of the French Revolution*, second edition, Cambridge University Press (1999); a reissue of the classic revisionist book with an introduction by G. Lewis.

G. Comninel, *Rethinking the French Revolution*, Verso (1987)

F. Furet and D. Richet, *The French Revolution*, Weidenfeld and Nicholson (1970) for a revisionist interpretation.

H. Gough, *The Terror in the French Revolution*, Macmillan (1998)

N. Hampson, *A Social History of the French Revolution*, Routledge (1963)

P.M. Jones, *The Peasantry in the French Revolution*, Cambridge University Press (1988)

G. Lefebvre, *The Coming of the French Revolution*, Princeton University Press (1947); a very readable Marxist interpretation.

G. Lewis, *The French Revolution: Rethinking the debate*, Routledge (1993)

C. Lucas (ed.), *Rewriting the French Revolution*, Clarendon Press, (1991)

J.M. Roberts, *The French Revolution*, second edition, Oxford University Press (1999)

G. Rudé, *The Crowd in the French Revolution*, Clarendon Press (1959)

G. Rudé, *The French Revolution*, Weidenfeld and Nicholson (1988); Marxist-influenced interpretation.

S. Schama, *Citizens, A Chronicle of the French Revolution*, Penguin/Viking (1989); lengthy but readable.

A. Soboul, *A Short History of the French Revolution 1789–99*, University of California Press (1965); the classic Marxist interpretation.

B. Stone, *The Genesis of the French Revolution: A global-historical interpretation*, Cambridge University Press (1994)

J.M. Thompson, *The French Revolution*, Hodder and Stoughton (1959)

M. Vovelle, *The Fall of the French Monarchy*, Cambridge University Press (1974)

G. A. Williams, *Artisans and Sans Culottes*, second edition, Libris (1988)

Napoleonic France

C. Barnett, *Bonaparte*, Wordsworth (1997)

M. Broers, *Europe under Napoleon 1799–1815*, Arnold (1996)

D. Chandler, *The Illustrated Napoleon*, Greenhill (1991); a military history.

O. Connelly, *Blundering to Glory*, Scholarly Resources (1988)

V. Cronin, *Napoleon*, Collins (1971); a readable pro-Napoleon biography.

C.J. Esdaile, *The Wars of Napoleon*, Longman (1995)

P. Geyl, *Napoleon For and Against*, Cape (1949)

P. Ingram, *Napoleon and Europe*, Stanley Thornes (1998)

G. Lefebvre, *Napoleon*, (1935); English version, Routledge and Keegan Paul (1969); a Marxist view.

M. Lyons, *Napoleon and the Legacy of the French Revolution*, Macmillan (1994)

F. Markham, *Napoleon*, Wiedenfeld and Nicolson (1963)

F. McLynn, *Napoleon*, Jonathan Cape (1997)

J.M. Thompson, *Napoleon*, Blackwell (1952)

J. Tulard, *Napoleon: The Myth of the Saviour*, Methuen (1985)

Bourbon France

J.P.T. Bury, *France 1814–1940*, Methuen (1949)

R. Tombs, *France 1814–1914*, Longman (1996)

INDEX